W9-BTT-117

TOTAL ACCESS

TOTAL ACCESS

A JOURNEY TO THE CENTER OF THE NFL UNIVERSE

RICH EISEN

THOMAS DUNNE BOOKS

St. Martin's Press ☆☆ New York

Questions from Wonderlic, Inc., have been reproduced and published herein with the express permission of Wonderlic, Inc.

THOMAS DUNNE BOOKS.
An imprint of St. Martin's Press.

TOTAL ACCESS. Copyright © 2007 by Rich Eisen. Foreword © 2007 by Steve Sabol. All rights reserved. Printed in the United States of America. No part of this book may be used or reproduced in any manner whatsoever without written permission except in the case of brief quotations embodied in critical articles or reviews. For information, address St. Martin's Press, 175 Fifth Avenue, New York, N.Y. 10010.

www.thomasdunnebooks.com
www.stmartins.com

Design by William Ruoto

ISBN-13: 978-0-312-36978-1
ISBN-10: 0-312-36978-6

First Edition: November 2007

10 9 8 7 6 5 4 3 2 1

To the thousands of prideful men who played this great game with honor and distinction, turning the sport of football into America's new pastime. Without them, this book would never exist.

CONTENTS

ACKNOWLEDGMENTS

There are several people who made this book possible. First and foremost, I want to thank my lord and savior, Steve Bornstein, the NFL's vice president of media and CEO of NFL Network. I tell Steve he's had the infinite wisdom to hire me twice: first, in 1996, at ESPN, where he was the most influential executive in its stellar existence, and then, in 2003, when he made me one of his first hires at NFL Network. Steve had (and still has) more confidence in my ability as a broadcaster than every single executive at ESPN combined, and, for that, I will forever be grateful. Because he hates being talked about, this will be the only mention of Steve in the book—along with the picture on the next page, taken with me, Deion Sanders, and Steve Mariucci prior to the 2006 regular season kickoff in Pittsburgh. That's Steve on the right. He's got a friendly smile. And I'm not just saying that because he's my boss. All right. Maybe I am.

I'd also like to thank the man on the left—NFL Commissioner Roger Goodell, whose support of NFL Network has been unwavering from the very beginning. Without his encouragement, the venture would not have been as successful. He is, quite simply, the man. Of course, I must mention his predecessor, Paul Tagliabue, without whom the entire project would have never gotten off the ground, period. By the way, Tagliabue has more of a sense of humor than many give him credit. I enjoyed discovering it for myself in the several conversations I was honored to have

(David Drapkin)

with Tagliabue, on and off the air. Others in the front office I'd like to thank for their support along the way include Joe Browne, Eric Grubman, Jeff Pash, Harold Henderson, Greg Aiello, Charles Coplin, Howard Katz, Kim Williams, Mike Pereira, Tracy Perlman, Seth Palansky and, for his compliance with the book, Derrick Crawford.

On the NFL Network side, there are countless people to acknowledge. First, I'd like to figuratively kiss the ring of Bill Creasy, without whose influence I would not be in the position I find myself today. I probably know of only half the things the man has done to help me in my career. Another major NFL Network contributor I'd like to thank is Geoff Mason. If I'm the face of the NFL Network (as some have called me) then executive producer Eric Weinberger is its heart and soul. His boundless energy and unique vision are the direct causes for the Network's immediate and long-term success. Thanks to him also for giving me the space to put my own stamp on our signature show, *NFL Total Access*. I also want to thank our director, Jennifer Love, for all the lovingly long single-shots she provides me on that show and others. Together, the three of us have been part of every single milestone show since the birth of NFL Network, a professional experience I will always treasure.

There are too many producers and production assistants to thank whose tireless hard work behind the scenes goes all too unnoticed, and I'm sure I'll leave some names out—so I thank them now en masse, which I hope they won't think is a cop-out. This book and the endless good times chronicled within would not have been possible without them. Thanks, as well, to the best camera, audio, makeup, and lighting crews in the business.

Eric and Jen flank me at our first Pro Bowl in 2005. *(Joann Kamay)*

(David Faller)

However, there is one co-worker I want to single out, although Joann Kamay is more than a mere co-worker. Joann is the primary stage manager for *NFL Total Access* and, without her, quite simply, my job would not be nearly as fun and enjoyable. Joann not only always has my back on the set every day, but also knows when to give me a swift kick in the ass when she thinks I'm acting like one. Which, of course, is quite rare, even though she might disagree. At any rate, in addition to being a first-rate person, Joann (below) is also a first-rate amateur photographer. She began snapping candid pictures of the crew on-set and behind the scenes from the very day NFL Network launched; much of her stellar work can be found in this book. Joann, you're the best.

As for the professional photogs whose work is also in the book, cheers to Kevin Terrell, David Drapkin, Amy Sancetta, and Upper Deck. I'd like to acknowledge my agent, Jeff Jacobs, of Creative Artists Agency, who hooked me up with the best literary agent, Rafe Sagalyn, of The Sagalyn Agency. There is no more tireless business manager in the business than

Reed Bergman of Playbook Inc. who has been a huge supporter of NFL Network since its inception. Thanks to my super editor Peter Wolverton of Thomas Dunne Books/St. Martin's Press and his fabulous assistant Katie Gilligan. This is my first book and their guidance was invaluable. They also helped talk me off the ledge several times.

On a personal level, I must thank my brother, Jeff, who was the first and biggest sports influence in my life. My parents, Joel and Eveline, stopped following sports when the Dodgers left Brooklyn and without Jeff, who knows, I might be writing a book about Judy Garland instead. Although I tend to doubt it. As for my parents, they've been there every step of the way, especially during the times I struggled writing book reports, let alone books. Now, I've written an actual book and it's officially in black-and-white how much I love them.

Lastly, and certainly not least, I want to thank my wonderful wife, Suzy Shuster, who always pushes me to strive to be better—at everything. We met at ESPN years ago, and, if you will, she had me at "hello." As her employers at ABC Sports, HBO, TNT, Fox Sports, and the NBA have already found out, Suzy's great at many things, especially on-air reporting, but perhaps they don't know she's also a superb copy editor. (She also came up with the idea and title for chapter 6.) I thank her for everything, but especially for her unwavering support for me in writing this book. As you'll soon read, the NFL season keeps me busy year-round, and Suzy endured several nights and weekends with me sitting at my office computer typing away. Honey, I love you.

Oh yes, I must thank our sweet rescue yellow lab-mix, Hudson, for sitting underneath my desk to keep me company the entire time. He got many treats and kisses. This book is also for Suzy and him. Hope you enjoy it.

FOREWORD

When I was a kid, TV was a miracle. At least it was to me. Just how the pictures—images is an adult word I never would have used—were made, or how they made their way to my house and our television set was beyond me. Probably even beyond my dad, and he knew pretty much everything. But I didn't care how it worked. I loved the shows. *Ramar of the Jungle*; *Kookla, Fran and Ollie*; and best of all, the cartoons Chief Halftown showed. The Chief was the host of a local kids show in Philadelphia. But I didn't know that. To me, he was the greatest TV personality in the world. He had a genuine buckskin shirt, a war bonnet with eagle feathers and his very own Seneca Indian chant to start the show: "*Ees sa sussaway.*" It meant "Let's begin"—and that was the clincher, Ees sa sussaway. No would would ever—could ever—top Chief Halftown. I was seven years old, and I was pretty sure about such things.

Turns out my tastes have changed. Forty-three years in the business will do that. While television isn't much of a mystery to me anymore, occasionally something extraordinary still occurs. I remember the last time it happened. It was November 4, 2003, the night NFL Network premiered. The moment I saw Rich Eisen on the set, a thousand questions disappeared. I knew the Network had a chance. Rich, as host of *NFL Total Access,* was smart and engaging. Polished with an easy grace. Don't ask me how, but he managed to bring gravitas to the launch of an entire network without losing the glibness that makes watching him like hanging out with a funny friend.

And that was just the first night. Since then, Rich has gotten even better. He isn't a fast learner but an instant one, soaking up whatever he needs to know. He can be both reverent and skeptical. He's earned two Emmy nominations as sports television's best studio host for the same reason he's so easy to watch. He gets to the heart of the matter. He's no blabbermeister. Whatever the issue, whoever he's interviewing, whatever event he's attending, viewers can always count on Rich for the prescient comment, the trenchant question, or the sly wisecrack that cuts through the noise and tells us what we need to know.

You can't fake dedication. Or talent. Not for long anyway. After four years of watching him every night, I think it's safe to say that Rich has plenty of both. Yeah, I'm a fan. In fact, I think Rich is just about the best host in the business today. He could cinch it with a little buckskin or a war bonnet, but that might be asking too much. *Ees sa sussaway!*

—STEVE SABOL

TOTAL ACCESS

INTRODUCTION

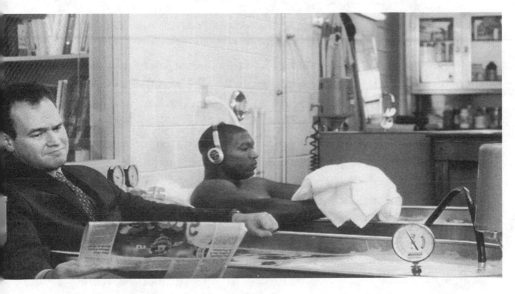

(NFL Network)

It all began in the hot tub next to Redskins offensive lineman Chris Samuels. Please allow me to explain.

It was September 2003, two months before NFL Network would officially launch into our cable and satellite lives forevermore. I had just left ESPN after seven fun years on the anchor desk at *SportsCenter* and had no idea what might lie ahead in my new all-football-all-the-time gig. All I knew for sure was this—a huge 310-pound Pro Bowl left tackle from Washington, D.C., sat chilling to my left in his own separate (very important distinction) metal tub.

Thankfully, we were just on a commercial shoot.

Like anything else being introduced to the unsuspecting American sports viewing public, NFL Network required a rollout commercial campaign defining what the very first sports network fully owned and operated by the National Football League was going to look like.

For better or worse, in the very beginning, it was going to look like a lot of me talking football. After all, this was the first 24/7/365 channel dedicated to covering the most popular sport in America. That's lots of time to fill, and as NFL Network's first and, at the time, only on-air hire, I was the one to fill it. That said, talk about your dream job. The concept for the commercial was simple. As host of NFL Network's nightly signature news and information program called *NFL Total Access,* I would be placed in the center of the NFL universe, and you, the viewer, would be taken along for the ride by merely tuning in.

So, to drive this point home like John Elway in Cleveland, the brilliant ad writers placed me in a wide variety of NFL settings: on a practice field, firing footballs from a Juggs machine to Rams Pro Bowl wide receiver Torry Holt; in a meeting room, reviewing plays on an overhead projector with Atlanta Pro Bowl quarterback Michael Vick and then–head coach Dan Reeves (who got edited out of the spot when he got fired midseason); at a team dinner with the New York Giants, reaching out, fork in hand, to stab a huge steak from a big plate of meat; grinning from the center seat of the head judge table during a tryout for the Raiders cheerleading squad (Hey now!); on the sideline, peeking under the hood of an instant replay booth as a ref watches in disgust; in a jewelry store, checking out a quality piece of bling with Saints running back Deuce McAllister; and, lastly, in the trainer's room, again, in my own *separate* hot tub next to Samuels. And, to complete the gag, I was dressed in my on-air attire—a business suit and tie—the entire time, even while I was sitting in the hot tub, which meant dry cleaning appeared on my very first NFL Network expense report.

To make matters even cooler, these scenes in the TV spot played out wordlessly under a familiar sound track—"Dear Mr. Fantasy" by Traffic. A stroke of genius, since being in the midst of all those terrific tableaus was, indeed, a football fantasy. Yet, we almost didn't get the rights to use the classic rock tune in the commercial. When NFL Network first came calling, lead singer Steve Winwood and the rest of the band hadn't spoken in years, and their apparently fractious relationship made getting all parties to sign off on releasing the song quite difficult. One of our backup songs was the theme to the 80s TV show *The Greatest American Hero*. You know, the whole "believe it or not, I'm walking on air" thing. Now, I'm a big Mike Post fan (I had the sheet music for the *Hill Street Blues* theme when I took piano lessons as a kid), but, thankfully, the boys from Traffic got their act together figuratively and literally. After finally agreeing to let us use "Dear Mr. Fantasy," the band planned to reunite but never did because lead guitarist Jim Capaldi got sick. So, a little part of me believes Traffic almost got back together thanks to NFL Network and its highly successful first advertising campaign.

It was also quite a prescient campaign. Because, once I hopped out of the hot tub, I quickly discovered that hosting *NFL Total Access* did, in fact, serve as my dream season pass. I also soon learned that, in the NFL, that season never ends.

What *do* you do in the off-season?

I get that question all the time, mostly from fans that don't yet have NFL Network. (Local cable operators are standing by!) Because if you watch NFL Network, you're immediately dialed in to the new reality of the football landscape: There really is no such thing as an off-season in the NFL anymore. The business of professional pigskin in America has so completely exploded in popularity that the NFL calendar can now be defined in two ways—a season in which football is played and a season in which it is not. To be blunt, it's absolutely crazy out there now.

Once the playing season reaches its stirring, confetti-laden conclusion in the Super Bowl, my job actually gets busier. Think about it: As the NFL regular season rolls on, more and more teams fall out of contention, meaning fewer and fewer teams with relevance remain. Once the final two teams play the final game in front of the free football world, all thirty-two franchises in the NFL become newsworthy once again. It usually doesn't take long for news to pop.

For instance, the league's near *billion*-dollar free agency period begins a mere three weeks after the Super Bowl. In between, serving as one luau of a distraction, you have the Pro Bowl, the league's annual All-Star game held in Hawaii every Sunday after Super Sunday. No fewer than ten days after the Pro Bowl comes the NFL Scouting Combine in Indianapolis, where every single draft-eligible player gets poked and prodded and tested and scoped and run about an empty RCA Dome under the watchful eyes of every stopwatch-wielding head coach, general manager, and scout in the game. It's where the talent evaluation process begins in earnest, because it's the first time in months when the coaches and general managers can take part in this process without that pesky thing called a playing season to occupy their time.

In March, the NFL owners have their day, not only with the aforementioned free agency sweepstakes but also with their annual meeting. Held approximately one month before the NFL Draft, the Owners' Meeting is where the elite meet (in only the finest of four-star properties) to discuss the pinstripe-suit business of football and institute esoteric rule changes for the upcoming playing season. It's where gray matter meets Grey Poupon.

"The spring comes when the crocuses are out," Commissioner Paul Tagliabue told me in his very first appearance on *NFL Total Access* at the Owners' Meeting in 2004. "But football comes when you get through the Owners' Meeting, then the Draft, then the Minicamps, and then you're there at Training Camp and the season. So, it's an exciting time of the year for us."

Not so fast, Commissioner. (Kapow! That sounded a lot like Adam West.) You missed a couple of important items on the calendar. After Minicamp (which is what it sounds like—a miniature version of Training Camp for all new rookies and returning veterans) comes the Rookie Symposium, a four-day summit at which every drafted rookie attends seminars and breakout sessions on all sorts of real-life topics, from choosing the right agent or business manager to avoiding trouble in nightclubs or in relationships. The NFL holds the Symposium every year in late June.

Only then does the bulk of the NFL actually take a vacation. I usually take two weeks off every July, just like many head coaches. In fact, in the fortnight around July 4, most team facilities are virtual ghost towns. Coaches, scouts, secretaries, you name it. Gone fishing. Late June/early July is typically wedding season in the NFL; assistant coaches who never have a chance for an extended getaway frequently plan their nuptials for this period. As for the players, they soak in their final moments of freedom. Because once vacation ends, everybody takes a deep breath . . . and exhales in February. If they're lucky.

By late July and early August, every one of the 32 teams has opened its respective Training Camp. Before you know it, you're in the Preseason, which kicks off with the traditional Hall of Fame Game in Canton, Ohio, on the first Sunday in August. That game also caps the annual Hall of Fame Induction Weekend, which attracts tens of thousands of fans to cheer on the latest collection of legends chosen for enshrinement in the Pro Football Hall of Fame. After *that* comes the rest of the Preseason, which, of course, leads up to the annual regular season kickoff extravaganza hosted by the reigning Super Bowl champs and, holy smokes, here we go all over again.

That's the basic concept of this book: I'm going to take you inside a football season that flat out never ends. Take you inside meeting rooms and draft rooms and into locales normally off-limits. They don't call my show *Total Access* for nothing. Thanks to our unique ownership structure, those on NFL Network are afforded entrée to places and events to which the rest of the media is, quite frankly, shut out. I am one of the fortunate few who personally attend nearly every single one of these events on the NFL calendar. You see, Joe Gibbs may go to the Scouting Combine and the Owners' Meeting, but he doesn't go to Hall of Fame Induction Weekend or the Rookie Symposium. I do. Donovan McNabb may go to

Rich on the job at Super Bowl XL in Detroit. (*Joann Kamay*)

the Pro Bowl, but he doesn't go to the NFL Draft, which NFL Network has broadcast alongside ESPN since 2006, or the very first Thanksgiving Classic night game. I do. Plus, I get to go to the Scouting Combine, the Owners' Meeting and the Pro Bowl, too.

And, through this book, so will you. Welcome to my hot tub. If you will.

I've got to be honest.

I grew up loving baseball more than I loved football. A New York native, I loved the Yankees far more than I did either the Jets or the Giants. When the Yankees lost, my mood swung. When it came to the Jets or Giants, not so much. So, when I left ESPN, other than bolting a sports TV institution available in nearly 100 million homes for a new start-up venture in about one-tenth as many living rooms, my biggest trepidation concerned covering just one single sport. All year round. And that sport wasn't even my favorite, to boot.

Not anymore.

Don't get me wrong. I still love baseball and other sports, but since NFL Network first went on the air on Tuesday, November 4, 2003 (in the middle of Week 10 of the 2003 season) the National Football League has completely won me over, lock, stock, and two smoking barrels. And it's not just because they're paying me. Really.

It's because the National Football League is not just a major sport, but rather a culture. It's a lifestyle. When the NFL regular season schedule gets released in mid-April (on a two-hour *Schedule Release Show* on NFL Network, by the way), fans across the country begin rearranging their lives to attend one of the few home games available. There are some who reserve hotel rooms in Green Bay for every weekend throughout the season and, upon learning the Packers' home schedule, merely cancel the rooms on the weekends Brett Favre is on the road and keep their reservations intact for weekends when Lambeau Field is jumping.

Since NFL games are played only once a week and, for most teams, on only 16 regular season weekends a year, fan anticipation reaches a frenzied boiling point by kickoff. I feel it, too. The power of the game and the intensity of the playing season are like no other. Now the NFL's supposed off-season has become equally incomparable. No American sport has ever enjoyed a day-in, day-out grab on the national consciousness quite like the NFL does now. Plus, as you'll discover through reading this book, every event on the now year-round NFL calendar has its own unique fingerprint, its own vibes and attributes, its own diversity or lush history.

Then there are the people. Of course, every sport has its share of intense head coaches or managers who live and die with each victory or loss. But, in the NFL, the game becomes intertwined in a coach's DNA. They're not the best-rounded people, for they live in a virtual bunker until game day. Former Giants head coach Jim Fassel once told me that, in his first season on the job in New York, he was home eating breakfast during a midseason bye week when he noticed the kitchen was darker. His wife told him she had it painted a different color. *Six weeks before.* "You're just never home during the day to see it," she said. There's also a great story involving the bubble world of the great Hall of Famer Don Shula. It goes like this: At the zenith of the 1980s TV show *Miami Vice,* actors Don Johnson and Phillip Michael Thomas were introduced to Shula, who then thanked them for all their hard work protecting the city of Miami. He had no clue that Crockett and Tubbs were fictional. I have no idea if that's a true story, but knowing head coaches like I now know them, it sure sounds believable.

As for the players, well, they're basically the most prideful athletes I've ever come across. They don't like to lose. At anything. To a man, when an NFL player walks on that field, he believes his opponents are trying to take food off his table and money out of his pockets, which means they're going after his wives and kids and maybe his momma, too. That's how badly they want to win. I also believe it's the only mind-set he can logically have when he's playing a game in which one single unfortunate pileup can instantly end his livelihood. That's why virtually every NFL player looks mad as hell before and during games. It's also why players get a real bad rap.

Granted, some NFL players are bad seeds, just as in every line of work. But I've found most NFL players to be gregarious, courteous, family-oriented, community-minded people who love meeting other people. They're also real sharp. While some NFL players excel at the same Wonderlic aptitude test as regular, white- and blue-collar professionals, I'd venture to guess few of those same nine-to-fivers would pass a 50-question, 12-minute exam on the West Coast Offense. With playbooks so thick you can let your fingers do the walking through them, it really does take a certain genius to succeed in the NFL. Several players are also smart enough to realize extra exposure doesn't hurt. Unlike other professional sports, NFL rosters are massively large—52 players strong—making it tough for most players to distinguish themselves, certainly since masks obscure them during their prime face time. Thus, NFL players are more prone to seek out media exposure than other professional athletes. NFL Network is all about providing that spotlight.

On *NFL Total Access,* NFL players aren't only interviewees; they're also interviewers. Over the years, we've had active NFL players serve as in-field correspondents during the playing season and in the capacity of in-studio analysts on bye weeks. During the off-season, our Los Angeles studio becomes a virtual turnstile as players pay us visits, sometimes for an entire week at a time. Many wisely view those appearances as auditions for a second career. And why not?

I've been fortunate to be able to call a bunch of retired NFL greats "colleague." NFL Network's first in-studio analysts were three-time Super Bowl–winning linebacker Ken Norton Jr. and three-time Pro Bowl linebacker Seth Joyner. Terrell Davis, Most Valuable Player of Super Bowl XXXII, joined us months later, and after Seth and Ken moved on, none other than 11-time Pro Bowl cornerback Rod Woodson enlisted with NFL Network. So did two-time Pro Bowl lineman Lincoln Kennedy, the personification of a gentle giant. (Recruitment works both ways. USC head coach Pete Carroll used his post-2005 Rose Bowl ap-

I'm on the *NFL Total Access* set in Los Angeles *(from left to right)* with Rod Woodson, Lincoln Kennedy, and Terrell Davis giving me the rabbit ears. *(NFL Network)*

Deion Sanders, Steve Mariucci, and I bring you your highlights every Sunday night on *NFL GameDay*. (*Joann Kamay*)

pearance on *NFL Total Access* to recruit Ken Norton for his staff. Carroll asked Ken to walk him to his car after the interview and on the way invited him to join the USC coaching staff. Ken still coaches there today.)

All-time leading rusher Emmitt Smith spent the 2005 season working Monday nights on *NFL Total Access* with Davis and me. In 2006, eight-time Pro Bowl running back Marshall Faulk joined our crew, along with Prime Time himself—two-time Super Bowl champion Deion Sanders, who is by far the greatest character I've met on the job. His occasionally outlandish garb puts the cherry on top of a consummate professional. By the way, if you're scoring at home, Deion says he has nearly 2,000 suits in his closet. In fact, you will rarely see him wear the same outfit twice. After one episode of *NFL GameDay*, the weekly Sunday night highlight show that we cohost with former 49ers and Lions head coach Steve Mariucci, Sanders mentioned that once he wears a suit on TV, it "kills" the suit for at least three years.

I struggled mightily over how this book should begin. In the end, I decided to kick it off with the ever-loving' lulu of them all—the Super Bowl. After all, it is the end of one season and kickoff to another. Plus, if the NFL held a convention just like any other industry, the Super Bowl would be it. Anybody who's somebody in professional football's past, present, and future makes an appearance of some sort at the Super Bowl. Because the not-so-dirty secret of Super Bowl Week is that it's really about everything *but* the game.

The NFL Network crew arrives at the site of the Super Bowl a good eight days before kickoff. The first *NFL Total Access at the Super Bowl* hits air the Sunday before Super Sunday, or one day before the rest of the media horde comes to town. When the media hits town, it's all about the media. With very little else to occupy our time, we spend all week talking about the game, not in terms of X's and O's, but in terms of "distractions." Which team will be distracted by the hoopla surrounding the game? Which coach can keep the team focused to avoid distractions? Any team with a player who pops off in the media is, you guessed it, a distraction. In other words, what we do in the media is talk about something, then beat it to death and wonder if it's a distraction for the Super Bowl teams because we're doing that.

It's not just the print and TV reporters wagging tongues. Virtually every sports talk radio host in America descends upon the Super Bowl city and sets up shop from something called Radio Row. Because so many morning zoos and afternoon drive-time programs cover the Super Bowl for their avid longtime listeners and first-time callers, the NFL puts them all in one place, a collection of row upon row of tables located in the Super Bowl city's convention center. Each radio program has a producer roaming the floor of the center looking to cherry-pick guests. No one escapes their grasp, including yours truly.

Plus, I'm easy to find. *NFL Total Access* places its largest Super Bowl set smack-dab in the middle of Radio Row. And when I say large, I mean silly. At our first Super Bowl, XXXVIII in Houston (New England vs. Carolina), we had a piano on our set. The next year, for Super Bowl XXXIX, in Jacksonville (New England vs. Philadelphia), we had a piano *and* a pool table, *and* a mini–football field. At Super Bowl XL, in Detroit (Pittsburgh vs. Seattle), we lost the piano and pool table but added a wet bar. For Super Bowl XLI, in Miami (Indianapolis vs. Chicago), we toned down our Radio Row set but added another outdoor set across from the Versace Mansion in South Beach.

I mean, it *is* the Super Bowl. There's no reason to hold back. And that's only the Sunday and Monday before the Big Game. We're merely just beginning to put our fingers in the dirt, people.

THE CONVENTION

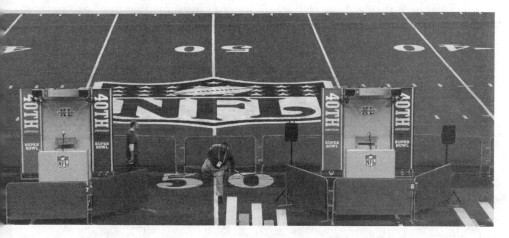

An NFL official stretches his quads before the media crush. *(Joann Kamay)*

TUESDAY

EVER THE PRECOCIOUS YOUNGSTER, I remember once wondering why there was no such thing as Children's Day. I mean, there's Mother's Day and Father's Day. Then you've got Veterans Day, Columbus Day, Presidents Day (on which, for some reason, we celebrate only two presidents), and even secretaries have their day once a year.

Why no Children's Day?

The answer always came back: "Because every day is Children's Day."

Well, the reverse logic applies to Media Day at the Super Bowl. How could there possibly be something called Media Day? Isn't every day media day at the Super Bowl?

Once a team arrives in the Super Bowl city, the head coach and his star players hold a press conference at their hotel. That's after they're greeted at the airport by a gaggle of media. The next day, each team holds its first Super Bowl practice, prior to which . . . there's a press conference. The same thing happens Wednesday. And again on Thursday, the final day players are made available to the media before the game. On Friday, the head coaches hold their final press conferences, prior to which both men pose in front of The Precious—the Vince Lombardi Trophy. It's a photo opportunity you see in your local paper every year: Both coaches are smiling, desperately trying to act nonchalant in the presence of the mythical item they've been chasing their entire lives. Neither touches The Precious because, well, the Football Gods frown upon such hubris. Never touch The Precious. More on that later.

Even with all that talking and questioning and answering and tape rolling and microphone shoving and follow-up questions to a question already asked and answered on Monday and Wednesday and Thursday and Friday, there's *still* something called Super Bowl Media Day.

It happens every Tuesday of Super Bowl Week. On Super Bowl Media Day all in the media are basically allowed to have their way with every single person playing or coaching in the game, and every single person playing or coaching in the game has to take it and like it. Well, they don't have to like it—but take it they must. Or get slapped with a hefty fine . . . although, by day's end, some of the players probably want to do some of the slapping.

Here's how Media Day works. The NFL makes each team available in separate sessions on the field of the Super Bowl. For the sake of our discussion, let's say the NFC team goes first. The entire NFC team appears and *everybody* must show—coaches *and* players, even the ones on injured reserve. The bulk of the team roams the sideline while 16 of the more popular participants in the Super Bowl take to 16 podiums spaced out from one goal line all the way down the field to the other goal line. The podiums face the stands that the media will soon stampede down like the tatanka from *Dances with Wolves*. You see, while the players get set up for Media Day, hundreds of reporters, scribes, bloggers, camera operators, and photographers are shepherded into the stadium's first-level concourse. When the clock strikes 10:00 in the morning, security lets the herd loose, and they literally come tearing down the stadium steps toward the field whereupon . . . they scatter! And get to ask everybody and anybody whatever question they wish for as many times as they wish for a period of one hour.

When I say "ask anything," I mean it. Super Bowl XXII was the forum at which Doug Williams, the first African-American quarterback in Super Bowl history, was famously asked, "How long have you been a black quarterback?" Or at Super Bowl XXXII in San Diego, where Broncos offensive lineman Gary Zimmerman was asked, "What's it like to be a Jewish lineman in the NFL?" (He's not Jewish.) Or at Super Bowl XXXIX in Jacksonville where Patriots running back Corey Dillon was asked no fewer than four consecutive questions about White Castle hamburgers. To this day no one knows why. The year before, one of the first questions for Tom Brady came from a Japanese journalist. "What do you say to all your fans in Japan?" Brady politely responded, "Hello?"

The media mostly gather around the podiums, usually one belonging to a quarterback, head coach, or any player with a brash gift of gab. Otherwise, the media grab any player found roaming the area between the podiums and the stands. Usually, an assistant coach or two is seated in the stands for good measure, and the media circle him in Section 125 or the like. From above the action looks like a scene from the movie *Antz*.

After 60 minutes, the media must leave the field and retreat to the concourse, where the National Football League serves them a not-so-sumptuous meal. But the meal is free, which is, quite frankly, really all the media want. In fact, all of us media folk live by the same dark, dirty motto: If it's free, it's me. We'd step over our own mothers for a bag of SWAG, which, for the uninitiated, stands for Stuff We All Get. Trust me. Anyone who denies that is full of it.

After lunch, the AFC principals take to the same hooded sideline podiums and a horn touches off another mad rush down the stadium steps for the fully-fed media now seeking to feed the beast. Sixty minutes more of virtually the same questions and . . . it's all over! Down goes the media! Down goes the media! Or at least back to their hotels or studios to write whatever stories or edit together whatever sound bites they gleaned from Media Day, which, to be truthful, isn't much.

That, my friends, is Super Bowl Media Day in a nutshell. For those who wish to learn more details on the free-for-all, read on. Everyone else, uh, please read on. I mean, this is the first chapter of the book. Stick with me here, people.

One of the more frightening aspects of Media Day is that anyone with a pulse gets a credential. Don't get me wrong. Anyone who applies for a Media Day press pass receives a stringent security vetting, but the league's philosophy behind the annual Super Tuesday media madness is simple: the more, the merrier. It's the biggest game on Planet Earth and requires a commensurate spotlight. So, whether you're from ESPN or the lone sports editor of a *Pennysaver* in rural Arizona, it doesn't matter. You're in. Got your own blog or ham radio operation and can prove it? You're in. If a TV station in Germany wants to send a crew to Media Day, then... *Willkommen!* France? *Bienvenu!* Mexico? *Bienvenido!* Especially if it's that hot blonde that TV Azteca sends to Media Day every year. *Ay caramba!*

Even Ray Lewis's Super Bowl press credential is intimidating. (*Joann Kamay*)

Indeed, folks from all walks of life comprise the media throng at Media Day. In addition to Señorita Azteca, there's a ponytailed guy from Hawaii armed at every Media Day with a minitape recorder and boxes of chocolate-covered Mauna Loa macadamias for his interviewees. There's also invariably someone from *Entertainment Tonight* handing out something called The ET Super Bowl Awards. At Super Bowl XLI in Miami, *ET* reporter and former ESPN *SportsCenter* colleague Kevin Frazier strolled up to podium number 16 in front of the rest of the gathered media and handed Colts placekicker Adam Vinatieri a piece of Lucite that served as "the first-ever Mary Hart Award." Why? Vinatieri and Hart are both from South Dakota. Because the people who first foisted Leonard Maltin on the unsuspecting American viewing public are apparently fair and balanced, *ET* also gave a member of the Bears special teams an ET Super Bowl Award. Punter Brad Maynard won the Justin Timberlake Award for Bringing Sexy Back.

"I don't know what's sexy about a thirty-two-year-old man, balding, married with three kids, but maybe that's sexy to some people," Maynard told *ET* (exclusively!).

Speaking of E.T. . . . . No, I've never seen anyone come to Media Day dressed as Spielberg's Reese's Pieces–loving alien, but someone did come to the Super Bowl XXXIX Media Day in Jacksonville dressed, for some reason, as the Green Hornet. The year the Panthers and Patriots played in Super Bowl XXXVIII, in Houston, Jimmy Kimmel sent a reporter—his famed cousin Sal—to Media Day in the uniform of placekicker John Kasay. I remember Sal winking at me as he passed the NFL Network set while running down the steps in the media stampede wearing the full Kasay uniform and a Panthers ski cap (with one of those fuzzy balls on top); he then proceeded to create a general ruckus on the turf, especially when he found the real Kasay. Like all good comedians, Kimmel perfected his craft—outdoing himself at Super Bowl XLI Media Day in Miami, for which his "correspondents" were the first two rejects on the 2007 *American Idol.* You know, the latest incarnations of William Hung—the guy Simon Cowell denigrated as resembling a bush baby and his portly compadre. They respectively roamed the Media Day turf in Brian Urlacher and Peyton Manning jerseys and accosted several of the Bears and Colts as well as members of the media (including your humble narrator and ESPN's Chris Berman) to sing along with them in a chorus of "Take Me Out to the Ball Game." I held my breath the night my

Your humble narrator delivers a pithy soundbite at Media Day. *(Kevin Terrell/NFL Network)*

makeshift *American Idol* moment aired on Kimmel, wondering if I would have a job the next day.

Now, it's not as if NFL Network is above this fray. Well, literally, we are—usually stationed on a set built into the stands on the 50-yard line for our live coverage of Super Bowl Media Day. Live, as in Brentson Buckner, the extroverted Carolina Panthers defensive tackle, was on live TV when he once flipped the bird at the camera at the end of his interview with our Media Day field reporter Kara Henderson. We also station reporter Solomon Wilcots on the turf. They ask as many questions of as many people as they can buttonhole while I sit on the set and anchor the coverage, occasionally dipping into the podium interviews. We have a camera and a microphone hookup at each one. And at Super Bowl XLI Media Day, in Miami, we even added a new feature: Podium Cam—a camera placed on the podium hood looking out at the gathered masses to give you viewers at home the player's view of the scrum from the podium. Last but not least, we also send our own correspondent into the volatile mix to tape a feature for Tuesday's *NFL Total Access at the Super Bowl*. Every year, that intrepid reporter is an actual NFL player who sadly didn't make the Super Bowl himself. Seven-time Pro Bowl defensive tackle Warren Sapp ably performed this role at Media Days at Super Bowls XXXVIII, in Houston, and XLI, in Miami, while five-time Pro Bowl receiver Torry Holt held down the fort at Super Bowl XL Media Day in Detroit. For the Media Day at Super Bowl XXXIX, in Jacksonville, our man on the scene was defensive lineman Simeon Rice, who wore a thick gray-and-white chinchilla coat for the occasion. While Rice's swapping his jacket with a TV reporter from an Eastern-bloc nation made for some good television, Sapp is our reigning king of the Media Day turf.

"It's crazy down there," he said after having at it in Houston. "I don't know how you guys do it."

Warren Sapp crashes the set on Super Bowl XLI Media Day. (*Joann Kamay*)

During his foray into the media mosh pit, Warren flirted with *Entertainment Tonight* correspondent and model Lauren Bush, got Danish lessons from a hand puppet–wielding TV reporter from Denmark, and pecked CBS analysts Dan Marino and Phil Simms on the cheek with his best Joe Namath impersonation: "I wanna kiss you!"

Yes, at Super Bowl Media Day even the media is made available to the media. The TV announcers broadcasting the Super Bowl pregame and game action hold a press conference of their own during the lunch session. At Super Bowl XL, in the Motor City—the final NFL broadcast on ABC after 36 years of *Monday Night Football*—the venerable Al Michaels was nearly as sought out at Media Day as Steelers running back and Detroit homecoming king Jerome Bettis. Starting the following season, *Monday Night Football* was moving to ESPN and Michaels had signed a deal with the cable giant to remain as its lead voice—but rumor had it that Michaels now wanted to jump ship with John Madden to call the new Sunday night package on NBC. It turned out to be true. Just four days after the Super Bowl, in one of the more bizarre transactions in sports TV history, ESPN "traded" Michaels to NBC for broadcast rights to the Ryder Cup, expanded access to highlights to other NBC events like the Olympics, and last, but definitely not least, rights to an old Disney cartoon character named Oswald the Rabbit. For those in need of a refresher, Oswald was the precursor to Mickey Mouse.

Apparently, NBC's parent company, Universal, had owned Oswald's rights, and for 79 years the Disney family had wanted him back. Al Michaels's desire to work for a peacock got a rabbit back in the Mouse House.

"I'm going to be a trivia question someday," Michaels said.

At Super Bowl Media Day, however, Michaels was mum. Virtually every member of the media, including your humble narrator, believed in miracles (to use the Michaels vernacular) and thought Al would crack under constant questioning about his future plans. No such luck. But, come to think of it, nobody ever cracks under the Media Day spotlight, which is the ultimate irony of it all.

We all try to get a rise out of the players and get very little in return. You see, most of the podium-worthy players are quintessential "go-to guys" for the media, which means they know how to handle the scene.

"It was fun," Lincoln Kennedy once said of his Super Bowl XXXVI

Do you believe in being coy? Yes! (*Joann Kamay*)

Media Day experience. "But, after it was over, I was glad it was over with because you get asked the same question over and over again."

Sure, a player's patience gets tried, but, to date, no one has ever blown a gasket. Nobody wants to be the guy who gives out bulletin-board material at a Super Bowl, either. Certainly a coach won't. Thus, no one in his right mind would take to a Media Day podium and blow the roof off the sucker. Not even Terrell Owens caused a stink or generally talked smack during his one-hour session at Super Bowl XXXIX Media Day. His podium (number 4, for those keeping score) was the most crowded one I've seen in all my Media Day days, with Peyton Manning's (podium 8, right in the middle) at Super Bowl XLI being a close second. With both teams reflecting the quiet reserve of their head coaches Tony Dungy and Lovie Smith, that Colts/Bears Media Day in particular was notable for, well, nothing.

"Nobody's saying anything!" lamented Deion Sanders, a noteworthy presence at two Super Bowl Media Days in his day. "Somebody say something!"

There is hope for the future. One player has sworn to me that we will bust up Media Day like we've never seen before. However, Chad Johnson has to make it to a Super Bowl first. But if the Bengals ever make to the big game, Johnson assured me he will attend Media Day, quote: "In a towel."

I informed Chad that the NFL might mandate that he wear his Super Bowl jersey on the podium just like every other player.

"I don't care," Johnson said. "I'm gonna step up to that podium in a towel and start talking."

Uh, what do you say to all your fans in Japan, Ocho Cinco-san?

Now, *that* will be a Super Tuesday.

WEDNESDAY

AS WITH ALL CONVENTIONS, you have days when attendees arrive in greater numbers. At the Super Bowl, that day is Wednesday. Certainly, if the Super Bowl is held at a destination spot like, say, Miami or San Diego, Wednesday is the day when many fans check in for a fat five-day weekend extravaganza. It's noticeable on the streets as traffic and security builds around town.

Wednesday is also the day the corporate-sponsor boondoggle hits a higher gear. Just like any sport, the NFL has its legion of "official sponsors." You know, the Official Beer of the NFL, the Official Outfitter of the NFL and so on. There're quite a few of them. More often than not, the sponsor's staff is fully ensconced in town by Wednesday of Super Bowl Week, setting up various parties and events and hospitality suites. Or making sure the hotel room is all set for the CEO flying in on Saturday. *And don't forget about Mr. Johnson's tickets to the tailgate before the game!* For each "official" league sponsor, there are countless other corporations with no "official" league business in town on their own Super Bowl boondoggles because—let's be honest—there's always a client in need of schmoozing, and what better place to schmooze than at the Super Bowl?

One popular way to make a client happy is to have said client tee it up with a real, bona fide NFL player before the Big Game. Thus, you see a considerable uptick in the number of former and current players strolling around the Super Bowl on Wednesday, the same day you notice more golf bags at the hotel valet. Of course, it's another sort of green that attracts players to a Super Bowl city in greater numbers. Many players hit town to pitch a corporate sponsor's product (Jerome Bettis for Degree antiperspirant!) or promote a corporate sponsor's Web site (for more, log on to Degree.com!) or pick up an award sponsored by, you guessed it, a corporate sponsor (Carson Palmer and LaDanian Tomlinson are this year's FedEx Air and Ground winners!). Radio Row becomes more crowded as all these players need a forum in which to sell whatever they're pitching, and the sports talk radio guys fall all over themselves to accommodate them because they need their afternoon drive-time hours filled. For an interview-driven program like *NFL Total Access at the Super Bowl*, it's manna from heaven. We also plug in to that gravy train and ride it—to the tune of five hours of live shows from noon to 5:00 Eastern time for three straight days . . . starting Wednesday. Every time I host one of those programs, I feel like ending it with "You'll Never Walk Alone."

But what an experience! On those days the *NFL Total Access* set on Radio Row becomes a revolving door of Who's Who in the NFL, past and present. For instance, in the 15 hours of live afternoon broadcasts from Super Bowl XL, in Detroit, the following luminaries sat down with us: Bart Starr, Lynn Swann, Chad Johnson, Takeo Spikes, Steve Sabol, Alex Smith, Mike Nolan, Jerry Kramer, Santana Moss, Cris Carter, Terry Bradshaw, Boomer Esiason, Steve Smith, Tony Gonzalez, Antonio Gates, Michael Strahan, then-Commissioner Paul Tagliabue, Tom Arnold (yes, the comedian), David Spade, Rob Schneider, Shawne Merriman, Cadillac Williams, Matt Leinart, Steve Young, Larry Johnson, Edgerrin James, Clinton Portis, and Willis McGahee. Just to name a few. And I'm not including those who served as my cohosts on the broadcasts: Rod Woodson, Terrell Davis, Lincoln Kennedy, former head coach Steve Mariucci, Ray Lewis of the Baltimore Ravens, and the guy with whom he won Super Bowl XXXV, quarterback Trent Dilfer.

I know. Name-dropper.

To be honest, it's freaking cool. And when we first started up NFL Network, we all hoped it would turn out this way. Of course, we never knew for sure—until the Wednesday of our first Super Bowl week in Houston for Super Bowl XXXVIII, the day that first defined NFL Network.

W hen word filtered out that George Bush Senior (a.k.a. Bush 41) might be stopping by the *NFL Total Access* set in the Houston Convention Center for an interview, I didn't believe it. At the time, NFL Network was only 11 weeks old and in only 12 million homes. In the television world, that's barely more than a Thousand Points of Light. Why in the

Chad Johnson (in backwards cap) is one of my all-time favorite guests.
(*K. Terrell*)

world would Poppy Bush leave the golf course to chat on NFL Network
with me?

Well, several reasons, apparently. Bureau producer Drew Ohlmeyer
explained that Bush attended Houston Texans games as the invited guest
of his good friend and team owner Robert C. McNair. McNair asked Bush
to make an appearance on NFL Network as a favor to him, to help promote
the host city and also give a boost to this newfangled television venture
launched by the NFL just two months before.

"There's a chance this may happen, so be ready," Drew told me
Tuesday night, after Media Day.

Be ready? I assumed the president knew more about Patriot defense
missiles than the Patriots defense against Carolina quarterback Jake Delhomme. I asked some people on the staff for ideas and questions, fully be-
lieving I wouldn't get the chance to ask any of them. But sure enough,
around 10:00 A.M. Wednesday (we didn't start going live during the day
until two Super Bowls later, in Detroit) a bunch of serious-looking dudes
straight out of *The Matrix* surrounded the set, talking into the cuffs of their
white button-down shirts.

The president had entered the building. This was actually going to
happen.

McNair and Commissioner Paul Tagliabue soon appeared as a welcoming committee. I was told I'd be interviewing the commissioner and McNair together later in the day, but I couldn't think of that at the moment: George Herbert Walker Bush had just arrived on the set of *NFL Total Access* at the Super Bowl. One of his concerned aides asked me what topics I'd be covering with the president.

"You know, the first Gulf War and the Star Wars defense initiative," I said.

The aide gave me a blank look.

"Just kidding," I said.

Eventually, the president sat down and we shook hands.

Now, occasionally people ask me what's the difference between con-

George H. W. Bush (a.k.a. Bush 41) on the set. *(Amy Sancetta)*

ducting an interview for a newspaper and on television. The answer is simple. If this were a print interview, I'd turn on a tape recorder or whip out a pen and off we'd go. However, when a subject sits down for a chat on TV, it sparks a whirlwind of activity. Lights get readjusted, cameras are repositioned, makeup is applied, microphones are clipped on, tapes roll. It takes maybe a minute. Honestly, it feels like an hour. As the interviewer, it's your job to make light chitchat to keep the interviewee talking and feeling comfortable until the cameras roll—but not too comfortable! You don't want the interviewee saying something off camera that you'd rather get on camera. It's a tough tap dance; toss in a literally and once figuratively sitting president of the United States, and it's downright nerve-racking.

Interestingly enough, an Associated Press photographer snapped off a picture of this very moment—the president's eyebrow arched as the makeup artist and our audio tech Rob Ohlandt worked on him. He's saying something to me. I wish I knew for sure what it was. We photocopied the picture and hung it over our watercooler when we got back to our Los Angeles set and held a "name the caption" contest. At any rate, as for the interview, here are some highlights. Please do feel free to read the president's lines in the voice of Dana Carvey.

ME: This is the greatest honor we've had to date at NFL Network. We are joined on our set here at the Super Bowl by George Herbert Walker Bush, the forty-first president of the United States. Thank you so much for joining us, sir.
POTUS: Well, I'm caught up in the Super Bowl mania here and I'm happy to be here.

ME: What do you think of the Super Bowl coming to your town here in Houston?
POTUS: Well, I think it's great, of course. What I really am interested in is what other people from out of town think. But I can tell you, this has captured the imagination of all Houstonians, whether they play football or not. And it's a great thing for our city. I happen to think we're a very hospitable city and I hope that's the lasting impression that the fans from all across the NFL feel.

ME: Well, the cab driver I had last night was very hospitable.
POTUS: Was he speaking English?

ME: He was very conversant in the language, no question about it.

POTUS: Yeah, good. They're great. The cab drivers here are really wonderful. They are.

And that's the way the interview started. I felt like we were drinking lemonade on the porch in Kennebunkport. We talked of his affinity for both owners involved in the Super Bowl, New England's Robert Kraft and Carolina's Jerry Richardson, and also chatted about a fellow Andover man in Bill Belichick.

ME: Who's the best football player you've ever met, Mr. President?

POTUS: Best one I've ever met?

ME: Mm-hmm.

POTUS: Well, if you put it this way, the one I feel I know pretty well is Roger Staubach. Not only was he a great football player, but then he went on to be very successful in life and our paths have crossed once in a while. I think I'd have to put Roger down. He's the one that I feel is up there on Cloud . . . way up there on Cloud Ten or whatever.

Now, he *really* began to sound like Dana Carvey.

ME: Did you watch the Super Bowl while you were at the White House as a sitting president?

POTUS: Oh, I'm sure I did. I just can't remember.

ME: Okay.

POTUS: I can't remember where I had breakfast yesterday.

ME: Okay.

POTUS: I'm almost eighty. So I can't remember any of the details at all.

ME: Your son, the current president right now—

POTUS: He'll be watching it.

ME: He'll be watching it?

POTUS: I'm confident he will.

I asked him which foreign leader was the biggest sports fan he'd ever met and he said Carlos Menem of Argentina, which I'm confident will be the only mention of Carlos Menem of Argentina in the history of NFL Network. We talked some about golf and how much his wife, Barbara, was giving him grief over his decision to celebrate his 80th birthday by jumping out of a plane with the Army Golden Knights.

POTUS: She said to me, "One way or another, this is going to be your final jump!" and I said, "Hey, phrase it a little differently will you?" People say, "Why do you [jump]?" Well, I do it for a lot of reasons. One, it's a physical thrill, but also it shows that when you get to be old that doesn't mean you have to stop having fun. It's why I like to go sixty miles an hour in my boat. Or why I love to root at all these ball games.

ME: It's the competition.

POTUS: That's right. And I think— You know, I'm sure I made plenty of mistakes as president, but I think part of my motivation came from the athletic experience. It's a lot like politics.

"All right, it's time to wrap it up," producer Eric Weinberger said in my ear. "Time to say good-bye to your new friend, the president."

I knew exactly how I wanted to end the interview.

ME: Can you do us one favor and call your son in the White House and have him call his local cable operator to get NFL Network? Would you mind doing that for—

POTUS: Maybe they've got it. I don't know. They've got almost every network I've ever seen when I go there.

ME: Then hopefully that's where he'll tune right after he watches the Super Bowl.

With that, we shook hands and the commissioner and McNair quickly mounted the stage to thank Mr. Bush. I stood there with the three mighty power brokers as they chatted until I suddenly realized I had no business being in this high-powered clique . . . and slowwwwwly backed away. There's another picture of that moment, too.

Later, when the commissioner and McNair sat down for their interview, I felt the need to get some brownie points with the boss.

What in the world am I doing in this conversation? *(NFL Network)*

"Not that I'm looking for anything extra in my paycheck, Commissioner, but when the former president was here I told him to call his son and have him call his local cable operator and request NFL Network."

"Well, that would be a positive thing," the commissioner said, "but you might have overreached with that suggestion."

For those not conversant in the language, that's commissioner speak for "smart-ass." Now, interviewing a commissioner and a president would be a full day in itself, certainly for a network not yet three months old. But there's so much more to tell you.

In between the Bush and Tagliabue chats, the lively quartet from CBS's *NFL Today* pregame show visited the set—Jim Nantz, Boomer Esiason, Dan Marino, and Deion Sanders, the last making his very first appearance on a network he would join two years later as an analyst. It became obvious the four had heard enough of each other all year long as they chirped at one another throughout the entire 14-minute interview. All holy heck broke loose when Nantz brought up his pet peeve, sudden death overtime. Nantz steadfastly believes the NFL should outlaw the coin flip and pass a new rule guaranteeing both teams at least one possession in overtime. For support, Nantz mentioned that venerable *New York Times* Pulitzer Prize–winning sports columnist Dave Anderson agreed.

Deion countered by saying he had never heard of Dave Anderson, but instead knew of "a guy back home named Pookie Anderson." Deion then challenged anyone on the set—crew included—to claim they knew of Dave Anderson.

Nantz was beside himself.

NANTZ: You know, I took Deion into CBS. The *first* time I took him into CBS, I said, "I wanna show you where Walter Cronkite announced that JFK had been assassinated." And he said, "Who's Walter Cronkite?" I swear to God.
DEION: You're lying. Quit lying.

NANTZ: You did.
DEION: That is a *lie.*

NANTZ: You did!
DEION: That's a— Come on, every brother in America knows who Walter Cronkite is.

NANTZ: Come on.

Guests collide: Jim Nantz and Boomer Esiason chat it up with Bush 41 before duking it out with Deion. *(NFL Network)*

DEION: Nobody don't know Dave Anderson. I know a bro back home named Pookie Anderson.

NANTZ: Come on.
DEION: And Pookie said, "The best team will win [in overtime], forget the coin toss."

NANTZ: This is nuts.
DEION: Forget [changing] the overtime [rules]. The best team will win. Pookie Anderson said that.

MARINO: Just let it play out [with a coin toss].
BOOMER: *(To Nantz)* Whoa, I'm telling you. You're fired up, man.

ME: This is great. It's Houston. The Super Bowl is in [Nantz's] town.
NANTZ: *(Not letting it go)* Walter Cronkite—

DEION: That's a blatant lie! That's a blatant lie that you told about Walter Cronkite.

To change the subject, I then asked the sartorially splendid Sanders if he had picked out his suit for the Sunday pregame show (not yet knowing he had almost 2,000 suits at home). Sanders said he wouldn't know until game day since he brought 12 different suits to Houston. Ever the needler, Boomer brought it back to Nantz and another unorthodox idea Nantz had apparently been espousing all year.

BOOMER: On a later show, you should talk to him about the laser light that he would like to have over the goal line to ensure the ball crosses the plane.
NANTZ: That would be amazing. That will seriously happen.

DEION: Sounds like Dr. Evil.
BOOMER: Right, exactly.

NANTZ: The football one day will be specially encoded—

MARINO: *(Exasperated, like he's heard it before)* So, when it breaks the plane—

NANTZ: *(Shouting to be heard)* The football will be encoded and so when the football crosses the goal line, we don't have all these ridiculous close calls! *(Everyone starts laughing.)* Seriously, it's no different than a photo finish!

MARINO: Right, so there's a satellite and you beam it off. Another beam comes back—

NANTZ: There's a chip inside the ball.

MARINO: A chip inside the ball. That's it.

NANTZ: Save me this tape. The technology is already being developed and your ultimate bosses *(Nantz pointed at me.)* are working on it, so that's all I'll say. I rest my case.

BOOMER: Dave Anderson wrote about that.

DEION: Pookie Anderson.

Fifteen minutes after the classic interview, I strolled into the CBS offices mere steps from our set to thank Nantz for the appearance, and he was *still* steaming about Dave Anderson. By the way, Wednesday was now only half over.

After lunch, I interviewed the three finalists for the (sponsored!) FedEx Air Award—Daunte Culpepper, Steve McNair, and Peyton Manning, the latter two had just split the 2003 MVP Award. At the time, we were beginning to experiment with our interview process—having the subjects ask each other questions rather than only me being the one to pose them. So I asked Peyton if he had a question for either of his two counterparts.

ME: I know I might be putting you on the spot, but you audible quite well.

MANNING: I guess I'll ask them both what's it like to be able to lower your shoulder and run over a middle linebacker like Ray Lewis or Zach Thomas? I would like to be able to do that. [At 6 foot 5, Manning is taller but still slighter in build than Culpepper or McNair.] Everybody asks me what it's like to get hit, but I don't know what it's like to hit anybody. So tell me what it's like after you run over a strong safety or a linebacker? Start with you, Steve.

MCNAIR: Well, you have to pick and choose when you do it. You have to catch them off guard a little bit, but it feels good because you're tired of receiving the hits—
MANNING : I hear you.

MCNAIR:—and when you have the opportunity to go out and, you know, catch a guy off balance and hit him and take advantage of that, it feels good. When you get up, and instead of them looking over at you, you're looking over at them, it feels real good.
MANNING: It's hard for me to hear these answers, because it's not gonna happen for me. Daunte, before you answer, I don't know what you're listed in the program, but what did you play at in Week 15, weight-wise, because you look like you're running the 4.4 40 out there, so I gotta know how much you weigh. And I want the truth here, on NFL Network, no holding back.

ME: This is the access we have on *Total Access*.
CULPEPPER: Well, you know, two hundred and sixty-five pounds, man.

Manning laughed.

MANNING: Okay, that's not even human. That's not human. But what's it like? I've seen you run over a lot of guys.
CULPEPPER: Man, it's just like Steve said. You get tired of getting hit, so when I get down the field, like you say, you gotta pick and choose. My rookie year, I'd run down there and take on two or three guys. But that's how you get injured because these guys get paid, too—to hit you hard. So I pick and choose. But when it's third and five and I come out of the pack and I see that first down mark, I gotta get it, you know?
MANNING: *(Nodding)* Go get it.

Manning sat transfixed. I did, too. And not just with the interview, but the whole day, which, believe it or not, was only *now* about to reach a stirring finale. Thirty minutes after the three quarterbacks departed the set, a three-time MVP quarterback arrived—none other than Brett Favre, winner of something called the (sponsored!) Snickers Hungriest Player of the Year Award. To spice up the interview, we had the following join in: Sterling Sharpe, Favre's first career go-to receiver; Warren Sapp, whose many good-natured on-field jawing matches with Favre are the stuff of legend, and Terrell Davis, who denied Favre a second Super Bowl ring by winning Super Bowl XXXII MVP for Denver against Green Bay.

Favre tapped Sterling on the knee.

"He raised me," Favre said, before tapping Sapp. "And you aged me."

I was just learning that everybody laughs when they're around Brett Favre.

"When I got to play with him, I had been in the league four years," Sharpe said. "And football wasn't fun. It was a job. And then to watch Brett come in the huddle and notice people in the stands and say, 'Hey, have you ever eaten at this restaurant?' you know, things that were the farthest away from trying to pick up a first down and score a touchdown. It relaxed you and allowed you to go out and make football fun again.

Brett Favre flanked by *(left to right)* Sterling Sharpe, Warren Sapp, and Terrell Davis. *(NFL Network)*

"That was probably the most important thing that I took away from the game after playing with him was the fact that it was never a job. It was never a business. It was always fun."

However, Favre had little fun during the 2003 season that was wrapping up in Houston with Super Bowl XXXVIII. His father, Irv, died of a heart attack in late December, leading to a *Monday Night Football* performance for the ages—four touchdowns in the *first half* against the Raiders just two days after his father's passing. The Packers instantly became America's Team. Millions rooted for Favre to win another Super Bowl for his dad. But Favre's season came to an end by his own hand—a brutal overtime interception in Philadelphia that cost Green Bay the game in the divisional playoffs. Favre hadn't spoken publicly since that loss—until he showed up on the *NFL Total Access* set in Houston.

"It's been obviously an up-and-down month and a half, but time sort of heals everything," Favre said when I asked about his father. "I miss my dad and will always miss him."

It kick-started quite a soliloquy.

"[The death] was a shock, not only to me, but to a lot of people. But, you know, I've dealt with it. I'd like to thank him the best way I know how, and that's to play football and play it at a high level. And I knew over time, it would feel a little bit better, but I'm still reminded of it every day. When I got home last week, I'm thumbing through my cell phone that I have at home. And I, you know, see Dad's number there. Just things like that and you know it's never gonna go away.

"Not that you want it to. I always want him to be in the forefront of my mind, but it would've been nice to continue on [in the playoffs]. And I know that the country, in some respects, was pulling for us. But we didn't do it. And that was unfortunate that [the season] stopped, 'cause then you have to kind of dwell on the negative things."

Sapp eventually took things over, revealing "I can't get you to talk to me no more" after a play. Favre revealed his offensive lineman forbade him from smack talking with Sapp because "they say it's tough enough to deal with you without me getting you all riled up."

Sapp laughed and cut to the chase: "How many more years do I get to chase you?"

Favre talked about loving the game and playing it only for one more ring, not for statistics. As we all know, Favre still feels the same way, toying with retirement every off-season since. Back on Super Bowl Wednesday 2004, after his father's death, he was particularly contemplative and offered insight that no doubt still has relevance today.

"I love doing what I do. And I like to think I do it the best of my ability, but when I get away from it, there ain't nothing like getting on a lawn mower and cutting a little grass. I mean, I never thought I would say that. I honestly never thought I would say that. But I'm saying it today."

The interview lasted 18 soulful minutes. Nobody wanted it to end, but it did, with Favre offering one last thought on mourning his father.

"You know that old cliché you hear all the time, 'He would want me to play.' I'd always heard that, too, and I never thought I'd have to deal with it. But I sat in my room [in Oakland] that night and I said, 'Here *I am* having to deal with this.' And I never— You know, that's the call you never wanna hear. Whether it's your father or anyone. And I don't wish it upon anyone. I mean, it was great the way the fans and the country rallied around that. But I don't wish it upon anyone. If I could trade it and throw fifty picks in that Oakland game and not make the playoffs, I hate to say it, but I would trade that right now."

And that was that. It's still the only time Favre has sat down in person on *NFL Total Access* in any venue.

By day's end, I felt just like the rest of the crew—spent but exhilarated. We had an American commander in chief and the NFL's commander in chief as our guests. And talk about your quarterback group: We welcomed Favre, Marino, Manning, Esiason, Culpepper, and McNair on the same set on the same day. With Deion Sanders, Warren Sapp, Terrell Davis, and Sterling Sharpe. Plus, we somehow managed to interview four actual Super Bowl participants that day, too—Carolina's Mike Minter and Michael Rucker and New England's Troy Brown and Richard Seymour, along with our special cohost for the day, then-Vikings head coach Mike Tice. It's a day we still talk about, referring to it as "The Big Wednesday."

Needless to say, Wednesday's two-hour Super Bowl edition of *NFL Total Access* couldn't contain it all. We bumped the Deion and Nantz smack fest to Thursday's show, which was already jam-packed, what with Sapp's old college teammate at Miami—Dwayne "The Rock" Johnson— visiting our set. Plus, Janet Jackson and the rest of the halftime entertainers were coming to town.

THURSDAY

To DATE, THE ONLY event that's caused more Americans to turn on their television sets for something other than a Super Bowl was Hawkeye Pierce bidding good-bye, farewell, and amen to his comrades at the 4077th Mobile Army Surgical Hospital in Korea. Yep, in terms of the highest average audience in TV history, your current Neilsen Media Service rankings look like this:

1. *M*A*S*H* series finale, 1983   50.15 million homes
2. Super Bowl XLI, 2007   47.48 million homes

And that Super Bowl between the Colts and the Bears isn't even the most-viewed Super Bowl in TV history. That distinction belongs to Super Bowl XXXVIII, for which an estimated total of 144.4 million people tuned in to watch the Patriots and Panthers go down to the wire—nearly 5 million more than the total audience that clicked on Super Bowl XLI. Now, if you want to go global, Super Bowl XL got beamed out to a record 234 countries on Planet Earth, including Kazakhstan and Vatican City. Yes, both Borat and Pope Benedict XVI (not to be confused with cornerback Marquez Pope or Super Bowl XVI) watched with the rest of us as Jerome Bettis bussed off into the sunset.

So, if no entertainment program can bring in the eyeballs quite like the Super Bowl, then why, one might wonder, would the Super Bowl require extra entertainment? Well, because it's the Super Bowl. Plus, every football game needs halftime entertainment, and, at the Super Bowl, that means no ordinary marching band will do. You've got to kick it up a notch with platinum-record artists or Rock and Roll Hall of Famers. The day those all-world musicians first hit town during Super Bowl Week is Thursday.

Their arrival completely overshadows the final media availability of the players for the week. After Thursday, the Super Bowl participants go into virtual lockdown. The media can no longer reach them. Therefore, you'd think a big deal would be made of the combatants' final comments prior to kickoff, but not when, say, Paul McCartney rides into town on the same day.

When McCartney arrived on Thursday of the Patriots/Eagles Super Bowl Week in Jacksonville, he dwarfed even the final media availability of Terrell Owens, which, as we know, is saying a lot when every member of the professional football media is amassed in one place. On that day, however, that place was Conference Room A of the Jacksonville Convention Center where the lovable former Mop Top made his first appearance at Super Bowl XXXIX. By all accounts it was, without question, the largest gathering for a Super Bowl press conference *ever*—and it had nothing to do with football.

Now, I know what you're thinking: *Duh! He's only one of the more famous people on the planet, Rich. Of course, he's going to attract a crowd.* True. But, at this event, McCartney served as the first Super Bowl halftime entertainer since Janet Jackson and Justin Timberlake forever baked the words "wardrobe malfunction" into our national lexicon the year before. In fact, according to a media research firm called Carma, the phrase "wardrobe malfunction" appeared in 5,028 stories in major U.S. consumer and business publications, newspapers, and major TV and radio broadcast networks in 2004. Media interest, shall we say, was high. Of course, McCartney had the press in the palm of his hand.

"I don't have a wardrobe to malfunction," McCartney said, flashbulbs popping with his every gesture. "Because we're going to play naked!"

At this juncture, your humble narrator was pacing in the back of the room. The NFL had actually put a clause in McCartney's contract requiring he make an appearance on *NFL Total Access*. Talk about huge. A sit-down chat with Sir Paul? That would make George Bush Senior look like Pete Best. I immediately called my high school friend and Fox News correspondent James Rosen, who, by his sobering stand-ups on the White House lawn, few can tell is an A-One Beatles freak. The guy's firstborn has a middle name of Lennon. James gave me about 20 ideas for questions. My head was spinning. I envisioned interviewing McCartney at the piano on the *NFL Total Access* set, sitting next to him like Stevie Wonder. *Play us a sad song and make it better as we go to break, Paul.* I could hardly sleep the night before. To paraphrase a line from Paul circa 1965, that was so unwise, ahhhh, the night before.

Because none of it mattered.

The closest I got to McCartney was three feet. He came out of the press conference surrounded by a posse of handlers and security and, within five minutes, was in a car speeding away from the building. What was the NFL going to do? Fire McCartney because he blew me off? Charles Coplin, the league's vice president of entertainment who also serves as NFL Network programming chief, looked despondent. He actually came over to me and offered an unnecessary apology.

"I'll make it up to you next year," he said.

Another Super Bowl Thursday, another explosion of flashbulbs. The Rolling Stones had just entered the room. Mick Jagger, Keith Richards, Ron Wood, and Charlie Watts, your halftime entertainment for Super Bowl XL, in Detroit—right there in the flesh. As expected, Jagger and Richards did most of the talking during the press conference.

"I lived in New York for a long time in the seventies and eighties and, in those days, I did follow football a lot," Jagger said when asked about being an NFL fan. "I mean, I can remember Lynn Swann, I can remember him playing. But I must say I haven't really been following football in recent years. I've been following soccer."

"Tiddlywinks is actually our sport," Richards said.

"Yes, that's Keith's game," Jagger retorted.

The media ate it up. So did I, because I was soaking in all the information I could for the separate sit-down interviews I was scheduled to have with Jagger and Richards after the press conference. Just me and Mick. Then me and Keith. At the Super Bowl.

"And this time, it *will* happen," Coplin assured me earlier in the day.

Sure enough, NFL Network stationed a camera crew in a room just one floor above the press conference in the Renaissance Center in downtown Detroit. I sat down in my chair and waited. Suddenly, a side door in the room opened up and, sure enough, in came Mick Jagger. We shook hands and our producer, Jason Wormser, locked the main door to the room.

"What are you going to ask me?" Jagger asked as he clipped a microphone to his shirt.

I had flashbacks to George Bush 41, perhaps the only time you'll ever see a comparison between these two men in black-and-white. I told Jagger that we'd talk some music and football. He nodded and clapped his hands together, which meant, in essence, start me up. So we did.

But wouldn't you know it! Right in the middle of Jagger's first answer, a thundering knock came from the locked main door. We all jumped. I couldn't believe it. The cameras stopped rolling, Wormser opened the door and we all craned our necks, including Mick Jagger, to see who the offending party was.

It was Charles Coplin. Of all people. The guy who made this happen had just busted it up. It's something I've since teased him about constantly.

"Sorry," he said.

Take two.

ME: Pleased to be joined by Mick Jagger. Thank you.
JAGGER: Hey, nice to see you.

ME: Thank you for joining us on NFL Network. You've never played a Super Bowl event before.
JAGGER: That's correct.

ME: Has that been something you've always wanted to do?
JAGGER: Not really. *(Laughs.)*

Yikes. What a way to start. I could feel everyone in the room cringe, especially my door-pounding friend in the back of the room who had spent much time and energy to sign the Rolling Stones to this gig that they, uh, apparently never really wanted to do?

ME: But it's something I guess you were offered to do and you guys said, "Sure."
JAGGER: Here we are. No, you know, these things have a momentum of their own and have a way of crossing, so you're on tour in the United States and the Super Bowl comes up. So you're asked to do it, and you can do it.

ME: Right.
JAGGER: I mean, I'm not sure if I was sitting at home in London and, you know, I would want to do it just on its own.

ME: Right.
JAGGER: But when we're on tour, it's a great thing to do.

I figured we'd better switch topics fast. So I mentioned soccer, which I know is his brand of football, and it got Mick, if you will, rolling. As it turned out, he knew a lot more about the current state of the

Mick and I talk American football. *(NFL Network)*

NFL than he let on in his press conference. With the Steelers getting set to take on the Seahawks, he brought up his Lynn Swann memory again and then, well, read for yourself:

JAGGER: But I think the thing about the Super Bowl is that it's super hyped up, of course.
ME: Yes.

JAGGER: Why shouldn't it be? And unfortunately, a lot of times . . . Well, it's the same with the World Cup soccer final, it . . . it tends not to live up sometimes to the lead-up to the games.
ME: Mmm. That's what happens, yes.

JAGGER: But this year, you know, I think it could be rather interesting. I mean, I'm sure you share my— I mean, I think both teams are kind of set up for really quite an interesting final.
ME: *(Pleasantly surprised)* Yes.

JAGGER: And for various reasons, you know. Because I think both teams can play both kind of games, you know.

ME: *(By Jove, he's got it!)* Right.

JAGGER: They can either pass or they can rush or whatever.
ME: I love it. I never thought I'd break down the Super Bowl with Mick Jagger before. This is fantastic.

JAGGER: Well, I'm not *(Laughs.)* . . . you can tell me more.
ME: No, no, you're doing very well on your own.

JAGGER: But that's why I think that this final— This Super Bowl could be . . . could be interesting. And you got, I mean, the Steelers were not really fancied this year.
ME: That's correct!

JAGGER: I mean, they were really not. But the Seahawks were really seriously fancied but yet here we are with the Steelers being the favorites I think, right?

I was floored. Mick freaking Jagger turning into Jimmy the Greek in front of my very eyes. I could hardly get out my words.

ME: It's— You are— You're on fire right now, Mick.
JAGGER: Well . . .

ME: I mean, if I could only play a musical instrument, I'd suggest we swap roles.

Despite the rocky start, the interview ended well after all. We shook hands, and as soon as Jagger left the room, a different woman from the Stones posse entered to prepare the room for Keith Richards. She placed a bottle of water along with an ashtray and a lighter directly at the foot of Keith's chair.

"You never know when Keith might be thirsty or want a smoke," she said.

I asked her if this was standard for every one of Keith's interviews and she said yes. Richards then rolled into the room, his nappy hair pushed back by his trademark headband.

"Hello, everyone!" he said, waving to the whole crew.

Indeed, the Richards interview had a much different tone than the one with Jagger. For instance, this was Keith's response to whether he had ever been to a Super Bowl:

"I've seen a few on TV, but it should be an experience. I feel like we're sort of taking the place of the ol' marching band. And apparently you can meet the cheerleaders that way."

Or whether he had a favorite Super Bowl memory from watching it on TV: "Only from certain friends being very joyous because they had just won some money. That's what I remember about Super Bowls, thinking '*This* is what's got the Americans going, huh?'"

At no time during the interview did Keith reach for his lighter or bottle of water. They went untouched. I thought of snagging the lighter. But then I thought about how pathetic that would be. When I got back downstairs to the *NFL Total Access* set on Radio Row, I told our stage manager Joann Kamay that I wanted the Keith Richards setup for interviews from now on. She rolled her eyes. But, sure enough, when I sat down on the set on Friday, my left foot kicked something. I looked underneath the desk and saw an ashtray with a lighter and a bottle of water.

"You said you wanted it!" Joann laughed.

Without question, the most bizarre Super Bowl Thursday I've experienced was the Colts-Bears one in Miami. Well, anytime giant paper flamingos ridden by people in full referee outfits and face paint take part in a Super Bowl press conference—that qualifies as bizarre. Indeed, Cirque du Soleil provided the pregame entertainment for Super Bowl XLI and enjoyed quite the colorful media availability.

Several "flamingos" crashed the stage, as officials from Cirque du Soleil doled out information never previously disseminated at a Super Bowl. Before the Colts and Bears could have at it, Cirque du Soleil would transform the Dolphins Stadium turf into a Salvador Dali painting. Their pregame performance included the following: 6 stilt walkers, 29 Cirque du Soleil artists, 48 salsa dancers, 54 "extreme cheerleaders," and one Gloria Estefan of Miami Sound Machine fame. They'd all perform on a massive set with 30-foot-long alligators, 15-foot-tall "bikini couples," and those giant flamingos with refs on top.

Alrighty.

Would you believe things could still get stranger? Well, The Stranger himself was coming to the podium. None other than Billy Joel then held

one of the odder Q&A sessions in the history of Q&A. Joel was perform-
ing the national anthem and seemed bewildered that singing a song that
wouldn't last 90 seconds necessitated a press conference. His acerbic
New York persona was on full display. The questions he got didn't help.
First up:

> **Q:** Hello, Billy. I'm representing Nippon TV from Japan. When you
> have a concert, do you think it's a similar feeling for the players going
> into Super Sunday?

Billy paused.

> **BJ:** I don't know. I've never played on Super Sunday.
> **Q:** All right, then, a tougher question.

> **BJ:** There's a tougher one than that?
> **Q:** Who's gonna win the game?

Another pause.

> **BJ:** Who's gonna win? I have no idea. I was rooting for New York,
> so . . .
> **Q:** Over here. I'm from Sky Sports in the U.K. Billy, your fans in the
> U.K. will be delighted to know that you're singing the national an-
> them. Do you have a message for your fans in the U.K.?

This pause lasted a full five seconds.

> **BJ:** I'm not really a message guy.

He then talked about the difficulty of singing the song—calling
"America the Beautiful" a better tune—and termed himself a "dinosaur"
since he had previously sung the anthem at the Stanley Cup, the World
Series, and Super Bowl XXIII.

> **Q:** How does it feel to be the first performer to sing the national an-
> them twice at the Super Bowl?
> **BJ:** I don't know. I haven't done it yet.

Q: Your expectations at least?

BJ: Expectations? I think it'll be fun. I mean, I'm just singing the national anthem. I ain't doing the halftime show. Prince is doing the work.

Q: Over here, Billy. You haven't put out an album in a while. Are the creative juices still there? And I don't know if anybody's ever said this to you before but you've kind of morphed into a much younger version of noted meshuggener comic Alan King?

I'm not kidding. An awkward titter came from the audience. Billy stared at the guy and took a swig of water.

BJ: Is that a question?

Q: Yes.

BJ: What's the question?

Q: Well, you just kind of look like him and I was wondering if anybody's ever told you that.

BJ: Yeah, I've heard that. Look, I ain't no matinee idol and I never have been, so . . . What was the first part?

Q: About the new album.

BJ: There's isn't a new album.

Q: Is there one coming?

BJ: I don't know. If I feel like writing an album, I'll write an album. Today I don't feel like writing one.

And this went on and on . . . and on. For 10 minutes. Eventually, a reporter from TV Azteca (not the blonde from Media Day) caught on to Billy's vibe.

Q: When you did the national anthem at Super Bowl XXIII, you didn't have a press crowd like this at the time. What do you think of the Super Bowl evolving into more of an entertainment show than a sports show?

No, Billy, I don't think you look like Alan King. *(Kevin Terrell/NFL Network)*

BJ: Well, I think people have always recognized that it is a form of entertainment. It's the biggest TV day of the year; it's the biggest event for that medium. No, I didn't do a press conference before Super Bowl XXIII, I just kinda went out and sang the song. I'm actually kinda surprised I'm doing this [press conference] to sing the national anthem. Prince is doing the halftime show. He's should be the guy to do all this.

Prince, however, wanted no part of the "all this" to which Billy referred. After the Joel press conference, a group of hurried workers removed the backdrop to reveal a set of drums, keyboards, and mikes. You see, Prince preferred to let his music do the talking with the media. Smart guy. It worked out so well, I wouldn't be surprised if halftime performers will only perform for, rather than parry with, the media on future Super Bowl Thursdays.

Before he took the stage, Prince, wearing a bright orange suit, walked past the NFL Network green room near the press conference room. The man could be 100 pounds soaking wet, and if he's 5 feet tall, then I'm the artist formerly known as Yao Ming. But what's jammed inside that package can not be quantified. Prince tore the roof off the place.

He performed three songs—"Johnny B. Goode," "Anotherloverholenyohead" and "Get on the Boat"—and, within seconds, had the hard-bitten media audience tapping their feet. Some even began clapping and singing along. After seven-plus minutes of flat-out rocking, he got a standing ovation. From the media. Now, *that's* a press conference.

"See you at the Super Bowl," Prince said.

Only three more days.

FRIDAY

THE CELL PHONE BUZZED in Steve Mariucci's pants pocket. He took it out to look at the caller ID even though he was on live television. Normally, that's a cardinal television sin. All cell phones and BlackBerry devices must be turned off prior to airtime. On the *NFL Total Access* set, we have a system of fines: Five bucks for a cell phone that rings. Ten bucks if it rings on the air. But, in this case, Mooch had a great excuse—he was waiting for a call from Brett Favre, who had just told a local Mississippi newspaper that he would be returning for a 17th NFL season in 2007.

"This is Brett!" Mariucci smiled and held up his phone.

"Well, go ahead and answer it!" said cohost Fran Charles. They were anchoring live wrap-up coverage of the State of the NFL Address delivered by the commissioner every Super Bowl Friday. During Commissioner Roger Goodell's press conference, Mariucci had left his old Green Bay pupil a voice mail to see if the report coming out of Mississippi was true. Mariucci flipped open his phone.

"Hey, Brett," Mariucci said as our camera zoomed in. "Is it true?"

You heard the buzz of Favre's voice through the microphone clipped to Mariucci's tie.

"Yep, he's coming back," Mariucci relayed, before laughing at something Favre said.

"Brett says he's watching us in his kitchen right now!"

If Mooch only knew how to work the speakerphone function on his cell phone. He's not well versed on that stuff. Earlier that season, he received the first text message of his life, but it took him three weeks to realize the yellow envelope on his cell phone meant he had a text waiting. It was from Deion Sanders, by the way.

At any rate, no one knows why Favre chose the Friday of Super Bowl XLI to let his cat out of the bag, but it makes sense. If I were a football player and wanted to make an announcement, I'd do it on Super Bowl Friday. Again, the Super Bowl players are no longer available to the media, who are officially looking for something on which to feast. That's why, one assumes, Emmitt Smith used the Super Bowl Friday platform in Jacksonville to personally announce his retirement from the NFL.

The league's all-time leading rusher brought his whole family to Jacksonville, where he held a tear-filled and star-studded news conference in the very same room where McCartney had appeared the day before. On the Friday before the Patriots and Eagles played Super Bowl XXXIX, Emmitt Smith ruled the news cycle.

His eyes still glistening from the good long cry he had had at his press conference, Smith strolled down Radio Row in the Prime Osborn Convention Center and right into our *NFL Total Access* set, where I interviewed him with longtime Cowboys safety Darren Woodson, who had retired himself just weeks before. I asked Smith if, when he first came in as a rookie, he had ever envisioned finishing up with an astounding 19,000 yards.

EMMITT: I didn't imagine nineteen thousand. I did imagine seventeen-plus. [Walter Payton held the rushing record for eighteen years, finishing with 16,726 yards.] My goal as a rookie—and I wrote it down—was to become the all-time leading rusher. Now, that was 1990 and I knew that Payton did it in thirteen [seasons]. So, I knew I had to do it at least thirteen years to get close to it or have a chance at doing it. And so, that was my goal. And once I got it, I just wanted to extend that [record] out and create another level of goal and pushed that number farther out.

ME: Where did you write it down? In a book?

EMMITT: I wrote it down on a piece of paper like I normally do every year. I create my goal list, of what I want to do as a team and then what I want to do as an individual.

ME: Then you just file that away? And you look at it later on or something?

As soon as he retired, Emmitt Smith *(center)* joined me and fellow former Cowboy Darren Woodson on *NFL Total Access.* *(Joann Kamay)*

EMMITT: File it away and look at it later on. Then come back next year and do the same thing again. My high school coach always told the team that it's only a dream until you write it down—*then* it becomes a goal. I've always dreamed of [breaking Payton's record]. So, I figured I'll write it down and it became a goal. And, now, I've actually physically done it.

ME: So what advice would you give to all the Tim Brown, Jerome Betties, and Jerry Rices of the world? [All three players were pondering retirement at the time.]

EMMITT: What I'm gonna say to Tim Brown is what Tim Brown said to me.

ME: Okay.

EMMITT: Just because you can, don't mean that you should. *(Laugh.)*

ME: He said that to you?

EMMITT: That's what he said to me last year. Last summer before training camp, I was over at his house, at his daughter's birthday party, me and my family. And we were talking how this might be our last year, et cetera, et cetera. He said to me, "Just because you can, don't mean that you should." And that was great advice. All those things just weighed on my mind throughout the whole entire year, so he planted a nice little seed in me at that time.

Interestingly enough, Brown retired later that off-season and so did Jerry Rice, but only after trying to hook up with the Broncos in training camp. Bettis stayed on with the Steelers one more year and retired in the manner every player dreams of—by winning the Super Bowl.

As for Smith's future, I asked him his plans. His answer is quite interesting in hindsight.

EMMITT: I look forward to spending a little bit of time with Roger Staubach in terms of trying to further my business relationships in the real estate market. I've talked with him and look forward to spending some time with him. But also, I look forward to perhaps even sitting in one of these chairs with y'all one day. Talking about the game of football or doing something with the Network period.

ME: I think the NFL Network executives in the truck just leapt out of their seats. They might be bursting through that door in a moment.

EMMITT: Oh, well. Okay.

ME: Look out. They might come at you.

EMMITT: I'm available for all kinds of conversation now.

Within seven months, Emmitt was indeed part of *NFL Total Access,* working with me and fellow league MVP Terrell Davis every Monday night before and after the ABC game. Now, he's talking football for ESPN. At the time, however, there was no mention of dancing. No one had any idea, Smith included, that he wasn't done winning championships—and by doing the cha-cha on national television, of all things.

Now let's get back to The Precious.

As I mentioned earlier, it's on full Friday display at the final head coach press conference of Super Bowl week. It sits there all beautiful and shiny on a table off to the side of the microphone podium. Perfectly polished, The Precious sparkles in the lights. Perhaps it mocks the head coach while it gleams in the periphery. After all, it's *right there*. Both Super Bowl head coaches just successfully negotiated twenty-six grueling weeks of training camp and regular season play and whatever hellacious January gauntlet the Football Gods had just conjured up—all to get at The Precious. By week's end, however, only one will touch it. Yet there it tantalizes, while the head coach stands at the podium mere feet away and answers the same question he's already been asked 30 times in the week with the very same answer for the 30th and final time.

Perhaps just to make it stand out even more, the league places the Lombardi Trophy in between two pieces of plastic—the helmets of both Super Bowl teams, each face mask pointed smack in its direction. The imagery could not be starker. A confrontation lurks. One team will make history and hoist The Precious to much fanfare while another gets to

C'mon Lovie! You know you want The Precious! (*Rogash*)

watch and never forget. It is why, as Bill Parcells once told his players, you lift all them weights.

I've had the good fortune to be around The Precious and feel its power. You see, for the first few days of Super Bowl Week, it sits right there on our set. Some sports shows use nice potted plants as their set dressing. On *NFL Total Access at the Super Bowl,* we've got the Lombardi Trophy. So, I've been around it for an absurd number of hours. More, probably, than most people who have ever won it. Hands down, it's one of the best perks of the job.

Because you were kind enough to purchase this book, I will now tell you all I know about The Precious:

- It stands 22 inches tall, weighs 7 pounds and takes 72 man-hours to create.
- It is made by Tiffany and Co. and is made entirely of sterling silver.
- Because it is made by Tiffany, it does indeed have its own blue bag.
- It has an estimated cost of $12,500.
- League personnel refer to it by its proper initials VLT—Vince Lombardi Trophy.
- I know. Calling it VLT does make it sound like a sandwich. I'll stop with the bullet points now.

When the actual Vince Lombardi hoisted The Precious, it was called the World Championship Game Trophy. Upon Lombardi's death in 1970, the league renamed the trophy in his honor, meaning the first official winning of VLT was by the Colts in Super Bowl V. Bart Starr, MVP of Super Bowls I and II (how's *that* for a résumé line?), once visited our set in Detroit. I asked him what Lombardi would say if he knew his name was on the trophy.

"He might tear up because a side of him that you probably never heard much about is he could cry rather easily," Starr said. "He had a great sense of humor, but he was very emotional. And I'm sure that if he could see that name on that trophy, he would tear up."

The Precious makes hard-ass grown men cry. The reason why it glistens in smudgeless glory is because the only people allowed to touch it with their bare hands are those who win it. Every other mere mortal on

Earth must wear a pair of white cloth gloves if they desire to handle the goods. To make sure no unsheathed grimy paws lay an oily finger on The Precious, two security guards are assigned to watch it around the clock.

No joke. It resides in its own blue bag in a nondescript black trunk brought to the set every day by security. Once the guards take VLT out of its packaging, their strict orders are to not let it out of their sight—and they do not mess around. The first day the Lombardi Trophy appeared on our Radio Row set in Miami, one of the guards physically stood over it *at attention* on the corner of the stage as we were going to air. Joann, our stage manager, had to shoo the man away, reminding him he could still stand vigil two feet away, off camera. In Jacksonville, however, one of the security guards ran onto the stage *on live TV* because Terry Bradshaw touched it without gloves.

The guard's name was Gwen. We all got to know Gwen during the week. Actually, we get to know VLT's security detail every year because of how much time they spend around the set. Gwen was a sweet lady, always smiling. Except for that time when Terry lunged for it.

Bradshaw was paying us a visit along with fellow *FOX NFL Sunday* analyst Howie Long à la Nantz, Deion, Dan, and Boomer in Houston the year before. Neither of them was taking a thing seriously, talking about chewing gum, my hair, Jimmy Johnson's hair, you name it. I tried to rein in the interview by pointing to our shiny set dressing, which they had won a combined five times in their playing days.

"As you know, there's nothing like hoisting that little Tiffany bauble right there. Do you guys ever miss that at all?"

Long said no and began to explain why, when Bradshaw suddenly leapt from his seat and crossed the set, heading directly for the Lombardi Trophy with his bare, outstretched hands. Gwen snapped to attention.

"Uh-oh. Oh, boy," I said. "You're supposed to have gloves with that."

Bradshaw reached and Gwen twitched. I felt compelled to call play-by-play of the scene.

"There's a security guard here and she just made a move. She just made a move. It's OK. It's OK."

Our director Jennifer Love zoomed in on Gwen.

"There she is. She almost went for you there, Terry."

At that point, Bradshaw, undaunted, plucked the Lombardi Trophy from the table.

The Precious as *NFL Total Access* set dressing. *(Rob Ohlandt)*

TERRY: There's not much to this.
HOWIE: What do you mean?

TERRY: There's no diamonds, no emeralds. Just a chunk of *stuff* that represents a wealth, you know, a wealth— I want to thank you.

Bradshaw then held VLT over his head, which was now officially too much for Gwen to take. She stormed the stage in her red Day-Glo security slicker. Four-time Super Bowl champion and MVP of Super Bowls XIII and XIV or not, Bradshaw was now waving The Precious around like it was made of Reynolds Wrap.

ME: Uh, oh. There she goes. She's on the set now.
HOWIE: What's your name?

ME: That's Gwen.
GWEN: I'm Gwen.

HOWIE: You packing? You got Mace, anything?
ME: Okay.

HOWIE: Yeah, you could take him.

Gwen wordlessly pointed at Bradshaw to put the Lombardi Trophy back down. Bradshaw backed down, put it down, and then sat down. Our stage manager, Joann, led Gwen back to her post. Everyone went back to their corners.

ME: There we go. There she goes. There goes Gwen.
HOWIE: Dance around, dance around him for two or three—

TERRY: For as much as that represents, what do you think that thing cost?
HOWIE: Twenty-four thousand dollars.

TERRY: Oh, like *you* know.
HOWIE: Yeah. About. Approximately.

ME: Well, it's peaked in value now that you've touched it.
TERRY: That's true.

Suddenly, someone finally got serious. Bradshaw had literally put the Lombardi Trophy back in its proper place. Then Long figuratively did so through the prism of one of the teams playing that Sunday.

"You know, at the end of the day, everybody talks about how the Patriots pay scale is around twenty-second in the league. And you take a guy like [New England linebacker] Tedy Bruschi, who re-signs for well below market value at that position. And some people in the league were a little bit disappointed, particularly agents. But really, when all is said and done, it's not about the house, it's not about the money, it's not about the cars. It's about the legacy, the ring, and winning."

You bet. It's about The Precious, which sadly gets taken away from the *NFL Total Access* set on the Friday of Super Bowl week. It has other places to go and people to see. The league puts it right in front of the coaches' noses at their final Friday press conference and then places it at the NFL Experience Fan Festival for the masses to behold. Eventually, the Vince Lombardi Trophy makes its way to the stadium on Sunday. Just like all of us.

SATURDAY

WITH THE WAY THE intensity ratchets up with each day of Super Bowl Week, you'd think Saturday would be completely off the charts—but you'd be wrong. Well, the party scene does get intense, thanks mostly to the popular Saturday night bashes held by *Sports Illustrated* (Is that Heidi or Petra?), *Playboy* (Is that real or fake?), and, most recently, the Hollywood-based Creative Artists Agency (There's TomKat!) That's all on the heels of the Friday night *Maxim* magazine bash, easily the best Super Bowl party held every year. (No offense to the others. I still need to get in to those parties. Plus-4, of course.) In Houston, the good folks of *Maxim* rented out an entire cattle ranch for their party and kicked it up a notch three years later in Miami, renting out the entire Sagamore Hotel on South Beach. When I say the entire hotel, I mean they turned the check-in desk into a bar and the lobby into the red carpet paparazzi spot. Out back, the pool area was wall-to-wall people stretching all the way to the beach several hundred feet away, where *Maxim* built a stage on which Fergie from the Black Eyed Peas performed. Now *that's* a Super Bowl party. It's tough to top on Saturday night, but many parties try, and most fans don't mind them trying. Thus, the day before the Super Bowl, things get a bit sleepy, literally and figuratively.

The Convention itself grinds to a virtual halt. The teams are hunkered down at their respective facilities, far from view. All the musical acts are busy in rehearsal. Because most sports talk shows broadcast only Monday through Friday, Radio Row suddenly becomes a ghost town. The current and former players who provided the listening fodder for Radio Row all week long are nowhere to be found; they're either on the golf course or pounding Gatorade after Friday night's festivities. But just when you thought there was nothing else to do except, you know, play the Super Bowl, the Pro Football Hall of Fame steps into the void and enshrines some people.

Well, the enshrining officially doesn't happen until the annual August ceremony in Canton, but the announcement as to who ultimately receives that honor is made every year on the Saturday before the Super Bowl. And, ever since 2005, your humble narrator has served as emcee for the press conference.

The day begins early in the morning when The Selectors—a group of 40 anointed members of the football media—convene in a room in the Super Bowl convention center and vote on which players should make it from a list of 17 finalists. I've never been to one of these meetings, but one must assume there is a spread or schmear of some sort. Maybe some coffee and danish. Why? Because the media likes to eat. And the voting process can take a *very* long time.

First, the finalist list—or Final Preliminary List as the Hall of Fame calls it—has to be narrowed down from 17 to 10. After that, another round of debates before another vote is taken to winnow the list down to six. Then everybody gives an up-or-down vote on the final six. Any remaining finalist who gets 80 percent of that vote is a freshly minted Hall of Famer. Got it?

It's also a very fickle process. You simply cannot predict what The Selectors might decide. In 2007, the recently retired commissioner, Paul Tagliabue, was a finalist, but didn't even survive the first cut, and these were the same writers who had placed him atop the Mount Rushmore of American sports leaders when he retired. Once Tagliabue eventually gets enshrined, will he be more worthy then than he was five months after his legendary stint as commissioner?

Just as with any major sports Hall of Fame, there are passionate cases to make concerning every finalist. However, this is the only voting process in which some of the finalists are actually in the same building, waiting for the official word, like the proverbial expectant father. I'm also waiting. So is the rest of the Super Bowl media, including NFL Network, to carry the event live whenever The Selectors finish their business.

Once that happens, Hall of Fame vice president of communications Joe Horrigan (one of the more affable fellows in all of football) enters the room and hands me an envelope. It contains two of the three final lists: those who made the cut down to 10 and those who survived the penultimate cut from 10 down to 6. It's my job to start the press conference by announcing that list. I'm not going to lie. I absolutely, positively, take a peek before the press conference begins.

It's a tremendous privilege, yet a terribly awkward one. That's because some of the game's all-time greats, greats that I grew up idolizing and watching on TV in the basement of my Staten Island home, are basically hearing from me that they didn't make it into the Hall of Fame. I think of that every time I read the cut list: I'm the Paul Revere of Disappointment.

Once I'm done bumming out the Art Monks and the Bob Kuechenbergs and the Andre Reeds of the world, the executive director of the Hall of Fame comes to the podium and announces which players of the final six—if not all six—have gained enshrinement. You can hear a pin drop. Then a fire drill breaks out.

Joe Horrigan hops on the phone to deliver the good news, going down his call sheet that—just in case—includes the home and cell phone numbers of all 17 finalists. If any of the finalists are in town, they're asked to come on down to the convention center as soon as possible to take part in the press conference. As I said, some of them are already in the house—guys like Troy Aikman, Dan Marino, John Elway, and Barry Sanders, all traveled to the Super Bowl site specifically for Hall of Fame Saturday. They were all sure-fire first-ballot locks and, thus, were in no risk of being jilted at the altar by The Selectors.

So, in Detroit, Aikman watched the announcement from his hotel room at the Renaissance Center Marriott and took an elevator ride down to the podium. In 2004, Elway and Sanders watched the announcement from the NFL Network green room in the Houston Convention Center (we got their reactions on camera, of course) and then walked down the hallway to the podium.

Other finalists, however, don't dare set foot in the convention center prior to the announcement—even though they're in town. That might anger the Football Gods. In Detroit, John Madden, on hand to call Super Bowl XL the next day, drove around town in his Madden Cruiser watching the press conference on NFL Network and refused to point his bus toward the Renaissance Center until he heard his name for real. That same year, Warren Moon, in town to call the game as part of the Seahawks radio team, sat in his hotel room and got a call from one of The Selectors who told him it would be a good idea to start heading toward the Renaissance Center. Moon still didn't believe it.

"It was snowing that day in Detroit, going down the freeway not knowing exactly where I'm going," Moon said days later.

Eventually, the same Selector called him again and told him to step on it—the news was official.

"I just kind of lost it," Moon said. "I got really emotional—and grabbed the wheel of the car."

Then there's Michael Irvin. The Selectors snubbed the famed Cowboys "Playmaker" in his first year of eligibility, the same year his beloved quarterback, Aikman, got the nod. In Detroit to cover the Super Bowl for ESPN, Irvin appeared at the press conference anyway to support Aikman, even though you could see the disappointment etched on his face. The following year in Miami, sensing The Selectors' change of heart, we offered Irvin the NFL Network green room from which to watch the press conference. He initially accepted, but eventually backed out. Heaven forbid that he should show up at the ball only to have The Selectors treat him like Cinderella again. They didn't. Irvin got in, but he must have been watching the press conference from Boca Raton because it took him nearly 45 minutes to get to the Miami Beach Convention Center.

That's when your humble narrator is forced to seriously tap-dance at the podium.

Once a new enshrinee arrives at the press conference, he makes a few remarks and takes questions from the media. If another new enshrinee hasn't arrived by the end of that Q&A, I'm forced to come up with my

Rich emceeing the Hall of Fame announcement at Super Bowl XXIX, letting down
Art Monk. Again. *(K. Terrell)*

own questions and tap-dance until another all-time great finally beats the
traffic and arrives on the scene. Sometimes, if a new enshrinee is out of
town, Joe Horrigan will get him on the phone and I'll conduct an interview from the podium with the conversation pumped into the room via
loudspeaker. In Detroit, Joe tried getting the great Giants captain Harry
Carson on the horn, but kept getting his voice mail. Many took that as a

sign that Carson was telling the Hall to stick it. After The Selectors snubbed him for a fifth straight time in 2004, Carson told Canton to take him off the eligibility list.

"It's only fitting that he puts the Hall of Fame on hold for a little bit," I said at the podium while Joe furiously redialed off to the side.

Carson, however, was sending no message. He wasn't getting the message, either. Carson was on a flight to Hawaii at the time. So, after all those years of waiting, Harry Carson found out he had finally made it into the Pro Football Hall of Fame from people who congratulated him at the baggage claim of Honolulu International Airport.

It's not a perfect process, but it's one for which I'm thrilled and honored to have a front-row seat. Sure, I may deliver some bad news to all-time greats, but I also get to stand on a podium within arm's length of other legends as they bask in the immediate afterglow of officially becoming Immortal. It's one of those many times on the job when I have to pinch myself. Then the Super Bowl is the next day.

SUNDAY

RAY LEWIS LEANED OVER and extended his fist, demanding that I pound it. I reached past Terrell Davis, Super Bowl XXXII MVP, and touched knuckles with Lewis, Super Bowl XXXV MVP. Now, our five-hour-long pregame show could officially begin.

Not a bad way to start a Super Bowl Sunday at Ford Field in Detroit.

After an entire week at The Convention, during which so many events have so little to do with the actual game, the arrival of game day truly provides a shock to the system. Nothing matches the energy inside a Super Bowl venue, and I've been fortunate to attend World Series, NBA Finals, and NCAA Final Fours. Alright, I've never been to a Westminster Dog Show, but I think you get my drift.

Because Super Bowl pregame shows last longer than *The Thornbirds,* they begin in complete silence well before the gates open. No fans. No blaring music. Nothing. Thus, from our set on the Super Bowl field, we watch the stadium fill up around us throughout the day and feel the energy build from zero to Spinal Tap 11. However, it usually takes all afternoon for the building to fill, thanks to traffic and the tailgate party thrown by the NFL.

Good seats were still available as *NFL Total Access at Super Bowl XLI* hit the air. (*Joann Kamay*)

The annual Super Bowl Tailgate is a monstrous, sprawling affair held usually within walking distance of the stadium. The league pulls out all the stops, providing food—with the menu either being a nod to the host city (ribs galore in Houston) or the Super Bowl teams (Chicago brats and Indy tenderloin in Miami)—and, yes, even more musical entertainment. Will Smith, Stevie Nicks, Gwen Stefani, the B-52's, and Lionel Richie have all performed at the NFL Tailgate. And it is wall-to-wall people. An estimated 10,000 fans attend the bash, attesting to the fact that the NFL Tailgate is a much tougher ticket than the Super Bowl. Trust me, I get more requests for help getting into the Tailgate than any event on the NFL calendar.

Those who need no help have their own VIP section: The league's owners, team presidents, corporate sponsor bigwigs, and celebrities all hobnob and rub elbows before the Big Game at the Tailgate. At one point during the Super Bowl XLI Tailgate in Miami, I saw retired commissioner Paul Tagliabue standing mere feet away from Justin Timberlake, whose presence shocked me. I know he's bringing sexy back, but he was once the NFL's Public Enemy No. 2, behind Ms. Jackson. Or Janet, if you're nasty.

As for the players, most arrive at the Super Bowl four hours before kickoff, just like it was any given Sunday. Except it's not. Very few NFL games start at 6:00 in the evening or, if the Super Bowl is on the West Coast, 3:00 in the afternoon. Players have to adjust their normal routine to the odd kickoff time and, eventually, to the absurdly long halftime show. I've been told the wait before a Super Bowl can feel like the proverbial eternity as the participants do their best to remain calm, although, as you'll soon see, pregame cookies can occasionally get tossed.

Ultimately, the players hit the field for warm-ups, the local honor guard presents the colors, the national anthem gets sung, military aircraft of some sort fly over the stadium and scare the bejesus out of everyone; invariably a former president officiates the coin toss, the players go back to their respective sidelines, the head coaches bark out their final instructions and the Super Bowl football gets placed on a tee, which *finally* brings an official end to The Convention. The time for talk and debate and Radio Row calls from longtime listeners and first-time callers and press conferences and promotional appearances and corporate outings and party hopping in stretch Lincoln Navigators is over.

It is time to play the game at the heart of the biggest American sporting event of the year.

In terms of flashbulbs popping throughout a stadium, the only event I've seen come close to a Super Bowl kickoff was Mark McGwire's at-bats in the 1999 All-Star Game Home Run Derby. When toe meets ball at a Super Bowl, a virtual strobe light ignites in every section of the stadium—which brings me to where I watch the Super Bowl.

Once the game starts, the NFL Network crew disperses to the press box, NFL Network green room, control room truck, or seats in the stands. Like many Super Bowl ticket holders, I go corporate and watch the first half from the suite of an NFL sponsor. For instance, at Super Bowl XXXVIII in Houston, the good folks of Gatorade welcomed me and my wife, Suzy, into their posh 25-yard line digs in Reliant Stadium. With all the great stars in their deep-down-body-thirst-quenching constellation—Derek Jeter, Michael Jordan, and Mia Hamm leap to mind—you'd think the Gatorade suite at the Super Bowl would be a veritable Who's Who. Instead, it's more like a who's that? Indeed, the Gatorade VIPs were the Ph.D.-educated scientists who study athletes' performance at something called the Gatorade Sports Science Institute. These on-staff personnel help you replenish your valuable nutrients with blue stuff called Gatorade Frost Glacier Freeze—and they know what they're talking about.

On that day, the Patriots and Panthers were struggling to put points on the board. In fact, a Super Bowl had never gone scoreless longer than Super Bowl XXXVIII—26 minutes and 55 seconds elapsed before Tom Brady found Deion Branch in the end zone to start the scoring. During the drought, one scientist turned to me and said, "These guys are going to be gassed by the end of the game."

When I asked why, the scientist pointed to the closed Reliant Stadium retractable roof. The league had hoped to keep it open, but the game-time temperature was an unseasonably cool (Glacier Freeze–like) 40 degrees. The scientist then remarked how neither sideline had a Cool Zone, those huge oscillating fans that spray frigid mist on players to prevent overheating. Mad Gatorade Scientist Guy was right. I looked on the Patriots sideline and noticed linebackers Willie McGinest and Tedy Bruschi splayed on the bench with a trainer literally waving a huge towel in their direction.

"See? They're already exhausted," he said.

"Well, at least they've got Gatorade to restore potassium and other important vitamins," I said.

Dr. Gatorade Xtremo Mango or whatever-his-name-was gave a wan smile that a guy with a Ph.D. would normally give a guy with a mere master's degree in journalism, but he was completely spot-on. By game's end, every defender was on fumes and the teams combined for a Super Bowl record 37 fourth-quarter points. The two teams combined for 868 yards of total offense, the second-highest total in Super Bowl history. Every defensive player from that game I've subsequently interviewed agreed at how completely tapped out everybody was.

Well done, Doc. Now tell me about the fragility of Velcro under those conditions.

Watching a Super Bowl halftime stage get put together is a sight to behold. Once halftime strikes, scores of workers rush the field carting huge pieces of the stage that had been sequentially lined up in a tunnel during the second quarter. Like a jigsaw puzzle, the stage quickly forms in front of your eyes. In Detroit, the Rolling Stones performed on a massive 35-piece, 5,800-square-foot stage in the shape of the band's iconic mouth and tongue logo. The crew had just six minutes to put it together. They did it in five. It amazes me every time. Same thing happened in Houston.

The crew required only five minutes to erect 4,500 square feet of staging that included six different 30-foot towers—and then Janet Jackson and Justin Timberlake took the stage.

Let's be honest. We all remember where we were when Janet's womanhood popped free and shocked the Rhythm Nation. I was sitting with my wife in the Gatorade suite half paying attention to a halftime show that was already noteworthy for its outrageous suggestiveness. From my vantage point, all I could see was Timberlake reach out and Jackson quickly grab her chest and bolt off the stage. I shot up in my seat.

"What the hell was that?" I screamed.

I got several blank looks from The Scientists. Suzy said she saw nothing. Everyone thought I was crazy. While you and the rest of world were already reviewing what TiVo calls the most reviewed moment in its history, all of us in the stadium were left wondering if we saw anything at all. It took about two minutes for word to slowly began to creep from the outside world into the Gatorade suite, starting with a text Suzy got from her cousin Jana that read: "Did you see THAT?"

Sure enough, BlackBerrys and cell phones started going off throughout the suite. I suddenly wasn't so nuts after all. Now, while the NFL isn't happy that Janet's starburst is the most popular snippet in TiVo history, there was some added benefit to it. You see, the first ad that aired after halftime was NFL Network's first-ever Super Bowl commercial— the one in which Bill Parcells, Jerry Jones, Warren Sapp, Terrell Owens, and other NFL stars sang the Broadway hit song "Tomorrow." Hopefully, the commercial and NFL Network got extra, uh, exposure thanks to Janet's.

Once halftime ends, the NFL Network crew reconstitutes in the green room to watch the third quarter on TV. For our first three Super Bowls, the NFL Network green room was a trailer in the parking lot. At Super Bowl XLI in Dolphin Stadium, however, our green room was actually the Florida Marlins indoor batting cage.

No fooling. Surrounded by thick netting, we placed two TVs and two leather couches and a coffee table directly in the area where the likes of Gary Sheffield, Devon White, Bobby Bonilla, and Craig Counsell have all taken warm-up major-league hacks. That's where Marshall Faulk, Deion Sanders, Steve Mariucci, I, and the rest of the NFL Network crew watched Peyton Manning pull ahead of the Chicago Bears for good.

Marshall Faulk, coordinating producer Aaron Owens and producer Bardia Shah-Rais chill in the Marlins batting cage during Super Bowl XLI. (*Joann Kamay*)

As the Super Bowl winds down in the fourth quarter, Joann comes to collect us in the green room and bring us to the field as quickly as possible. We've missed a couple of big moments during that walk—Ike Taylor's interception of Seattle's Matt Hasselbeck on Pittsburgh's 5-yard line with 11 minutes to go in Super Bowl XL and Jake Delhomme's 85-yard touchdown pass to Mushin Muhammad to put Carolina up by one with six minutes left in Super Bowl XXXVIII. On each occasion, we hit the turf and wondered, "How did Pittsburgh get the ball back?" or "How did Carolina take the lead?" But I'm not complaining. There's nothing like watching an NFL game from the field. Watching a fourth quarter of a Super Bowl from the field is, as they say in the MasterCard commercials, priceless.

I watched from the back left corner of the end zone in Reliant Stadium as Tom Brady methodically led the Patriots down the field away from us for the eventual game-winning Adam Vinatieri field goal against the Panthers. Each time Brady let the ball go, it appeared—from my vantage

Mooch, TD, Ray and I soak in the final moments of the Steelers victory in Super Bowl XL. (*Joann Kamay*)

point—that he was throwing it directly to a Carolina defender. Each time, however, one of Brady's receivers swooped in at the last moment to make the reception. After I saw that happen twice, I realized what was occurring: The incredibly accurate Brady was throwing the ball to a spot and his receiver was running a perfectly precise route to that spot. No wonder Brady's a two-time Super Bowl MVP and the Patriots a three-time winner. It was clockwork.

Now, if you ask me what happened at the end of Super Bowl XLI in Miami, I have absolutely no clue. I was trapped in a small plastic hut, you see.

As we all know, Colts vs. Bears was the first rain game in Super Bowl history. So, Joann led us to our set in one corner of Dolphin Stadium, and there we sat until the awarding of the Lombardi Trophy was over. If it wasn't raining, we could have turned around and watched the end of the game and ceremony, but because it was pouring, the set required protection on all sides by plastic sheeting, underneath one big plastic roof that had to be collapsed to its lowest level so as not to block the fans' view of the field. So there we had to sit—Deion, Mooch, and I—hunkered down in plastic until we could literally raise the roof and start our show.

Our best postgame experience to date came in Detroit after the Steelers won Super Bowl XL—and for a couple of reasons. First, the soulful, charismatic Ray Lewis was part of our broadcast team, and second, it was the first time in NFL Network history that a winning head coach visited our set after the Super Bowl. In our first two Super Bowls, Patriots head Bill Belichick, quite frankly, blew us off. Both times Belichick kindly visited our Radio Row set during the week, but puzzlingly refused to sit down with us after the victories in Houston and Jacksonville. So when an emotional Bill Cowher chatted with us after his victory, it was an emotional moment for many of us on NFL Network, too.

With director's chairs placed directly atop the Steelers logo in their Super Bowl end zone, we enjoyed a postgame show for the ages. Before Cowher appeared, team owner Dan Rooney—son of Art "The Chief" Rooney—sat down for an interview. After Cowher left, the entire Jerome Bettis clan stopped by for a visit. Without question, the gregarious running back known affectionately "The Bus," was the feel-good story of the

Hey, Mooch—can you see through the plastic? (*Joann Kamay*)

week. Bettis is a Detroit native and was reaching the end of his career. He dodged retirement questions all week long. You would be hard-pressed to write a better script than winning your first Super Bowl and retiring in your hometown. Once that Hollywood story actually played out, Bettis immediately announced his retirement. Minutes later, with at least two dozen members of his family standing behind us, Bettis sat down on our set with his newborn daughter Jada on his lap. It's an interview I'll never forget—Bettis and his family on the verge of tears, with Lewis placing his trademark passion squarely on his sleeve.

> **RAY:** Everyone says, every *teammate* says: This one's for "The Bus." What does it feel in your heart for your teammates to come out and fight for you the way they did today?
>
> **JEROME:** You know what? That meant everything. [linebacker] Joey Porter, when we were walking down the tunnel [before the game], he said: "Hey, it's only fitting for you in your hometown to bring us out." And we wanted to come out as a team, but he said, "No, no. We're *gonna* come out as a team, but you're gonna lead us. So, you go. I'm gonna hold the guys and we're coming out behind you." And when he said that, that—

The Bus and his passengers. (*Joann Kamay*)

RAY: Look at that smile.

JEROME: —it brought a tear to my eyes.

RAY: Look at that smile. Look at that smile. Go ahead. *(Laughs.)*

JEROME: It was unbelievable.

MARIUCCI: You know, Jerome, this is such a perfect ending, but I want to ask Mom and Dad, how are you feeling right now?

GLADYS BETTIS: I'm ecstatic. I think I'm still crying.

MARIUCCI: Oh, yes.

JOHNNIE BETTIS: Yeah. I'm ecstatic. I got over my crying spell. I'm okay now.

GLADYS: Best ever.

JEROME: You know, it's great for my family to be here. They've been with me every step of the way. [It's true. Jerome's parents attended *every single game* of his college and professional career.] And for them to be able to see me finish like this here, I mean, I couldn't ask for anything more.

RAY: There's been a lot of stories written. If I can end my story, I want to end my story like Jerome ended his story today.

JEROME: Well, you know what, coming from you, a great player like yourself, Ray, I mean, that's an honor. So, hopefully, you know, when you get that opportunity, you better believe I'll be there.

RAY: Let me always tell you this, through the years of me competing against you, every time I looked at you, I knew of what respect you and me had for each other.

JEROME: No question.

RAY: I love you, man.

Terrell Davis then turned the conversation to Bettis's decision to retire. He didn't just mail in the 2005 season. Bettis served as the Steelers' emotional leader and also led the team with nine rushing touchdowns. When TD asked about playing more, Bettis turned and pointed to the people behind him.

JEROME: You know, I have to think about my health, my daughter, my fiancée, my new family. And so it's important for me to now go to the next level and next stage of my life. That's critical.

TD: You're not gonna change your mind?

JEROME: No. Trust me. I mean, because in April, May, June, when it's time to go out there in that 100-degree weather, *that's* the hard part. And that's something that I was willing to do to win a championship. Now, I've won it, and The Bus is in the garage now.

ME: And if you go into TV now, Jerome, will your parents go to every single one of your broadcasts? Is that gonna happen?

RAY: That may cost a lot.

GLADYS BETTIS: If you take me, I'll go. *(Big laughs from the family.)*

ME: Okay. If he takes you, you'll go.

RAY: Follow him, Mama. Follow him, Mama.

JOHNNIE: I might miss a few.

Everyone laughed. But, in hindsight, that last line rings more melancholy than anything. Ten months later, Johnnie Bettis died of a heart attack. At least he was there to watch his son in his greatest moment. Once the Bettis clan departed, Hines Ward, the first Steelers receiver to win the Super Bowl MVP award since Lynn Swann, sat down, making it a troika of Super Bowl MVPs on our set.

TD: Welcome to the club, okay? M-V-P! Do you realize what that means yet? Have you thought about that?

HINES: No, I haven't. I mean, because coming into this game, I never came in saying I want to win the Super Bowl. I just want to come out and make plays and . . . I dropped that one touchdown play, you know. The great ones on this stage make all the plays and I still left some plays out there. So, to win this award knowing that I still left some plays on the field is very gratifying. And it is just good that I helped contribute to the team's effort to win the Super Bowl.

RAY: You know what, it's so special. And I wish every young kid stayed up just to hear your interview. A man just won the MVP, just won the Super Bowl, and he's upset at himself because of the drop of a touchdown. I walked up to you before the game; I said, "Hines, how are you feeling?" You said, "Ray, I've never felt this feeling before." I said, "Just let it go and just be you." And tell me, just tell me, what happened after you went back in the locker room?

HINES: Oh, man, I almost threw up, actually. I was *that* nervous, and, you know, seeing the whole media, the fans, this is what it's all about. As a little kid, you dream about playing in the Super Bowl and when I saw you guys [TD and Ray] over there, you guys experienced it, I said, "Is it bad to be nervous now?" You said, "No, it's time for you to just let it all out," and actually I walked to the locker room, I got light-headed and went to the bathroom and did my thing, but it's gratifying now. I can say that I won the Super Bowl.

RAY: Welcome to the club.
HINES: Oh, I appreciate that. Thanks.

ME: I like this. Everybody's welcoming everybody to the club.

With that, we suddenly had only one more segment of television to execute from Super Bowl XL in Detroit. Over 100 hours of live television in the books. Now only one final three-minute portion remained from confetti-strewn Ford Field, which, by this point, was virtually empty. I turned around during the commercial break and saw the Lombardi Trophy podium being taken down. The Convention and its game were finally over.

Fittingly, Ray Lewis had the final word. Typically, he drilled it.

"You know, sometimes you try to put certain things with words and that's what I was trying to express with Jerome when he was sitting here. The childhood dream is so true and most of the time you try to find the perfect storybook ending. And the way Jerome went out, the way his team respects him as a *man,* the way his team dedicated this Super Bowl to Jerome, nothing else can be said at the end of that book, nothing else can be written to make that story any better. That is a class act. He's a guy that I go to battle with. I've gone to battle with Pro Bowlers for the last ten years of my career. And just like I told him, every time I put on my shoulder pads, I just knew all I had to do was nod at him as a man, because I knew the respect that we had for each other. So seeing a true warrior like that leave the game, it makes your heart warm just to understand that one day, my day will be coming just like that. And if it's anywhere close to the way his story ended today, I think my mom will be happy."

Amen.

We all stood up from the director's chairs and hugged each other. By the time we got out to the production trailer, it was well past midnight and only one car remained to take us back to the hotel 10 blocks away. We all crammed into the sedan: me, Steve Mariucci, Ray Lewis, Terrell Davis, Kara Henderson, and Jennifer Love, with executive producer Eric Weinberger navigating the streets of Detroit with occasional brazen maneuvers. As you might imagine, Ray can take up space. A major laugh fest broke out when someone's cell phone began buzzing and no one knew whose it was because we were so piled on top of each other in the backseat.

Once at the hotel, we spilled out like clowns from a circus car. Somebody suggested heading to the NFL postgame party (yes, one final party!) being held somewhere in the hotel. It was nearly one in the morning and I hadn't packed. I had an early flight in the morning, but I hit the party anyway. Why not? It's the Super Bowl. Plus, I needed a minute to unwind. For, believe it or not, my road trip was only half over.

WHAT'S YOUR ROOM NUMBER?

Donovan McNabb came strutting through the pool area, proudly pushing his baby carriage. Peyton Manning lounged at a table off to the side with some high school buddies he had flown out for the occasion. The roar of the blender at the outdoor bar nearby drowned out their conversation. Across the way, John Lynch and his family caught some rays near Bill Cowher and his family, while Tony Gonzalez, towel draped over his shoulder, sauntered down the beach to where, just off-shore, Torry Holt sat in a paddleboat having a grand old time.

Welcome to the Pro Bowl.

Or, more appropriately, Aloha.

Yes, the National Football League holds its annual All-Star Game one week after the Super Bowl on the sun-kissed island of Oahu in our nation's picturesque 50th state. And it places all of the game's stars in one luxury resort hotel sequestered 20 miles west of Honolulu to create a de facto NFL Club Med—with the Turks being the players and the Caicos being, well, who cares? You're in Hawaii for a full week with the cream of the NFL crop, for crying out loud.

Pro Bowl Week is a just reward for those who spent the previous 26 weeks sacrificing considerable amounts of blood, sweat, and tears proving they're the absolute best of the best. I'm also talking about the NFL Network crew. Sure that's hokey, but, to heck with it. The Pro Bowl *is* a major event on the NFL calendar, which means, gee whiz, *NFL Total Access* has got to cover it, right?

Twist my arm. And pour me a mai tai. *Mahalo.*

While the bulk of Super Bowl observers are still picking confetti out of their hair, heading to Disney World or sleeping off the previous night, I'm already on a flight across the Pacific to the Pro Bowl. The year the Super Bowl was held at Ford Field, I believe I became the first person to fly from Detroit to Honolulu for work since Thomas Magnum, P.I. The great thing about the gig—as if one aspect could possibly be singled out—is that NFL Network kindly embeds your humble narrator directly into ground zero of this beach boondoggle at the same hotel as the Pro Bowl principals, the JW Marriott Ihilani Resort and Marina, where the Pro Bowl players and coaches stay and practice for the game at week's end in Aloha Stadium in Honolulu. In between, they enjoy heavy helpings of golf, sunbathing, swimming, snorkeling, fishing, and general poolside revelry with their coterie of guests. And talk about your all-star roster—the Pro Bowl guest list is a menagerie of moms and dads and wives and young children and babies and girlfriends and best friends and childhood friends, all on the scene to celebrate the Pro Bowl selection of their son, husband, boyfriend, best friend, dad, or sugar daddy.

Then there are the Pro Bowl coaches—the staffs of the two teams that lost the conference championship games two weeks before. It's the Mother of All Consolation Prizes.

"Hey, thanks for playing. Sorry you didn't make the Super Bowl. But you're not leaving empty-handed! Tell them what they've won, Johnny!"

"You've won seven days and seven nights in beautiful, luxurious Hawaii! And a brand-new car!"

All right, maybe not the brand-new car part. Although the Pro Bowl MVP does win one of those. Nevertheless, Pro Bowl coaches are fired up because they're on the ultimate busman's holiday—one full week in the sun and sand before heading back into the bleak bunker for the Scouting Combine, free agency, and the NFL Draft. With the pressure of the playing season in the rearview mirror, the trip to Hawaii serves as one big release. And bless the league for creating the perfect bubble environment by reserving all 387 guest rooms and 36 suites at the remote JW Marriott

Ihilani for the entire week. In other words, the Pro Bowl is gadfly-free—no interlopers, hangers-on, or autograph hounds to disrupt anybody's mojo.

Therefore, guards go down, good times roll, and everything flows freely. Conversation. Dominoes. Lava. Well, not an actual molten rock but rather a thickly blended frozen concoction called a Lava Flow that must be, without question, 2,000 calories per serving. It's a drink that eats like a meal and it is churned out en masse by the overtaxed crew overserving the masses that flock to the Ihilani pool bar, which is, without question, the nexus of fun the entire week.

Yet, that is also where evil lurks. Like the TV show *Lost,* those new to the island must be vigilant of considerable danger. For this peril of which I speak can be very costly. It can sneak up on you in many ways, but it always arrives in the form of the same seemingly benign four-word question: What's your room number?

Thankfully, on my first trip to the Pro Bowl in 2005, I had a trusted veteran on my side—11-time Pro Bowler and *NFL Total Access* analyst Rod Woodson, who kindly gave me the lay of the land on the long flight out to Hawaii from Jacksonville. Just like everything else in the NFL, the Pro Bowl features a form of rookie hazing: Get the room number of an unsuspecting newbie and start putting your entire tab on his room. In other words, you must guard your room number with your life because at the Pro Bowl the veterans are Fletch, the rookies are the Underhills, and the tab is way more expensive than a steak sandwich . . . and a steak sandwich.

"Any time you get a rookie coming here for the first time, you kind of just sit beside them, by the pool or something," Rod said, "and they give out their room number to the waitress, and then you've got him. Baptized into Hawaii."

I was concerned. What could be more fresh meat than the NFL Network guy at his first Pro Bowl? Rod agreed. His advice could not have been blunter: Even if the hotel was *on fire* and someone called to say my belongings could possibly be saved, I *still* shouldn't cough up my room number.

I'm telling you. The Pro Bowl spies are out, and that wolf is in sheep's clothing. Miami linebacker Zach Thomas got stuck with a $4,000 bill at his first Pro Bowl—thanks to the wily 12-time Pro Bowl linebacker Junior Seau. Upon Thomas's arrival from the mainland, Seau acted as if he was taking the young Dolphin under his wing.

"Seau told me practice begins real early in the morning and he didn't want me to oversleep because of the jet lag and all," Thomas told me. "So Seau says, 'I'll come by and knock on your door to make sure you're up. What's your room number?' So I gave it to him."

Game over.

Like running into a special teams wedge for the very first time, Pro Bowl rookies must keep their heads on a swivel. Because even coaches will nail them. In 2007, Saints and NFC head coach Sean Payton got the room number of Cowboys quarterback and Pro Bowl rookie Tony Romo and then announced it to the rest of the team in practice. Just how Payton pried the all-important digits loose from Romo is, quite frankly, downright cold.

Payton and Romo go way back. Payton was the Cowboys passing-game guru and quarterbacks coach when Romo arrived in Dallas from Eastern Illinois, which is also Payton's alma mater. So it was quite believable when Payton approached Romo at the first NFC team meeting of the week and told him this touching tale: Payton's six-year-old son Connor was so excited about Romo playing on his dad's Pro Bowl team that the young lad had drawn a poster of Romo in honor of the occasion. Real sweet. Except for the fact that no such drawing existed.

"I told Tony about this poster and how Connor was all excited," Payton said. "So I say, 'Hey, why don't I have him bring the poster by your room. What's your room number?' And he says, 'Have him come by Room eight-fourteen. I'll sign it for him.'"

Using his young son as bait, Payton had Romo hook, line, and sinker. Even worse for Romo, so did longtime Cowboy and now-49er Pro Bowl offensive lineman Larry Allen, who was sitting directly next to Romo in the meeting and overheard the whole conversation.

"Larry's like this old alligator in the swamp that doesn't move for anybody or anything anymore," Payton said, crouching down and acting out his words for effect. "But once he heard Romo's number, Larry slowly rose from the swamp . . . and turned his head . . . and looked around . . . and *snapped* at the bird sitting on his back."

At NFC practice the next morning, Romo's room number spread like wildfire. Payton had the players huddle up and turned the stage over to Allen, who broke practice with this hands-in chant: "Everybody, eight-fourteen on three."

The 2007 NFC Pro Bowl squad then gleefully responded: "One-two-three! Eight-fourteen!"

Romo knew disaster loomed. Fortunately, he also had a trusted Pro Bowl veteran to serve as counsel, none other than the freshly minted Super Bowl XLI MVP himself, Peyton Manning, who suggested Romo immediately set his room bill up on a cash-only basis. Thus, if anybody threw around Romo's room number at the pool or at one of the restaurants at the Ihilani, they now had to pony up cash on the spot. No more tab. Crisis averted.

Not that Manning's above the fray. Quite the contrary. Upon his victorious arrival from the Super Bowl in Miami, Peyton needed all of about two hours before he acquired the room number of Titans rookie quarterback Vince Young and started abusing it. Vince was in Room 704, for those keeping score at home.

Now, don't get me wrong. There *is* work to do at the Pro Bowl. Each team holds a one-hour practice every morning on a makeshift field off to one side of the Ihilani, and NFL Network carries each practice live. After practice, we interview a handful of players and broadcast those taped chats on that day's edition of *NFL Total Access at the Pro Bowl*. Sometimes we interview the guys on the field. Other times, we bring the players down to a couple of lounge chairs set up on the beach. Actually we interviewed both Donovan McNabb and Terrell Owens on that beach set—separately, which, to be honest, came as a surprise at the time. It was the 2005 Pro Bowl, right after the Eagles Super Bowl loss to the Patriots in Jacksonville, and we asked McNabb and Owens to sit down for the beach interview at the same time, but both refused. It was the first indication our crew had that something might be amiss between the two stars. As we all soon found out, there was a lot amiss.

Mostly, though, players visit our end-zone set, from which we enjoy quite a view. Turn around and you can see the glistening Ko Olina lagoon. Face front and you've got clouds hovering over the top of the Waianae Mountain Range that perfectly frames the practice field on which the greatest NFL players of the day become teammates for a week.

It is awesome to behold. These are the absolute best of the best practicing together after spending the entire year trying to beat each other's brains in. When, say, Tom Brady dumps off a pass to Jerome Bettis or Shaun Alexander takes a handoff from Brett Faure or Carson Palmer play-fakes to LaDanian Tomlinson and throws deep to Marvin

Take your shoes off, T.O. Stay a while. *(Joann Kamay)*

Harrison, you can't help but think: Man, that is cool. And the real neat thing is the players feel the same exact way.

"I really enjoy getting to spend some time with guys that I'm trying to beat during the season," perennial Pro Bowler Peyton Manning said on our Pro Bowl set in 2006, the year he set the record for most touchdowns in a season with 49. "I've really gotten to be good friends with people like John Lynch and Tony Gonzalez, guys that you don't really see much besides when you're playing, so this is always a special week for me. If the fans and the players and coaches keep voting me in, I'll always come. I'll never not come, because it is special."

Throughout that special week, camaraderie is the order of the day—on the practice field, by the pool, or in the late-night establishment at the Ihiliani called the Hokule'a Bar, or as I've come to call it, the Ed Hochuli. After all, Hokule'a does sound like the Hawaiian name of the league's most muscular referee, and any zebra who wears a shirt one size too small specifically to show off his pythonlike arms should have a place of distinction at the Pro Bowl.

But I digress.

Deep down, the Pro Bowlers are all fans. You should see the swag they all ask of each other—hats, jerseys, gloves, cleats, helmets—and most of them autographed. Whether it's for their personal collection or for a silent auction at the slew of charity golf tournaments many Pro Bowlers host in the off-season, these guys flat out load up. Before the 2007 Pro Bowl, we spotted Falcons cornerback D'Angelo Hall dragging a huge duffle bag full of the stuff across the Aloha Stadium turf.

"I just spent the last fifteen minutes in the AFC locker room," Hall said. "I got an Antonio Gates autographed jersey. I got a hat from LaDanian Tomlinson, Chad Johnson, you name it. I may need to go back in there."

Not a single Pro Bowler is jaded. Eight-time Pro Bowler Marshall Faulk likes to tell the story of entering his first Pro Bowl huddle and getting blown away by the sight of John Elway. He says one word leapt to mind: *Whoa.* Manning had a similar reaction at his first Pro Bowl when he realized he was teammates with then-Raider Jerry Rice. In fact, when Manning entered his first Pro Bowl practice huddle, AFC lineman Lincoln Kennedy had to tell him to relax. Manning had no idea he was screaming. Eventually,

If Peyton looks relaxed, it's because he's in Hawaii and just won the Super Bowl.
(*Joann Kamay*)

though, Manning found his bearings and, throughout the week, lobbied then-AFC head coach Jeff Fisher to be the guy under center in the red zone rather than another AFC Pro Bowl quarterback—Rice's normal Oakland teammate Rich Gannon.

"I said 'Coach, if it happens, share the love a little bit. Rich Gannon gets to throw to Jerry all the time on a lot of touchdowns'," Manning said. "So we were creating all kinds of plays to get me down [near the end zone] to get to Jerry, but I never quite got it to him. But I did throw two touchdowns to him in practice."

Manning readily admitted the experience got to him.

"You see a lot of kids out here taking pictures with their favorite players. Heck, I was out here going, 'Hey, Jerry, Mr. Rice! Can I have a picture?' A lot of players, especially the younger players, turn into fans because it really is special for us. I don't think people realize just how much respect the younger players have for the Rod Woodsons, the Jerry Rices. Those are special memories for me."

The funny thing? Now *Manning* is the old graybeard who provides the butterflies. In his final Pro Bowl season as a Charger, Drew Brees made no bones about which AFC teammate he looked forward to playing with the most.

"Playing with Peyton . . . he's a guy who, with him being in Indianapolis and me being at Purdue [in college] very close by, I had a chance to follow him and kind of become a Colts fan, a Peyton Manning fan. Now, to be playing with Peyton in the Pro Bowl, that's a neat experience because, obviously, he's going to go down as one of the best ever. I'm looking forward to picking his brain a little bit and see how he works and prepares."

Which brings us to another fascinating Pro Bowl subtext: Brain picking is also the order of the day. Trade secrets do not exist in Hawaii; players constantly provide tips to one another. In fact, if you don't use the Pro Bowl as an opportunity to get better, you're considered foolish. In 2006, Hines Ward and Chad Johnson stood in the lobby of the Ihilani talking about blocking, something at which Ward is generally considered one of the league's best among wide receivers. So when Johnson appeared on *NFL Total Access* (in an interview Rod and I held with Chad, who was in shades, by the Ihilani pool) the subject of the unique lobby summit came up.

"There's much more room for improvement [with blocking]," said Johnson, whose renowned playfulness actually masks a consummate

Rod, Chad, and I chill poolside at the Ihiliani. The steps in the background lead to the Ed Hochuli. *(Rob Ohlandt)*

perfectionist. "I'm just basically doing what I do off of—I don't want to say raw talent—but I've got a long way to go."

"Can you learn something from a guy like Hines?" Rod asked.

"Oh, yes. Most definitely," Johnson said. "They [my AFC team-mates] don't even know. I'm taking notes out there on the practice field. We're not even going full speed, so I'm stealing stuff. I'm getting coached up at the same time by the best—Champ."

Champ, as in Bailey, the Broncos Pro Bowl cornerback, who, during one AFC practice, gave Johnson a surprisingly revealing pointer. Chad said Champ pointed out to him "something I was doing that was giving away a route. Something so small I didn't even know I was doing it."

I was stunned. If Johnson was doing something that would tip off the type of route he was about to run, wouldn't Bailey want to keep that to himself? That's like Barry Bonds telling Roger Clemens he knows when a fastball is coming. I posed the question to Chad: Perhaps Champ was just setting him up for the next time the Broncos play the Bengals?

"Yeah, maybe, but Champ is one of the best, one of the greatest," Johnson said, "and to pull me aside like that and notice something like that in my game just shows where he is as a person and, also, his level of playing, how much he pays attention. To notice something so small, I didn't even know it."

Plus, it was a moot point anyway, according to Chad, because, armed with Champ's new information, "once I straighten this out, man, it's a wrap."

As in—nobody can stop him. Ocho Cinco. The one and only Chad Johnson. That's right. Pro Bowl Week is chock full o' smack talk as well, with Cincinnati's No. 85 leading the charge. One day in 2007 when the NFC held its morning practice first, an AFC player stationed himself outside their locker room to offer words of warning to anyone who would listen.

"Man, it's like eight o'clock in the morning and I'm walking into the locker room and Chad is already there screaming, 'You better get ready. How you gonna stop eighty-five?' and stuff like that," said D'Angelo Hall while he was miked up and wearing an earpiece under his helmet for the NFL Network broadcast of NFC practice.

"So what did you say back to him?" asked Marshall Faulk from our set.

"I'm like 'Don't you have someplace else to be? It's eight o'clock in the morning! You don't practice till later. What's the matter with you?' That dude is crazy, man."

After the practice, Marshall and I taped a couple of interviews on our end-zone set for *NFL Total Access* with Panthers wide receiver Steve Smith, a well-known smack talker in his own right, and Chargers running backs Lorenzo Neal and 2006 MVP and single-season touchdown king LaDainian Tomlinson. With Faulk being the San Diego State legend that he is, I called our set collection "perhaps the best backfield in the history of San Diego backfields."

The interviews in the can, we were famished. Marshall, Joann, Kara Henderson and I took the two-minute walk from the stage to the pool area for lunch.

"Do you want four separate bills or put everything on one check?" the waitress asked.

"One bill is fine," I said, not realizing what I was walking into.

"Okay," the waitress said. "Then I need your room number."

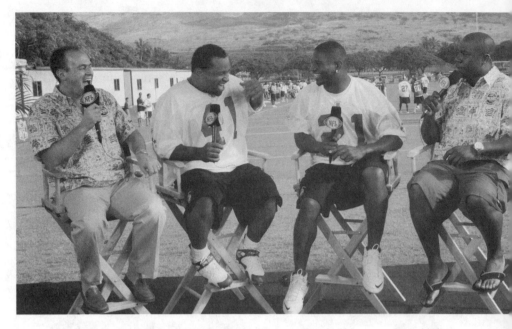

Marshall and I laugh it up at the 2006 AFC practice with Chargers running backs Lorenzo Neal and NFL MVP LaDanian Tomlinson. (*Joann Kamay*)

Marshall immediately shot up in his chair, keen to hear my answer. He had the classic Faulk you-know-what-eating grin I had come to appreciate since the eight-time Pro Bowl running back landed on injured reserve with the St. Louis Rams prior to the season and into our studio as a full-time analyst for *NFL Total Access*. Except, did I appreciate that look now? Not so much.

"Give me a pen," I told the waitress. "I'll write it down."

Marshall slapped his knee, laughing. I shielded the waitress's pad with one hand and quickly scrawled the top secret information: Room 636.

"Got it!" Marshall screamed with glee. "I know your room number!"

"How could you possibly know? I had my hand in front!"

"I can tell what numbers people are writing just by watching the movement of their pen."

Now, I knew Marshall had a reputation for being ultraperceptive, but that's ridiculous.

"You are so totally full of it," I said.

"Oh, yeah?" Marshall said. "The first and third numbers [of your room number] are the same and the middle one is half."

Yikes. He did have it. And Faulk's the type of guy to hold that over me all week, even if he really had no intention of running up my tab. I immediately tried to play it off.

"Whatever. Nine, four-and-a-half, nine is not my room number," I said.

"Oh, yeah. OK. Believe what you want to believe," Marshall said.

Joann, our stage manager, came to the rescue.

"I don't believe *you*," she said to Marshall. She grabbed a pen and wrote down 9-1-4-5-8 on a cocktail napkin.

"Nine-one-four-five-eight," Marshall said from across the table.

"Try one more," Kara said, enjoying every minute of the fact my room number could be, like the *Mission: Impossible* NOC List, out in the open.

Joann wrote down three more digits. Marshall nailed it again.

"Still, you don't know my room number, buddy," I said. "Trust me."

Marshall laughed and let it drop. He's way too smart to be thrown off the trail. Of course, he was also way too smart to get caught with his pants down in the room-number game at his first Pro Bowl, but that doesn't mean Marshall doesn't have the greatest rookie Pro Bowl story of all time. Check this out: In his first year with the Indianapolis Colts in 1994, Faulk ran for 1,282 yards and 11 touchdowns and also caught 55 passes, one for a score. Good enough to make the Pro Bowl as a rookie. So, when Marshall hit Hawaii for his inaugural Pro Bowl, his agent hooked him up with an exotic car rental that had our man Faulk tooling around Oahu all week in a sleek yellow Lamborghini Testarossa.

Come game day, Marshall missed the AFC team bus from the Ihilani to Aloha Stadium. So did Chargers running back Natrone Means. Thus, the sweet Italian ride had to serve as Marshall's chariot to his first Pro Bowl. With Means riding shotgun, Marshall hit the highway toward Aloha Stadium when a heavy rain swept through Oahu. Suddenly the Lamborghini hit a puddle. Marshall quickly lost control of the car and it hydroplaned—boom!—right into a cement stanchion. Both Faulk and Means were fine, but the car wasn't.

The future Hall of Fame running back was now stranded on Oahu's Interstate H-1 in a rainstorm with Pro Bowl kickoff fast approaching.

"We waited a while for the police to come, but nobody came. And we had to get going," Marshall said. "So we hitchhiked."

Thus, the future Hall of Fame running back was now riding in the *back of a pickup truck* with Natrone Means down Oahu's Interstate H-1.

The windswept duo arrived at Aloha Stadium just as the Pro Bowl players were being introduced to the sellout crowd of 49,121. But when Marshall and Means entered the locker room, they were greeted by three very angry people—AFC head coach Bill Cowher and two members of the Hawaii State Police who were wondering whose creased yellow Lamborghini was left on the side of the road. The famed Pittsburgh Jaw and Hawaii 5-0 on the case together!

Marshall explained how what happened was a one-car accident and circumstances left him no choice but to leave the scene. Remember it was 1995. How many of you had a cell phone then? Cowher persuaded the police to continue their interrogation after the game and sent Marshall out on the field, where he flat out tore it up.

Marshall proceeded to break O. J. Simpson's record for most rushing yards in a Pro Bowl and replace it with a mark that still stands today—an astonishing 180 yards rushing, including a 49-yard touchdown on a

Lurking beneath his Pro Bowl towel, Marshall Faulk plots his next move. *(Joann Kamay)*

fake punt Cowher called with the AFC leading 34–13. Apparently, the coach was taking his pregame anger out on the NFC. So, despite smashing up his Lamborghini and thumbing it to Honolulu in a pickup, Marshall Faulk owned the game and was named the 1995 Pro Bowl MVP for which he got, you guessed it, a brand-new car.

After the on-field MVP ceremony, Marshall returned to the locker room and the police were nowhere in sight. He hightailed it out of Dodge, no worse for wear. I defy anyone to come up with a better first Pro Bowl story than that.

Cut to 12 years later: Marshall is back in Hawaii and involved in a new caper—getting my room number.

After lunch, we headed to the elevators. We got on and both of us waited for the other to press a button first. I finally pressed 6. Marshall let his finger linger over the panel of buttons before finally pressing 8—and then gave me that *look.*

The sound of children's laughter echoed from one end of the Ihilani beach. About a dozen small kids were playing a game of touch football, and the official quarterback was an adult whose identity could not be mistaken. It was Steelers safety Troy Polamalu; his trademark, flowing, and curly locks identify him from 1,000 yards away. It's no surprise that Polamalu—fresh from having won the Super Bowl over the Seahawks in Detroit days before—would spend his valuable off time in that manner. The spiritual Polamalu and his wife have been known to look around a restaurant, seek out a dining couple that appears to be as in love as they, and quietly pick up their check.

Recreation is truly the order of the day at the Pro Bowl, since practices last barely an hour. Otherwise, the players revolt. Rod remembers the 1993 Pro Bowl, when AFC head coach Don Shula went old school on the guys and wanted a two-hour practice *in pads.*

"We declined the pads. We told him the first day we'd do the two hours, but not the pads," Rod said.

Shula acquiesced but tried for another two-hour practice the next day.

"The guys who were there for ten years or so, they were like 'No way. This is not happening again.' Now, I'm a young guy, it was only my fourth year there, so I'm like, 'Yeah, I'm with you guys," Rod said.

So a contingent of the veterans went to members of Shula's staff and told them the players would do one hour max.

"Somebody had to tell Don," Rod said, "and I don't think he liked it at first, but he went with it."

In 1999, Bill Parcells bailed out of coaching the AFC in the Pro Bowl, producing a letter from the Jets team doctor and his cardiologist saying the wear and tear of the season had taken its toll. Thus he handed over the reins to his assistant, Bill Belichick, who, Marshall recalls, once stormed off the practice field because the players weren't going full speed. Eight years later, however, a totally different Belichick showed up to coach the AFC squad, chuckling and casually twirling his whistle string throughout each practice. At one point, our microphones caught New England's modern-day Lombardi talking about the Rolling Stones with some of the players. But you can't teach an old dog completely new tricks: Belichick didn't make Peyton Manning one of the AFC's captains even though he had just (finally) won the Super Bowl and Super Bowl MVP. Not enough seniority.

"I had to go with Marvin [Harrison] because he had more years," Belichick told Manning as he stretched before practice.

Of course, Manning understood, and the two seemed just fine the next day as they formed the most fascinating poolside table of the week—Manning, Belichick, NFC coach Sean Payton, Minnesota guard Steve Hutchinson, Broncos safety John Lynch, and Shannon Sharpe and Phil Simms, both of whom were in Hawaii to call the game on CBS. Those guys sat at their table off to the side of the pool bar for hours, talking who-knows-what. Your humble narrator wasn't invited over, but did think of crashing the table wearing Ravens safety Ed Reed's skintight Under Armour beanie just for the joke of it. I'm telling you, after a while, those Lava Flows have a bite to them.

Apparently, so did the fishing lines of Belichick and Payton. The two coaches had just come back from a deep-sea fishing trip with their staffs, the Saints and Patriots coaches putting lines in the Pacific together. The year before, NFC head coach John Fox and AFC head coach Mike Shanahan appeared to be having a grand time, too. Both coaches virtually took over the Ed Hochuli Bar one night, with Shanahan and his offensive staff sitting at one table with Manning (if you haven't guessed, Manning is far and away the most popular and sociable player of Pro Bowl Week) while Fox and members of his defensive staff sat a few feet away.

A huge laugh came from the Shanahan table. Broncos assistant head coach Mike Heimerdinger, whom Shanahan had just hired away from the imploding New York Jets, had told everyone: "Congratulate me! I'm the only coach at the Pro Bowl who went four and twelve this year!"

Fox was hanging with his defensive line coach Sal Sunseri, whom Fox had taken surfing earlier in the day. Sunseri is a tough Pittsburgh guy who clearly had never been on a board before, but Fox is a different story. He grew up on the coast of Virginia before moving to San Diego and is a surfer. Thus, we convinced him to hang ten and let us videotape it for *NFL Total Access*. The shoot became an instant joke among our staff because of the local cameraman hired for the shoot. His name is, well, Hugh Gentry. Go ahead. Say that one out loud—sounds like he should be starring in *Boogie Nights*. At one point during the surf session, Coach Fox wiped out into the camera and he landed on top of, uh, Hugh Gentry.

Now, here Coach was, chilling in the Ed Hochuli. Neither of us really knew Fox, but he seemed cool enough. Kara Henderson thought Fox would appreciate the story of Hugh and his whereabouts on certain parts of the shoot.

"Let's find out," I said.

Well, Kara regaled Fox with the tale, and to say Fox loved it is a huge, if you will, understatement. Coach could not tell enough people the name of the guy with whom he had become entangled in the Oahu surf. "Hugh Gentry!" Fox screamed. "How about that one, Sal? Hugh Gentry!"

Even the next day, once Fox saw us at NFC practice he yelled out, "Huuuuugh Gentry!"

In fact, at the NFL Scouting Combine two weeks later in Indianapolis, I ran into Fox and Seattle head coach Mike Holmgren on the field at the RCA Dome. Fox got a big smile on his face and said, "Hey, Mike, you've got to hear this story . . ."

R ay Lewis could not have been more insistent. He wanted to teach me how to tackle. We had only one more segment in that day's *NFL Total Access,* for which Lewis was the guest Pro Bowl analyst for the week. The ferocious five-time Pro Bowler and Super Bowl XXXV MVP had been with our show since the previous week at the Super Bowl in Detroit. The man was as spiritual and professional on our set and in our show meetings as he appeared to be on the field with the Ravens.

Usually, the final segment on *NFL Total Access* is time for a game of "Four Downs," in which I ask our analysts four rapid-fire questions (first

Ladies and gentlemen: the legendary Don Ho. *(Joann Kamay)*

down, second down, etc.) and they answer with the first thing that pops into their minds. With a setting as unique as the Pro Bowl, however, our final segments in Hawaii are usually reserved for shenanigans. To wit, in previous shows, I've danced the hula with Miss Hawaii and sung "Tiny Bubbles" with Don Ho, who had us all rolling when he declared, "I'm so sick and tired of that song."

I've caught punts on the practice field with Rod Woodson, whose first Pro Bowl appearance in 1990 was as a special teams return man. (I caught one of three punts. It was windy and the football knuckled.) I've also ridden in an outrigger in the Ihilani lagoon with Rod and fellow *NFL Total Access* analyst Lincoln Kennedy. We finished another show by having Rod's five kids bury me and Lincoln up to our necks in the sand. It took nearly an hour for the crew to dig a big enough hole for the two of us.

On this particular day, however, we had about forty-five seconds remaining in our show and Ray Lewis, the most ferocious hitter of his day, suggested we grab a sand-filled tackling bag from the practice field and he'd teach me how to hit and wrap. Rod Woodson said he'd hold the bag while I hit it. Talk about a pinch-me moment—two future Hall of Fame

Lincoln Kennedy and I are in it up to our necks. Literally. *(Joann Kamay)*

defenders were about to give me pointers on tackling. During the final seconds of the commercial break, I wondered how many thousands of dollars such a lesson would fetch at a charity auction.

Lewis told me to keep my knees bent so that when I hit the bag, my motion was going upward as well as forward. In other words, I should hit the bag with my chest.

"Fifteen seconds left," producer Mike Muriano told me in my ear.

"Okay, so in the last ten seconds of the show, I'm finishing up by taking a big charge at this."

"Yeah," Ray said.

"Big charge," Rod said.

"Alright, look out, Rod."

I leapt toward the Weebles-like bag and smoked it—and then went *through* it, flying toward the ground on the other side. I hit the grass and rolled over my right shoulder as my watchband unsnapped on my wrist. The microphone pack hooked to my belt went flying.

"That's it, Rich!" Ray shouted.

"What time is it?" I yelled, mimicking the chant Lewis bellows out to his fellow Ravens before every game. Then I did the Terrell Owens eagle arm-flap dance as the show faded to black.

Ray and Rod were literally rolling around on the ground in hysterics.

Lewis finally caught his breath and said: "You went right through it!"

I pointed out that Rod had played Lucy to my Charlie Brown and let go of the bag.

"You told me to let it go, so I let it go," Rod said.

I never did. To this day, Rod Woodson and I argue about that. Regardless, I was now officially the tackling dummy because, 15 minutes later, my right shoulder began to throb. Three hours later, I could hardly move it. That night, I got no sleep. Now, hardly anybody gets hurt at the Pro Bowl and certainly nobody in the media gets hurt at the Pro Bowl. Nonetheless, I had clearly done something serious to my shoulder.

When I showed up for work the next morning, Ray, Rod, and the crew were still howling over the segment. Mention of my wounded wing only intensified the laughter. Joann gave me Advil; I gingerly slipped on my NFL Network golf shirt and hit the set for our live broadcast of NFC practice. To add insult to injury, during the practice Ray and Rod could not talk about my injured shoulder more, and from the truck, Muriano decided to roll in the video of my tackle from the previous day in *slow motion*. Then he called for the NFC trainer to visit the set to check out my shoulder on live television.

Sure enough, Carolina Panthers trainer Ryan Vermillion came up to the stage.

"We have not seen any injuries yet, and the tempo of practice has been great, so this will be the first thing I've looked at since I've been here," he said.

Unbelievable that I would be the NFC trainer's first and only patient.

"Have at it, Doc," I said.

Vermillion grabbed my right arm and began to move it around.

"Did he hurt his interviewing arm, Ryan? Because he might have to take it to the left hand the whole time," Rod said.

"Ow!"

It hurt. Ray Lewis held his microphone to Ryan's mouth for the prognosis.

"I think you've have an AC joint sprain," Vermillion said, referring to that bump at the top of your shoulder. "We may have to pad you up on game day."

"Do you have some sort of balm or something in the interim?" I asked.

Using my good arm to point to the monitor to show Rod, Ray, and Carolina trainer
Ryan Vermillion how I hurt myself. (*Joann Kamay*)

"We can put a balm on, but for more contact drills you're going to
need to have that thing padded," he deadpanned.

In all seriousness, Vermillion said I truly had hurt my shoulder, and
with rest and frequent icing I'd be able to regain normal use of it in two
to four weeks. Muriano quickly placed a graphic on the screen: "Rich
Eisen, sprained AC joint—Questionable." I was in disbelief.

"I sprained my AC joint at the Pro Bowl!"

Ray Lewis was laughing again.

"All right, Rich!"

Unlike most game weeks in the NFL, Pro Bowl Week gets more and
more relaxed as it progresses. The final AFC and NFC practices before
the game take place at Aloha Stadium in front of thousands of screaming
fans. Without question, it's the most lax session of the week. The teams
stay on the field for maybe 40 minutes, and the players wear ball caps instead of helmets. In 2007, Sean Payton wore a microphone, which overheard him calling for a play called "The Last Mango"—a halfback pass by

the retiring Tiki Barber. Payton said the idea to have Barber heave one in his final game was given to him by the singer Jimmy Buffett while they were deep-sea fishing the week before the Super Bowl in Miami on Buffett's boat named . . . *The Last Mango*. Overhearing an NFL coach call for a trick play conceived by a Parrothead and named after his boat? It can't get any more laid back than that.

Well, maybe.

The AFC practice ended early, so we asked the commissioner of the National Football League, Roger Goodell, to stop by for a chat. His one condition was that he share our set with a player, since the focus of Pro Bowl Weekend should be on them. Fair enough. So we chose the defending MVP of the game, 10-time Pro Bowl linebacker and model citizen Derrick Brooks.

I asked both a question and it became time for Marshall to jump in.

"Hey, Commish," Marshall said.

Commish? This wasn't Michael Chiklis we were talking to here.

"I can call you Commish, right?"

"I think you just did," I said.

"Sure you can," said the Commish, I mean, commissioner.

"I just want to make sure it was OK," Marshall said.

Rich with (*from left to right*) NFL Commissioner Roger Goodell, Derrick Brooks, and Marshall Faulk. (*Joann Kamay*)

"As opposed to what?" laughed Goodell.

"Roger?" said Brooks.

"You could do that, too," the commissioner said.

As if he weren't cool enough, the commissioner was wearing a Hawaiian shirt, too. Commissioner Bahama. I'm telling you—lax.

Moments later, we were interviewing Tennessee's Vince Young, the first rookie quarterback to play in the Pro Bowl since Dan Marino following the 1983 season. After watching Peyton Manning, Zach Thomas, and half the AFC use his room number as a punchline all week, I could not let him go without asking him the obvious.

"Are you afraid to check out and see your bill?"

"Oh, my goodness," laughed Young. "I definitely don't want to see my bill right now. I think it's gonna be pretty bad."

"It's going to be double for someone like Vince," Marshall said.

Clearly, Young was taking his lumps like a man. Realistically, he had no choice.

"I'm going to accept that because they were talking about tying me up the pole," Young said, pointing to the goalpost behind our set. "And I don't want that at all so I said, 'I'll accept the bill.'"

When it came for the show's wrap-up, we had a whopping two minutes to fill—more than enough time for a full segment of "Four Downs." Topics for the segment usually come from issues brought up during the show, so on the heels of our chat with Vince Young one of the four questions for Marshall was "Whose room are you charging things to?"

Marshall's eyes lit up. I thought: *He wouldn't dare.*

"Well, I'm not saying," Marshall said, getting that look on his face again. "But there is a person in Room six-thirty six—"

"That's an outrage," I blurted out.

"Now, I don't know who that person is," Marshall said, growing more sarcastic by the second.

"Yeah? Who is that person?"

"I don't know . . . I don't know."

"Maybe that person is Marshall Faulk? You're giving out your room number, which I think is really odd."

"Could be my room . . ."

My room number was now *completely* out in the open. Marshall had just mentioned it on national television. I tried my best to play it off, but I knew there could be someone watching at the Ihilani with excellent inference skills and very bad intentions. I also knew that, on the ride back to the hotel, I could not let Marshall think he had me. At least not before I hit the front desk and got that Tony Romo cash-only option applied to Room 6-3-6 posthaste!

Marshall knew that, too, and really turned up the heat once we got in the van to head home.

"Now, if you just tell me now that six thirty-six is your room number, I won't say another word or do another thing," he said. "But if you don't say anything, I'm going back to the hotel and start putting *everything* on Room six-three-six and, Rich, I promise you it will not be pretty."

"Whatever, Marshall," I said.

"Rich, look at me."

I didn't budge.

"Rich, I'm serious. Look at me."

Finally, I relented.

"It's going to be *bad*."

I paused.

"Marshall, I can't believe you'd give out your room number on the air like that."

One of the greatest all-purpose running backs in the history of the National Football League then let out a laugh that could only be categorized as an evil cackle.

The ride home felt like an eternity. Finally, the van pulled up to the Ihilani and I casually disembarked. I sauntered to the lobby and loitered until Marshall disappeared from view . . . and then pounced on the first front desk representative with a pulse.

A sweet-looking girl with a name tag that read Ki'ane smiled at me.

"Aloha," I said, not quite knowing how best to make my request.

"Ki'ane, you know how things work around here right?"

Ki'ane's eyebrows furrowed.

"Listen, I'm the anchor for NFL Network and one of my colleagues just gave out my room number on the air and I need to change my room to a cash-only—"

Ki'ane's eyes began to dart off to the side. I slowly turned to my right and there was Marshall Faulk, smiling the biggest Cheshire cat grin.

"*Do you mind?*" I said.

"Go on," Marshall said. "Please."

The jig was up. Pride does not taste better when swallowed with poi.

"All right. This is the guy who gave out my room number on TV. I need a cash-only option on Room six thirty-six, please."

"*Yes!*" Marshall screamed, raising his arms in victory.

I may or may not have dropped an f-bomb on him at that point. My room bill protected, I stormed off to the elevator. Marshall followed. I jabbed at the number 6. Marshall did his usual song-and-dance at the button panel . . . before pressing number 7 and letting out another cackle.

Game day at the Pro Bowl is just like at the Super Bowl—completely anticlimactic. Thanks to a week's worth of frivolity, you almost forget, Oh, yeah, there's a game. Same goes for the players, who usually wake up around halftime and realize there's some cash at stake.

Ah, yes, the prize money. There's a considerable chunk of it on the line at Aloha Stadium. Each winning player receives $40,000, while each losing player gets $20,000. Depending on the size of one's entourage, winning or losing the Pro Bowl is the difference between breaking even for the week or walking away with some quality walking-around money. Seriously. Let's say Player A has a typical Pro Bowl posse that includes Mom, Dad, Brother, Wife, Two Kids, and some teammates as a "thanks for a great season" present. When you add up the cost of flying everyone out and putting them up for the week and then toss in golf, meals, Ihilani pool bar ancillaries, a night or two at the Ed Hochuli, and the inevitable Waikiki shopping spree or three, Player A basically *needs* to win the Pro Bowl. That's why all the players are holding up four fingers in the air after the third quarter. They want that 40K.

Thus, the fourth quarter of a Pro Bowl is usually when you see a blitz or two—verboten according to the Pro Bowl rules. Indeed, to keep everyone healthy at the Pro Bowl, the league installs certain statutes to lessen the speed and intensity of the game. The defense cannot blitz except in short-yardage situations and otherwise cannot perform fancy pass-rush stunts on the line of scrimmage. No rushing a punt or a kick, either. Cornerbacks can only play man-to-man coverage and not bump-and-run, except inside their own 5-yard line. At least those are the rules. Many times they're, shall we say, ignored. There's a famous story about Junior Seau, who would frequently blitz in the Pro Bowl only to claim he didn't mean it.

"I thought it was a run [play]!" he would say to the ref.

In every Pro Bowl I've witnessed, each head coach spends the day screaming his head off at the referee to throw a flag on the opponent for blitzing. Either that or they're blowing a gasket over a bad call that can't be reviewed because there is no instant replay at the Pro Bowl. Sure, it's an exhibition game, but every person on that sideline is there because he's successful, which, in the NFL, also means he's outrageously competitive. Despite the relaxed nature of the week, juices begin to flow. I know, because, during the Pro Bowl, my job is to roam both sidelines and conduct occasional interviews for broadcast on the Aloha Stadium Jumbotron.

It's an incredible vantage point. During the regular season and playoffs, most teams don't allow people to watch from the sideline. At the Pro Bowl, we have full run of the joint. *NFL Total Access* places an analyst directly on the sideline, free even to sit on the bench during the game and conduct interviews for later use. Terrell Davis, Ray Lewis, and Marshall Faulk have all done it while I ran around with that Jumbotron microphone and otherwise listened in.

At the 2007 Pro Bowl, I was so close to NFC coach Sean Payton that I heard him call for "The Last Mango." It happened in the first quarter. Sure enough, Tiki Barber took the pitch from NFC quarterback Drew Brees and heaved one down the field . . . into double coverage. Ravens ball

Carolina defensive end Julius Peppers says cheese for the Aloha Stadium Jumbotron. (*Joann Kamay*)

hawk Ed Reed picked it off and returned it halfway up the field. Later that night, I saw Coach Payton at the pool bar. "I've fired Jimmy Buffett as my offensive coordinator," he announced.

The first quarter of a Pro Bowl can be a bit intense, too. That's when the offensive starters get their shot at the grand prize—the MVP award and its accompanying brand spanking new red Cadillac convertible. Most Pro Bowl starters play three series at the most, and few of them return to the game thereafter. Thus, those guys have only a handful of snaps in which to make a most valuable impression. For instance, on "The Last Mango," you're fooling yourself if you think Barber or Reed didn't have a fleeting thought about that convertible when trying to make their respective plays.

Of course, pride plays a considerable role, too. That said, a car and 40 grand helps turn on the jets in the fourth quarter. Invariably, the MVP Award goes to whichever offensive player has the most touchdowns, like Marshall in 1995 or Peyton Manning and his three touchdowns in 2005, or a defensive player with a game-turning interception, like Brooks and his 59-yard pick-six in 2006.

In 2007, Bengals quarterback Carson Palmer threw two touchdowns and nearly a third for the victorious AFC, thereby sending him to the MVP podium. After the ceremony, Palmer visited our live postgame show for a segment we began with onfield reporter Adam Schefter who had just conducted an interview with Chad Johnson, who caught one of Palmer's touchdowns. Schefter asked Chad how he felt about winning a Pro Bowl with his year-round teammate winning the MVP.

"Feels good," Chad said. "But it feels even better because he said I could have the car, so I got me a new Cadillac to ride home in."

"Carson said you could have his car?" Schefter asked.

"Most definitely. You need to talk to him and make sure that you reiterate that and let him know the car's coming with me."

Palmer wasn't wearing an earpiece, so he was watching that interview on our set monitor with no sound. Thus, I brought the 2007 MVP up to speed.

"Chad just said you said he could have your Cadillac."

Palmer rolled his eyes, let out a soft chuckle, and said, "Whatever."

Schefter tossed it back to me.

"Thanks, Adam. Pro Bowl MVP Carson Palmer now joins us on our set and, Carson, Chad Johnson just said that you would give him your brand-new car. Is that true?"

Palmer wasted no time. "It definitely is not, and I want to go on record as saying that. But I'm not surprised to hear him say that. I should have expected that out of him, but he is definitely not getting that car."

"Can he at least borrow it since he caught one of the touchdowns that you threw today?" Marshall asked.

"You know, it would be one thing if Chad had only one or two cars, but Chad literally has ten, eleven, twelve, thirteen cars, so I don't think he needs a new car anyway."

Palmer wasn't lying. One spring, Chad spent an entire week as a guest analyst on *NFL Total Access* and had no fewer than three exotic cars garaged in the Los Angeles area alone. And his main off-season hangout is in Miami! By the way, one of the three cars is a lavender Hummer H2 with a lavender interior that Johnson nicknamed "Barney."

We finished the Palmer interview, finished the show, and that's when reality hit. It happens every year when we wrap up our last program at the Pro Bowl—the stark realization that the playing season is over. That the next NFL game with NFL players won't come until August at Hall of Fame Induction Weekend. That the long season we just covered has noth-

Carson Palmer would not give up his ride to Chad. (*Joann Kamay*)

ing left to cover. That our Sundays are now suddenly free. It's one big exhale for the entire crew, with most of us thinking the same thing: I want to go home.

Your humble narrator resides in that camp. The Hawaiian paradise is a paradox. Sure, the sunsets are breathtaking and the Lava Flows scrumdelicious, but by the end of Pro Bowl Week, which comes on the heels of Super Bowl Week, which is on the heels of Senior Bowl Week in Mobile, Alabama, I'm ready to be wheels-up and flying east. I miss my dog and my wife (clearly not in that order) and I miss sleeping in my own bed. It is time for the boondoggle to end.

Marshall felt the same way. We were both scheduled to leave the next morning, but Marshall found a couple of seats on a flight back to Los Angeles scheduled to leave Honolulu that night and we pounced on it.

"Let's all meet at the pool for dinner around six," he said to me, Kara, and Adam as we rode together back to the hotel.

"Well, I would offer to buy . . . but my room has a cash-only option on it," I said.

Marshall laughed and promised to pick up the check.

The night of every Pro Bowl game, the NFL holds a luau at the Ihilani, and most players and coaches attend . . . for a bit. Eventually, everyone hits the pool bar for one last hurrah, and on this night it was jammed. To our right sat the entire Bulger family, from Rams quarterback Marc to his dad and brothers and sister and so on. To our left sat Seattle linebacker Lofa Tatupu and his father, Mosi, a hellacious running back who played 15 years in the NFL. Behind us were Steve Hutchinson and his wife, Landon, who are grade-school sweethearts; they had just returned from the luau. Time flew.

Marshall headed upstairs to pack. I had already done so, which allowed me to squeeze one extra drop out of pooltime. Suddenly, it was time to go, so I went to grab my bags. As I made the long walk from the elevator to my room, I noticed someone on his cell phone heading toward me. It was Marshall.

"Yeah, I'm headed off to the airport now," he said into the phone, walking briskly past me.

I kept walking and saw a bellman in the distance, jamming several bags onto a cart. When I got to the bellman, I looked up. We were in front of Room 635.

"Whose room is this?" I asked, already knowing the answer.

"Mr. Marshall Faulk," he said.

"That son of a . . ."

Marshall was right next door to me. In Room 635. The whole time!

I stormed downstairs, got in the car, looked at Marshall, and let the silence carry the moment for a moment. Then I may or may not have dropped another f-bomb.

"Room six thirty-five? Are you kidding me?!!"

Marshall cackled all the way to the airport.

Aloha.

THE COMBINE

It may well have been the most exciting NFL playoff game of the decade—Peyton Manning and the Colts coming back from 18 points down to finally beat their New England nemeses and make the Super Bowl. Exactly one month and three days after that Game for the Ages, the entire league's principal power players were back in the RCA Dome in downtown Indianapolis with even *more* reporters in attendance than those who covered that AFC Championship Game—yet, you could hear a pin drop.

All you could hear was the light hum of air-conditioning along with occasional beeps from the scores of digital stopwatches being brandished in the stands. One by one, more than two dozen hulking offensive linemen were quietly running the 40-yard dash, rumbling down a roped-off strip of turf behind the sideline where, 34 days before, Manning and Marvin Harrison and company mindlessly tossed away their empty Gatorade cups. Now, however, it was quite a valuable piece of RCA Dome real estate. Because when 6-foot-6, 311-pound Wisconsin offensive tackle Joe Thomas ran his 40-yard dash in a blistering (for a 311-pound man) 4.92 seconds, he secured himself several millions of dollars.

Well, some believe Thomas earned himself a sizable NFL signing bonus the minute he left college, what with that whole stellar All-America career thing and that Outland Trophy he received as the top offensive lineman in college football. Yes, all that is nice and well and good, but, in

Joe Thomas made serious coin with this dash. *(K. Terrell)*

the minds of NFL talent scouts, coaches and general managers (hereafter to be referred to as The Evaluators) that only tells one part of the story— a story that became only more legit thanks to Thomas's 4.92 40-yard dash. And his 33-inch vertical leap. And his 9'2" standing broad jump. However, any star collegian who posts such solid numbers (what The Evaluators call "measurables") could also have a major medical problem or mental flaw or personal history issue (what people call a police record) that sends said player's draft status plummeting straight to Hades.

Regardless, it's all eventually going to come out in the wash at the NFL Scouting Combine. Because the NFL Scouting Combine *is* a car wash. Or, in the eyes of the players who must endure it, a meat market. For The Evaluators, however, it's an extremely important exercise in due diligence because you simply can*not* afford to make a mistake on a player in the NFL Draft. The wrong decision in the wrong spot can send a franchise reeling for years and put an Evaluator on the unemployment line faster you can say Ryan Leaf. Or Tony Mandarich.

Thus, every year in late February (usually 10 days after the Pro Bowl), the league "invites" more than 300 draft-eligible players to Indianapolis to take part in what is, in essence, one massive weeklong standardized football test with every single NFL scout, trainer, doctor, assistant coach, head coach, general manager, and team president serving as the proctors. Sometimes, even team owners show up to inspect the goods.

For those who also covered the Pro Bowl, it doesn't take long to realize you're not in Hawaii anymore. Nothing is more hard core than an NFL Scouting Combine.

> *Run the 40-yard dash!*
> *Bench press 225 pounds as many times as possible!*
> *Lift!*
> *Jump broadly!*
> *Leap vertically!*
> *Now, run around these cones!*
> *Run around this bag!*
> *Leap over that bag!*
> *Run to that bag, leap over this bag, and then run through those*
>   *cones!*
> *Throw that ball!*
> *Throw it again!*

Run that pattern!
Catch this ball!
And that ball!
Run that pattern, then catch this ball!
Run backward through these cones, then catch this ball!

No, that wasn't a haiku, but you get the drift. All this and more goes down in what The Evaluators call field drills on the RCA Dome turf with coaches and scouts sitting in the otherwise empty stands, clocking everything with their stopwatches, taking note of absolutely everything from attitude and body language to manufactured speed and ankle flexion. Don't worry. You'll be an expert on this stuff by chapter's end.

Before any player puts a single toe out on the field, the medical staffs get ahold of him. He is then subjected to a regimen of testing that makes *One Flew over the Cuckoo's Nest* look like a stroll in the park.

Stand on that scale.
Hold that hand up to a ruler.
Step into that machine for a minute.
You might feel a little bit of pressure once we start.
Say ahh.
Take this cup with you.
We want you to take an MRI on a knee you've never hurt.
You sure you didn't sprain this shoulder back in high school?
If Mr. McMurphy doesn't want to take his medication orally,
　I'm sure we can arrange that he can have it some other way.

You got me. That last one was from *Cuckoo's Nest.*

That's only the physical portion of the diagnosis. Each and every player at the NFL Scouting Combine also takes a lengthy psychological exam along with a 12-minute, 50-question inquiry that tests their intellect called the Wonderlic. As if these poor guys aren't mixed up enough once they've been measured and weighed in front of a ballroom full of coaches and scouts with nothing on but a pair of shorts. That would send me over the edge, I'll tell you that.

If the players don't feel sufficiently stripped of their identity, they're literally stripped of their identity. Upon arrival, each player gets assigned a group and a number within that group. For instance, Notre Dame quarterback Brady Quinn may be the most famous quarterback in Indiana this side of Peyton Manning, but at the 2007 NFL Scouting Combine he was simply known as QB11. Heisman Trophy winner or not, Ohio State's Troy Smith was QB14. The previous year, the artist formerly known as Reggie Bush was RB25.

If all this poking and prodding and testing and retesting sounds like a deeply intimate if not outrageously overwrought process, well, that's because it is. Again, there's too much money and prestige at stake when choosing the next face or standard-bearer of an NFL franchise. Plus, it's about more than just snagging the right prospect in the first round of the NFL Draft. When you can draft a guy like Tom Brady with the 199th overall pick, you'd best do every last piece of due process, with every *i* dotted and every *t* crossed and every *p* and *q* minded to make sure you know who's available and what they can do on a football field when your team is called on Draft Day. Fortunes can literally change and the Scouting Combine is the only time when virtually every potential prospect is under one roof for every team to get the same look at him.

Therefore, this is serious business, and those who run the Scouting Combine do their best to keep it private. In fact, if it weren't for the 370 credentialed members of the media milling about in the hallway leading to the entrance to the Scouting Combine, you could waltz right into the Indiana Convention Center and never even know it existed.

The first time I walked into the Convention Center for a Scouting Combine, in 2005, only two signs stood in plain sight:

MIDWEST HOME BUILDERS ASSOCIATION, INDIANA CHAPTER—WELCOME!

CHEER AND DANCE NATIONALS THIS WEEKEND IN CONVENTION CENTER HALLS D AND E

Combine? What Combine?

Once you get past the phalanx of media milling outside the lone Combine press room (where most coaches and star prospects are made available at 15-minute intervals throughout the week) you see a big blue curtain at the end of the hall with two nondescript security guards (is there such a thing as a descript security guard?) standing watch next to a

sign that reads CREDENTIALS ONLY. There is zero indication the biggest
future stars of the biggest game in America being scouted by the biggest-
name coaches in the game are in the house. In other words, pay no attention to the men behind the blue curtain.

The NFL Scouting Combine is the only posse-free event on the entire National Football League calendar. No agents allowed. No handlers
allowed. No publicists or buddies from back home allowed. Now, agents
do show up to Indianapolis en masse. With every single NFL coach and
general manager on site, it's too juicy a target to resist. Factor in the fact
that the annual free agency period begins mere days after the Combine
and that an average of $270 million dollars in long-term contracts have
been given out on the first day of the last two free agency periods and
you've got yourself an agent orgy. In fact, the NFL Players Association
has begun to hold an annual meeting with its accredited agents at the
Combine because so many of them are already there. But allowing agents
inside to view the workouts? As Drew Rosenhaus would say: Next question. Basically, the RCA Dome and several rooms in the adjacent Indiana
Convention Center become the National Football League's hermetically
sealed laboratory for the entire week.

The NFL Scouting Combine. *(NFL Network)*

For years, the Combine would not allow a single member of the media to set foot inside the inner sanctum. That is, until 2005, when NFL Network began broadcasting the drills on the field and the reps in the weight room with *NFL Total Access* originating from inside the RCA Dome every night of the Combine. Now, one might think that airing young men navigating cones or lifting metal or running 40 yards as fast as they can might not be the most compelling television, but . . . Silly rabbit, think again. This is the NFL. Our ratings for the NFL Scouting Combine indicate people are transfixed (thank goodness)—and just three weeks after the Super Bowl, when they've supposedly been so oversaturated with all things pigskin that the last thing they'd want to do is watch a squat middle linebacker run a three-cone drill on TV. Watching the Scouting Combine is a lot like watching the Yule Log. You stare at it for hours on end and, at the end, wonder what in the world kept you so glued for so long. That said, NFL Network's exclusive coverage doesn't leave you humming "The Little Drummer Boy" afterward.

It's gone so well that the only group we know of that doesn't fully appreciate NFL Network's presence in Indy is the hard-core beat writers. Basically, they give their lifeblood to covering the sport only to be barred from the inner sanctum and then we come waltzing in with our highfalutin high-definition cameras. In 2007, a small pool of print reporters was allowed inside the inner sanctum for the first time, but for everyone else the line in the Combine sand remained.

And it has to stay that way. Essentially, when a coach sits in the stands at the RCA Dome to watch the workout, he is working. He doesn't need an agent or marketing representative or money manager chirping in his ear about his client who swear-on-his-mother's-life/hand-to-God is the next best thing. Plus, if an agent were allowed access to the field, he might somehow coach the NFL prospect and, therefore, muddy any true evaluation of said prospect. No single player in recent Combine memory illustrates this better than Maurice Clarett.

For those in need of a brief refresher: The 2002 Big Ten Freshman of the Year ran for an Ohio State freshman record 1,237 yards and 18 touchdowns, including the game winner in double overtime against Miami in the 2003 Fiesta Bowl. The youngster from Youngstown was the BMOC of The Ohio State University. That is, until Clarett was later charged with filing a false police report claiming that more than $10,000 in clothing, CDs, cash, and stereo equipment was stolen from a car he "borrowed" from a local dealership. Lots of ugly questions surrounded the car and cash and clothes, and suddenly the toast of Columbus was toast in Columbus, suspended by Ohio State for the 2003 athletic year.

Instead of trying to rehab his image or transfer elsewhere, Clarett turned his attention toward trying to get into the National Football League early . . . by suing his way in! The NFL's long-standing rule on eligibility clearly states that only players at least three years removed from high school are allowed to enter the league. Clarett got some high-priced lawyers and took the NFL to court on the highly charged subject, which, let's just say, is not the best way to ingratiate oneself with the National Football League.

Armed with an initial court victory, a 20-year-old Clarett got invited to the 2004 NFL Scouting Combine, which he attended. He went through the whole medical dog and pony show, but did not work out, claiming his legal battles prevented him from being in the proper shape, which, let's just say, isn't the best way to ingratiate oneself with The Evaluators.

Eventually, Clarett lost in court, and Clarett spent a second consecutive year out of football. So, when he arrived at the 2005 Scouting Combine one could say he did so with a bit of baggage. However, he also showed up leaner and, perhaps even more important, contrite.

"When I looked at myself sometimes I kind of looked like a joke. I guess it was a part of growing up and becoming who I am today," said Clarett at his media appearance in The Combine pressroom adding, "It's a humbling thing being humble."

Maybe things *could* be different this time. The next day, after two years of battles in court and with his demons, the time came for Maurice Clarett to run the most important 40-yard dash of his life.

When timing a 40-yard dash at the NFL Scouting Combine, you've got a handful of valuable vantage points. Obviously, the finish line serves as a crucial viewing spot, so you can nail that stopwatch button as soon as the sprinter breaks the tape. The starting line is also a good place to sit because not only can you hit the stopwatch at the runner's very first twitch, you can also get a good, close look at the athlete before he bolts down the field. See his physique. Check his burst off the line. Watch how he handles the pressure. That's one of the main reasons why Al Davis always sat in the first seat nearest the goal line at every NFL Scouting Combine in Indianapolis.

Now, there's no such thing as an assigned seat at the Scouting Combine, mind you. With the RCA Dome holding a capacity of 57,890, the hundreds of coaches at the Combine have a lot of space in which to spread out. Wherever coaches sit, they usually sit in the same area each and every workout session, give or take a row. Carolina's John Fox likes to sit midway up the end-zone section in an aisle seat. Cleveland's Romeo Crennel is usually across the aisle two rows up in another aisle seat. New England's Bill Belichick frequents the side opposite the 40-yard dash course. I once saw the Jets' Eric Mangini actually sitting in the upper deck. For years, Section 119, Row 1, Seat 1 at the RCA Dome was reserved for one man and one man only. That would be the Lawd of the Oakland Raiduhs himself: Al Davis, for whom the trip to Indy eventually became too much. He now watches the proceedings on NFL Network, but during his time in the RCA Dome, Section 119, Row 1, Seat 1 was Davis's bailiwick, and only two people were usually permitted to sit with him—Bill Parcells and longtime Cowboys player-personnel man Gil Brandt.

"I've known Al forever," Brandt told me, "and Al and Bill are good friends. They talk all the time."

Brandt said the three would be able to tell which players had properly worked out for the Combine just by the way they'd get down in their starter's stance for the 40. The Combine prospects would spark lengthy reminiscing sessions.

"Bill has a great memory. He'd say something like 'This guy reminds me of [Broncos running back] Otis Armstrong,' and Al would say, 'That guy reminds me of [Redskins tight end] Jerry Smith,' and I'd chime in. Now, I'd rather sit there, and Al and Bill would rather sit there, than just sit somewhere else and have a whole bunch of guys ask you questions: 'What did you think of this guy? What did you think of that guy?' "

Did anyone ever dare crash the row?

"No one crashed, although sometimes someone would come and sit down. If Al didn't want him there, Al would say, 'Can I help you?' And the guy got the idea to move."

One place the ejected coach might move is 20 yards to the right in order to get a split time for the 40. And, believe it or not, there is one last crucial location from which to time a 40-yard dash: the 10-yard line. Offensive linemen rarely run 40 yards at a clip during a game, but they frequently have to burst off the line to block for a screen pass or get out in front of a run. Thus, scouts meticulously measure an offensive lineman's

NFL coaches mill about between drills as Seattle coach Mike Holmgren chats with Bill Parcells in the famed "Al Davis Row." A Raiders coach serves as a Davis's seat holder next to Gil Brandt. *(NFL Network)*

10-yard time down to the one-hundredth of a second to determine how fast they can move from a stationary position. I'm not kidding. It's called an initial quick. Don't worry. The jargon lesson's still coming.

So, when it's time to run the 40-yard dash at the Combine, coaches form four columns in seats running from the first row of the lower bowl to the top along the goal line, the 10-, 20-, and 40-yard lines. Meanwhile, the *NFL Total Access* crew sits (like Al Davis) in the same location every year—on our set in Suite 216A, luxury accommodations right on the 20-yard line above the 40 course. In other words, a perfect viewing station from which to witness the whole scene when somebody like, say, Maurice Clarett puts his hand and cleats in the turf with all 32 franchises of the NFL watching.

As Clarett settled in to run his 40, I settled into the row of seats in Suite 216A next to my Davis—*NFL Total Access* analyst and Super Bowl XXXII MVP running back Terrell Davis.

The Evaluators take their seats for the 40-yard dash. *(NFL Network)*

"How do you think he'll do?" I asked.

"I don't know," TD responded, "but he does look thinner."

Off Clarett went and so did the stopwatches. *Beep!* You could hear the squish of his shoes and occasional grunt. He hit the 20 mark. *Beep!* And then soon: *Beep!* Just by the look on Terrell's face, I could see the beeps didn't come fast enough.

"That looked slow," he said.

It was. A good 40-time for a running back is 4.5 seconds. Any running back who runs a 4.4, like Auburn's Ronnie Brown in 2005, will see his stock skyrocket, as Brown's did. He was taken second overall by the Miami Dolphins in the 2005 NFL Draft, ahead of fellow running backs Cedric Benson and Cadillac Williams. Maurice Clarett's 40-time? 4.72. Yikes.

About 15 minutes later, Clarett ran his 40 again . . . and clocked in at 4.82 seconds. Molasses. An audible murmur rose from the stands, where coaches were turning every which way to compare readings with their neighbor. Even worse, Al Davis and Bill Parcells sat there stone-faced. It was the first time all day they weren't chatting. Clarett finally had his shot to show his stuff in front of the NFL world and officially spit the bit.

So he quit.

Soon after the 40, Terrell and I noticed Clarett had put his gray sweatshirt on over his running shirt, which, at the Scouting Combine, means you're no longer working out. The running backs group still had several more field drills to complete for The Evaluators.

"What's he doing?" Davis asked me.

"I don't know. Maybe he's hurt," I said. "His shoelaces are untied."

Sure enough, Clarett had unlaced his shoes, the clearest indication yet that he was done for the day. Word soon filtered from the field that Clarett was, in fact, not hurt. Clarett had indeed quit . . . and he *watched* his group run through the rest of the day's work. Not the sort of image one should project to The Evaluators, who put large premiums on dealing well with adversity because, in the NFL, adversity arrives in bunches every single Sunday.

Now, then. Had Clarett's agent been allowed in the stands, he would have no doubt called Clarett over and told him to take off his sweatshirt, tie his shoelaces, and suck it up. Any agent worth his salt would have reminded Clarett he had a personal workout day scheduled for The Evaluators three weeks hence and *forced* Clarett to run the rest of his group's drills to try and impress. Instead, Clarett was left to his own devices and thereby gave everybody a very clear window into his personality.

Now you know why no posses are allowed at the Scouting Combine, and why the Indiana Chapter of the Midwest Homebuilder's Association gets top billing in the Convention Center.

Had Clarett's agent also been inside the RCA Dome, he would have probably also forbade him from making an appearance on *NFL Total Access.* While the running backs were still working out, a despondent Clarett arrived on our set and sat down for an awkward yet fascinating conversation. I asked him why he had put on his sweatshirt. Clarett let out a long sigh.

"Man, I've been working on this thing for a long time. A lot of times waking up at five in the morning and . . . *(sigh)* I mean, going back to the gym at twelve thirty, then at seven, and just working probably twenty times harder than I did last year, and to get here and just totally bust out, it's kind of like, 'we're through.' It's extremely frustrating."

TD tried to lift his spirits by telling Clarett that *he* ran a 4.6 40-yard dash at *his* Combine and got drafted in the sixth round only to go on to great things.

"It just goes to show you—I mean the Combine, I believe, is only a small percentage of being a football player," Davis said.

"Well, it's easy to say once you've been through it," said Clarett, his eyes beginning to water. "I've been working a lot longer than a lot of people here, and I think that's the most frustrating part. I had a lot of time to work on it. I worked on these skills and these drills and to go out here and kind of mess them up was like . . . it kind of put me in the tank a little bit. But I got another day to look forward to it, and hopefully my career ends up like yours."

It didn't. Of all teams, TD's Denver Broncos picked Clarett, shocking the entire free football world by using their third-round pick—the final pick of the first day of the 2005 draft—to do so. Clarett never made the team; he was cut in training camp in August. In September 2006, Clarett was sentenced to seven and a half years in prison on various robbery and gun charges.

Yet to this day, former 49ers and Lions coach Steve Mariucci swears the one player with the best football smarts he ever encountered at the Scouting Combine was Maurice Clarett.

Open the Bod Pod bay doors, HAL. *(NFL Network)*

* * *

Once you get through the blue curtains and enter the inner sanctum, there's a long, double-wide hallway that eventually leads to the revolving doors of the air-pressurized RCA Dome. As you walk down the hallway, look to your right and you will see the cavernous White River Ballroom, in which all the players are weighed and measured topless in front of a capacity crowd of coaches. In the back of that room are five white, egg-shaped machines out of 2001: A Space Odyssey. They're called Bod Pods and each player steps into that machine to have his body fat measured. Look to your left and you'll notice a string of Orthopedic Stations, in which players are brought for examination by each team's medical staff. X-rays, training tables, entire medical histories—you name it, they've got it. If they don't have it, they send the players down the street to Methodist Hospital for an MRI.

Keep on walking and halfway down the hall you'll begin to hear it:

"UP! UP! UP!"
"Arrrrrrgh!"
"C'mon now, gimme one more! I want one more! Push it!"
"AAAAARRRRRRRRRRRGGGHHHHHH!"
"Lock it! Lock it!!"

Welcome to the bench press at the NFL Scouting Combine.

The all-important Weights and Reps sessions take place in Rooms 150 and 151 of the Indiana Convention Center. The Combine removes the partition between the two rooms and turns it into the personal pleasure dome of the most excitable strength coach in the National Football League, John Lott.

Just as the 40-yard dash is crucial to the so-called skilled position players, (running back, defensive back, wide receiver) the 225-pound bench press can help make or break an offensive or defensive lineman— and Coach Lott knows it. So, each year at the Combine, Lott stands over the bar as the spotter and bellows and cajoles and begs and screams and needles and demands, coaxing every last drop of a rep out of the kids. With his native Texas drawl, he's part drill sergeant and part preacher and once you enter his weight room, your ass belongs to him. Although Lott wouldn't say ass. He doesn't use foul language.

He's the genuine article. Before he "allows" any of the lifters into the Weight and Reps area, Lott gathers the group outside in the hallway for a pep talk. He wants to make sure, to use his parlance, they get their stinking minds right before they lift. Here is a speech he once gave to a defensive line group before they began their lifting session, verbatim:

> *Every defensive line coach in the National Football League is over in this stinking next room, okay, guys? The biggest thing about this, fellas, is it's the first impression. It's the first time we're going to see you eyeball to eyeball, get hit in the face, and see how you react to it. Hey, you have an opportunity here. You have a stinking opportunity here. Let's take full stinking advantage of it, okay, guys? I'm not going to give you stinking hype. I'm not going to sit up here like some stinking mannequin, so get these stinking lethargic eyeball looks off your face and get your minds right. This is coaching right here now. This ain't no stinking test, okay, guys? Get your stinking minds right, show you belong here. Fellas, you've got a window of opportunity and it closes up, all right? It's time to lift, so if you can lift, we're gonna make you lift. Let's do this thing, right? All right here*

John Lott runs a real tight ship in the Weight and Reps room. *(NFL Network)*

we go: hands in. Hard work on three, hard work on three. One,
two, three, hard work!

Yes, it's time to lift. One by one the players enter the Weight and Reps room in which the Combine places two large risers of seats, one on each side of the room, from which the coaches observe the lifting. They're always filled to capacity. A bench with a bar weighing 225 pounds sits in the middle. Lott stands on a riser behind it while Broncos strength and conditioning coach Rich Tuten sits in a chair at the player's feet. It's his job to make sure the lifter keeps his back flat on the bench, doesn't bounce the bar off his chest, and locks his arms out to complete a full, legitimate rep. Tuten has the authority to actually remove a rep from a lifter's total. Throughout the whole process, Tuten hardly says a word. He's the straight man. Ren to Lott's Stimpy.

"Say your name and your school, son," Lott says to the next lifter.

The player responds. If he's not loud enough, Lott will tell him to say it again.

"And be proud. It's the name your momma gave you."

Let's say he's from Iowa State.

"I hear you, Iowa State," Lott might say as the player takes the bench. "Let's see what you got, Cyclone."

My favorite one was when a lineman from Kansas lifted and Lott called him Toto the whole time.

At any rate, when the player grabs the bar, a deafening silence fills the room. It's time to lift. All you hear is the sound of the metal weights grinding against each other with Lott murmuring the number of reps one by one under his breath.

Speaking of breath, the lifter's soon gets very heavy. That's when Lott kicks in.

"Keep going. Don't you stop!"

A couple of more reps and and we see, soon, the first signs of struggle.

"One by one now! Here we go, Cyclone! One by one. *Up!*"

Meaning, just take it one rep at a time.

"*Up!* Gimme one more. UP!"

Lott gets one rep.

"Another! I want another! UP!"

Series of deep breaths and a slow push up of the bar.

"Lock it! Lock it! Lock it!"

The arms lock to complete another rep.

"Gimme another! Gimme another! Push it!"

The player's face is now completely beet red and invariably this is when he'll let out a William Wallace–like yelp straight out of *Braveheart.*

"AAAAAAAAAAAAAAAAHHHHHHHHHHHHHHHHHHH"

"Don't you quit! Don't you quit on me! I know there's one more!"

Slowly, the bar teeters up from the chest, with biceps and triceps bulging, neck veins and eyes popping and sweat gushing out of every pore. That's when Lott bends completely over at the waist so he can look down and make direct eye contact.

"UP! UP! UP! UP! UP! *UP!*"

The player just has nothing but fumes left. That's when Lott will grab the bar and say the same thing he always says when he grabs the bar away.

"Awwwww, shoot this thing!"

"Twenty-eight!" Tuten screams out to the room.

"Twenty-eight, way to go," Lott says, slapping the lifter on the side.

It's on to the next lifter. And the next. And the next. For six straight days. And they best all have their stinkin' minds right. Long live John Lott!

The biggest buzz at the 2006 Scouting Combine had nothing to do with any drill or physical attribute. It concerned the Wonderlic test score of Vince Young, the studly quarterback from Texas who had just whipped USC in the Rose Bowl with perhaps the most breathtaking performance in college football history.

The Wonderlic Personnel Test is a 12-minute, 50-question test that, according to the Wonderlic Web site, "measures cognitive ability or general intelligence, the strongest single predictor of employment success." It's normally used by human resource managers across the spectrum of American businesses—including (who knew?) the National Football League.

Players despise the Wonderlic in the same manner virtually every 15-year old hates algebra. Under what possible circumstances could this be useful in everyday life? It's not a football test; it's a "short-form measure of cognitive ability." Although, wouldn't it be great if, just once, a law firm candidate cracked open a Wonderlic and saw a question about a single-high safety shading to his right in a Cover Two defense?

Sharpen those No. 2 pencils. *(NFL Network)*

Well, that's the way most players feel when they've been poked and prodded by the medical staff for hours, only to be plopped into Room 152 (next door to John Lott's room!) at the Indiana Convention Center and handed a No. 2 pencil. Most of The Evaluators, however, swear something useful can be gleaned by a football player's Wonderlic score. Since a normal NFL playbook can be as thick as the Yellow Pages and feature more arrows and X's and O's than a DNA chart, the player with his nose in said book needs to be somewhat intelligent. Thus: *Take the Wonderlic, son. You've got twelve minutes. Good luck.*

Here are some sample Wonderlic questions as printed with permission from the good folks at Wonderlic.

1. **Assume the first 2 statements are true. Is the final one: 1) true 2) false 3) not certain**
   The boy plays baseball. All baseball players wear hats. The boy wears a hat.

2. Paper sells for 21 cents per pad. What will 4 pads cost?

3. How many of the five pairs of items listed below are exact duplicates?

Nieman, K.M.	*Nieman, K.M*
Thomas, G.K.	*Thomas, C.K.*
Hoff, J.P.	*Hoff, J.P.*
Pino, L.R.	*Pina, L.R.*
Warner, T.S.	*Wanner, T.S.*

4. PRESENT RESENT—Do these words
    1) have similar meanings 2) have contradictory meanings
    3) mean neither the same nor opposite

5. A train travels 20 feet in 1/5 second. At this same speed, how many feet will it travel in three seconds?

6. When rope is selling at $.10 a foot, how many feet can you buy for sixty cents?

7. The ninth months of the year is
    1) October 2) January 3) June 4) September 5) May

8. Which number in the following group of numbers represents the smallest amount?
    7   .8   31   .33   2

9. In printing an article of 48,000 words, a printer decides to use two sizes of type. Using the larger type, a printed page contains 1,800 words. Using smaller type, a page contains 2,400 words. The article is allotted 21 full pages in a magazine. How many pages must be in smaller type?

10. Three individuals form a partnership and agree to divide the profits equally. X invests $9,000, Y invests $7,000, Z invests $4,000. If the profits are $4,800, how much less does X received than if the profits were divided in proportion to the amount invested?

11. Assume the first two statements are true. Is the final one:
    1) true   2) false   3) not certain?
    Tom greeted Beth. Beth greeted Dawn. Tom did not greet Dawn.

12. A boy is 17 years old and his sister is twice as old. When the boy is 23 years old, what will be the age of his sister?

Answers:
    1. true; 2. 84 cents; 3. 1; 4. 3; 5. 300 feet; 6. 6 feet; 7. September; 8. .33; 9. 17; 10. $560; 11. not certain; 12. 40 years old

It's seemingly simple, but a test is a test. I don't know about you, but I absolutely tanked my first shot at the SAT. Supposedly, Vince Young knows the feeling. The day after his quarterbacks group took the test, word began to spread like wildfire that Young had posted a whopping dud of a Wonderlic score of 6. Out of 50. I've been told the average Wonderlic score for any Wonderlic testee is 21, and the average for an NFL quarterback is in the mid-20s, which equates to an I.Q. of 100. Evaluators would love for a quarterback to nail at least 15 correctly; that way they'll still feel comfortable looking the other way if the prospect is otherwise tantalizing. I mean, Dan Marino is said to have scored a 16 on his Wonderlic.

But not even to crack double digits?

Young's alleged score served as fresh red meat for the media throng standing outside the blue curtain. One outlet even tracked down the president of Wonderlic Inc., named Charlie Wonderlic (and the Wonderlic Factory!), and asked for his comment: "A score of ten is literacy; that's about all we can say." Young's agent, Major Adams, received a large dose criticism for apparently not preparing his client for the test. Each of those stories pointed out how Adams was a longtime family friend of Young's and actually had never before *been* an agent. Thus, Young's alleged score not only cast a poor light on his book smarts, but also his judgment in choosing such green representation in the first place.

"He didn't take the test on campus [in previous years]," one scout was quoted as saying in *USA Today*. "That raises a red flag. He's got that agent and that posse. It makes you wonder."

This is how quickly things can spiral out of control at the NFL

Scouting Combine. Over one single solitary score . . . on an aptitude test! Even for a top, blue-chip talent like Vince Young, although the Longhorn didn't help himself by not working out in Indianapolis.

Again, players are "invited" to the NFL Scouting Combine, which isn't really called the Scouting Combine if you want to pick nits. Its official name is the National Invitational Camp as called by the organizer of the event, a scouting company, National Football Scouting. They're the ones who run the show in Indianapolis, with heavy guidance from the NFL's Competition Committee. At any rate, National Football Scouting identifies the top prospects from all schools around the country and "invites" them to the NFL Scouting Combine to work out. For those who play at small schools or in the backwaters of America, an invitation to the Combine is a major thrill and an even greater opportunity. In fact, Dick Vermeil once told me many NFL head coaches get phone calls from small-school head coaches asking for help in getting their player on the invitation list to Indianapolis.

On the opposite end of that spectrum sit the Youngs, Brady Quinns, Matt Leinarts, JaMarcus Russells, and Reggie Bushes of the world. Their NFL draft status is virtually cemented by their superb college careers and, in their mind, cannot be improved by throwing a ball or running a 40-yard dash or a three-cone drill at the NFL Scouting Combine. So, they show up in Indianapolis to step on a scale, get measured, run through the medical gauntlet and interview with the select number of teams at the top of the draft with a ghost of a chance to take them. Otherwise, they stand around on the field during the group's position drills in a sweatshirt. If an NFL scout wants to watch him work out, he'll have to schlep to the player's Pro Day—the workout session all colleges hold for NFL scouts to come check out their draft-eligible players. Because players get to wake up in their own beds, throw to their own receivers in a workout run by their own coaches on their own college campuses, the blue-chippers prefer to work on their colleges' Pro Day.

Needless to say, The Evaluators hate that.

Pro Days are like primaries in a presidential election: Several get held on the same day. One Pro Day in March 2007 read like a Super Tuesday: Alabama, Connecticut, Montana, Tennessee, Texas. So, how in the world can teams scout all those players on different college campuses on the same day? They can't. That's why The Evaluators feel it's essential for players to work out at the Scouting Combine. It shows *them* respect, and that the players recognize the value of The Evaluators' time. The subject makes Dick Vermeil's blood boil; he said he would frequently get in the faces of kids who didn't work out at the Combine.

"I'd tell them they had all thirty-two coaches of the National Football League and all their staffs in one building and to make the most of it," Vermeil told me. "And if they thought we would all get our butts on a plane to go fly out to their college Pro Day just to see them, they were totally mistaken."

So, when players don't work out for The Evaluators, they give The Evaluators something else to talk about—like, in the case of Young, his weird arm angle when he delivers the ball. Or a dreadful Wonderlic score. Suddenly, Young's breathtaking performance in the Rose Bowl was fading from view.

The offensive lineman group goes through the vertical leap. Top draft choice D'Brickashaw Ferguson (leaning against wall) wears a sweatshirt to indicate he isn't working out. *(NFL Network)*

Team Young quickly went on the offensive. Young's agent said there had merely been a problem in the scoring of Young's test. Word spread that Young would be allowed to take the test again. Even the NFL, which never comments on such matters, felt compelled to clear the air.

"I can tell you absolutely that the score that has been reported on the Internet is inaccurate," a league spokesman said at the Combine. "I spoke to the person who graded the test, and he assured me that that number was not correct."

As for what happened next, no one knows. Either Young retook the Wonderlic or his original test got retabulated, because eventually Young's unofficial score of 6 had an official 1 in front of it: 16. No more red flag.

Less than 10 months later, everyone was talking about another Vince Young 6—the points he scored in his breathtaking 39-yard touchdown scramble in overtime to lead the Tennessee Titans past the Houston Texans in his hometown of Houston. Nobody mentioned the Wonderlic.

In case you haven't noticed, scouting an NFL draft-eligible player is one big jigsaw puzzle. One guy may be slow, but could be real football savvy. Another guy could jump out of the gym, but not tell the difference between a Will linebacker blitz and a Will Smith movie. A guy could test real well at the Wonderlic and run the 40 like the wind, but have some baggage that pops up on the psychological test. Or the medical staff may be concerned about the shoulder he dislocated two years before. And so on.

That's why a lot of coaches like to look the player in the eye and see what he's made of. After all, that's what coaches do. You can almost hear the thought clanking from underneath their Motorola headsets: *To heck with this Wonderlic and those damn X-rays. Let me get this kid face-to-face and see what's what.*

That's where the job interview comes into play at the NFL Scouting Combine.

Sure, these kids are about to become millionaires at age 21 because they're skilled at a highly specialized craft, but they're just like everybody else coming out of college—looking for a job, which means there's an interview process to go through with a prospective employer. So, once the prospects are done with their drills for the day in the RCA Dome, they're sent to their hotel. There, the teams are all waiting to chat with them through a highly organized and regimented process that, once upon a time, was like the Wild, Wild West.

Back in the Combine day, once drill work was complete, teams were free to grab whichever player they wanted to interview and keep him for as long as they wanted. Legend has it that the New York Giants would take the longest because they administered their very own psychological test straight out of *The Parallax View*. Thus, other team scouts waiting to interview the player the Giants had in their clutches for nearly an hour would line up outside the Giants door and pounce on the poor player once he exited. I'm told that, frequently, shouting matches and occasional fistfights would break out between scouts, with such playground retorts as "I was here first!" bandied about.

Therefore, National Football Scouting stopped the insanity. Nowadays, each NFL franchise submits an advance list of 60 players they wish to interview at the Combine. National Football Scouting makes up a schedule and hands it out to each team and each player and, voilà, it's now far more civilized.

However, sophisticated it's not. The interview area is the entire first floor of the players' hotel—the three-story Crowne Plaza Hotel across the street from the RCA Dome. It's one of those hotels where the rooms have no windows, unless you count the window facing the atrium of the hotel as an actual window. Each team is assigned one of those rooms for its interviewing area. So, if you've ever stayed on the first floor of the Crowne Plaza Hotel in Indianapolis, your two double-bed deluxe could be the same place where the Dolphins have been searching for the next Marino the last decade.

I'm not joking. The Steelers once let me peek into their interview room and the surroundings were quite Red Roof-ian. To create space for the coaching staff, the Steelers removed the two double beds from their room and placed two white folding tables about eight feet in length in their stead. The headboards from the double beds were still attached to the wall. Behind one table sat none other than Hall of Famer "Mean" Joe Greene, currently Pittsburgh's special assistant of player personnel. In front of the two tables, the Steelers placed two of what can only be described as those comfy, puffy chairs found in every hotel room on Planet Earth.

"I sit in this chair," said Head Coach Mike Tomlin, "and that other one is the hot seat."

Placed next to said hot seat was a large white grease board—a crucial part of every interview at the Combine. Every team asks the interviewee to "get on the board"—meaning walk up to the grease board and show off your football acumen. For instance, Tomlin might ask a linebacker to draw his favorite blitz play on the grease board. Running backs and tight ends are asked to draw up protection schemes against certain blitzes a defense might show. Quarterbacks spend most of their interview time on the board. It's a high-stakes game of Win, Lose, or Draw because through this process a coach can easily tell if a player not only knows his X's and O's, but has a passion for the game. Some guys may run like Forrest Gump and lift like Hercules, but get them "on the board" and they're dumb as a stump. Adios, climbing stock. Other guys may run drills poorly, but get them to the grease board and they're Da Vinci. Once again, Mariucci said the best player he's ever seen on the board was Clarett. Mooch swears he was like Rain Man with protections, routes, schemes, you name it. Go figure.

However, the best Combine interview story I ever heard was told to me by the great head coach Jim Mora Sr., best known for his postgame rants at the media. (*Playoffs?*) The winningest coach in Saints history, Mora had just been hired by the Indianapolis Colts and faced a whopper of a decision in his first draft with the team. The Colts needed a quarterback and owned the first overall pick in the 1998 Draft and there were two rocket-armed guys coming out of college: Peyton Manning and Ryan Leaf.

Of course, we *now* know the subsequent success stories of each: Manning will have a bust in Canton while Leaf became synonymous with the word "bust." Nevertheless, at the 1998 NFL Scouting Combine, Mora and his staff had no benefit of hindsight. Leaf and Manning were neck and neck in their evaluation, with Leaf coming off a stellar performance in the Rose Bowl against Michigan and Manning completing a wonderful four-year college career during which, however, most people noted he never won a big game.

So, the Colts brought both quarterbacks in for separate interviews.

Mora put both quarterbacks on the board and eventually asked them the same question: "If we make you the first overall pick in the draft, what's the first thing you're going to do?"

Manning replied he would immediately ask for the Colts playbook so he could learn it as fast as he could. That if the Colts so honored him by making him the first overall pick in an NFL Draft, he would do everything in his power to be their starting quarterback as soon as possible so they could start winning.

Impressive.

Mora said when he asked Leaf the same question, Leaf also gave an immediate answer.

"Oh, man. If I'm the first overall pick in the draft, the first thing I'm gonna do is call up my buddies and we are going to *Vegas!*"

Now, if you think that's when the Colts made their decision to choose Manning over Leaf in the draft, think again. Mora says their evaluation still went up to the last minute. Again, when I say the NFL talent evaluation process is outrageously overwrought, I mean it.

Pieces to a puzzle, my friend. Pieces to a puzzle.

All the time allotted to each team for this crucial interview portion of that puzzle is 15 minutes. National Football Scouting places two of its staff members at a table in the middle of the Crowne Plaza Atrium with a timer and an air horn. After 13 minutes of an interviewing session, one of the guys picks up the air horn and . . . WAAAAAAAAAAAA AAAAAAAAAHH. A two-minute warning that could be heard in Kentucky. Two minutes later, it's time for the session to end and . . . WAAAAAAAAAAAAAAAAAAAAAAHH! (In case you're wondering, it's the same number of A's and H's in my air horn onomatopoeia.) Suddenly, all the doors to the double-occupancy, first-floor nonsmoking rooms open up; the players come out and head in an orderly manner to their next interview room, be it down the hall or even, yes, on the other side of the in-ground family pool at one end of the atrium. One scout told me that a player once got so confused as to where he was headed next, he didn't notice the pool and took a direct header into it. No, the time it took for the player to get out of the pool was not considered a "measurable."

Ah, yes, now to the jargon! The Evaluators speak a language all their own. They use it when watching the prospects work out on the field.

They use it when watching game tape of every single player. Now, thanks to NFL Network draft and talent evaluation expert Mike Mayock, you, too, can sound like one of The Evaluators! Amaze your friends! Or, in the case of the many ladies that I hope bought this book because of the unadulterated heat generated by the cover photo, shock the men in your lives! Learn these key phrases and sound like you know what you're talking about! Here are Mike Mayock's key words of talent evaluation in the National Football League! I'll occasionally include uses in the form of a sentence for help!

Without further ado.

MEASURABLE: Anything you can take a measure of and attach a number to it: height, weight, speed, jump, etc. Mike says scouts tend to hang their hats on measurables. For proof, look no further than 49ers tight end Vernon Davis at the 2006 Scouting Combine. Davis set Combine records for a tight end in the 40-yard dash (4.38), standing broad jump (10'8"), vertical leap (42"), and bench press (33 reps). Davis immediately jumped from a middle first-round pick to the sixth overall pick in the Draft.

Example: Vernon Davis! That guy's measurables are mind-blowing! (EDITOR'S NOTE: *Ladies, be very careful how you say that sentence.*)

CHARACTER GUY: A player with character issues, whether it be problems meshing well with teammates and coaches or a spotty criminal record.

Example: He's got good measurables, but he's also a character guy, so you have to be careful.

HIGH CHARACTER GUY: Based on the previous term, you'd think this was a player with many character issues, but it's quite the opposite. A High Character Guy has lots of character and, thus, a great way about him. So, in the parlance of the scouts, you stay away from a Character Guy but draft the High Character Guy.

PREMIUM ROAD GRADER: A great run-blocking offensive lineman. When I asked Mike Mayock what a great pass-blocking offensive lineman is called, he said without hesitation, "Millionaire."

KNEE BENDER: An athletic offensive lineman, because good offensive linemen bend at the knees instead of the hips.

Example: That guy Joe Thomas is a knee bender and he certainly isn't a . . .

HEAVY-LEGGED WAIST BENDER: An offensive lineman who bends naturally at the waist instead of having the proper flexion to dip his hips and naturally bend at the knee. Thus, the lineman's feet won't move quickly enough, causing him to look . . . heavy-legged.

HIP FLEXION: Bending properly from the hip so you don't become a heavy-legged waist bender.

Example: Check out the hip flexion! He moves so well for a big man!

ANKLE FLEXION: Yes, there's more flexion! Good ankle flexion allows a lineman to keep his entire foot down on the ground, which gives him a bigger base with which to . . .

PLAY WITH LEVERAGE: Mike says the man who gets the lowest to the ground wins in football. So if you can get lower than your opponent in blocking or tackling, it's a good thing. OK. Now, let's put it all together.

Example: He once was a heavy-legged waist bender, but after working with a trainer on his hip flexion and his ankle flexion, he's now a knee bender who plays with leverage. On run plays, he's a premium road grader. I think he'll go on the first day.

FIRST DAY: As in first day of the two-day NFL Draft. The first three rounds are held on the first day with the final four rounds held on the second day. Thus, if you say a guy is a first-day pick, you think he'll go in the first, second, or third rounds.

Example: I can't believe the Broncos made Maurice Clarett a first-day guy.

WORKOUT WARRIOR: A player who doesn't play up to what his physical attributes suggest. The Mother of All Workout Warriors was Boston College defensive lineman Mike Mamula, who blew the doors off the 1995 Combine. The Eagles swapped first-round picks and gave two second-round picks to Tampa Bay to move up five spots to draft Mamula seventh overall. Mamula suffered an injury-riddled career, playing only 77 games in six seasons for Philly.

FUNCTIONAL SPEED: Normal playing speed in pads as opposed to the shirts and shorts in which the players at the Combine work out.

Example: Jerry Rice may not have run the fastest 40, but nobody had better functional speed.

MANUFACTURED SPEED: Many players go to special speed camps to work on their agility in order to get faster for the 40-yard dash at the Combine. Those guys have manufactured speed.

Example: Sure, the guy ran a 4.5, but is that manufactured speed as opposed to functional speed? Ladies, definitely drop that one on your unsuspecting guy and see his reaction. It's fun for the whole family!

QUICK TWITCH: A skilled player with initial explosion and acceleration off the line of scrimmage.

Example: Reggie Bush is a quick-twitch athlete.

INITIAL QUICKS: An offensive or defensive lineman with explosion and quickness off the line of scrimmage.

Example: This guy has initial quicks. He can really get off the snap.

MOTOR: Someone with incredible energy.

Example: Look at the motor on that guy!

SPIN: A quarterback throw that comes out of his hand naturally well.

Example: I tell you, JaMarcus Russell can really spin it. That's one term you can use all year round, even during the regular season.

HAPPY FEET: When a quarterback gets nervous in the pocket and causes his footwork to get all out of whack, he has happy feet.

BURP THE BABY: The quarterback burps the baby when he taps his hand on the football way too long and gets rid of it too late. This one is a personal favorite.

COLOR IN THE HOLE: A free safety in the middle of the field. A quarterback needs to read color in the hole prior to a snap. Mike Mayock says scouts scrutinize just how quickly a quarterback can recognize that safety and react with his throw.

Example: The quarterback didn't see the color in the hole there and that's gonna be a mark against him. He may just be a second-day guy.

SECOND-DAY GUY: See First Day.

Example: A second-day guy may not be as good as a first-day guy, but he's certainly better than . . .

JAG: Just a guy.

Here endeth the lesson.

There is one last person who runs the 40 every year at the NFL Scouting Combine that I've yet to mention. That person is me.

One day at our first Combine, I was slumped in a seat in Suite 216A waiting to tape a final segment and I stared out at the empty field of the RCA Dome, the long day's drills complete. That's when the thought hit me. Maybe I should go down there and run the 40-yard dash just for you-know-whats and giggles. As some of you may have surmised by now, the subject matter at an NFL Scouting Combine can be, at times, a bit dry and technical. Somebody had to shake things up. If it's not going to be John Lott, then, by golly, let me at that 40 . . . in my suit and tie. I wasn't going to run the darn thing in shorts and a shirt with proper shoes. I'm no track athlete, but to try to run in my three-button, high-performance Zegna suit, now that's a challenge. And, in my mind, good TV.

So I got up and went downstairs to the field. James Lytle, the fabulous steadicam operator for *NFL Total Access* since Day One, was on the field and quickly grabbed his camera. The tape operators in the truck hit the record button. I put my hand on the turf . . . and off I went! Arms flailing wildly, coat spread out wide, legs splayed out behind me, tie flapping in the wind, and *whoosh!* I crossed the finish line. Well, "whoosh" may not be the most appropriate word. I clocked in at 6.77 seconds.

Still, I was proud of my achievement—and played my running of the 40 for legendary Washington Redskins head coach Joe Gibbs when he appeared on *NFL Total Access* the next day. Who's better to get feedback from than a Hall of Fame head coach?

"There is one forty that is run here at the Combine that I think you need to evaluate, Coach," I said, as the truck rolled the tape. "Tell me if you think this guy can help the Redskins."

"I think you need to work on your form a little bit there," Gibbs deadpanned.

The next day, Lions president and former Raider and 49er linebacker Matt Millen came on the show and *during his interview* demanded to see my 40-yard dash. Word had spread among the scouts, he said.

"I can understand why there's a buzz," I responded, as the truck rolled the tape again.

Millen said his favorite part was when I hitched my pants up by my belt at the finish line. So, imagine my surprise that when I walked through the blue curtain for the first time at the 2006 Scouting

Jim Mora Sr. and Redskins coach Joe Gibbs *(center)* are clearly awestruck while they watch my 40 run on tape. *(Joann Kamay)*

Combine, a startling number of coaches and scouts asked me when I was running my 40-yard dash again. Clearly, I had to give the people what they wanted.

So, three days into the 2006 Combine, I took to the turf again, coat neatly pressed and tie tightly knotted. This time, however, I made one crucial change—lace-up dress shoes. I realized I had made a crushing measurable-altering mistake by running the previous year in loafers. James focused his camera just as I did the same on the line and . . . off I went again! Arm swing a bit more controlled, tie still out of control, belt staying put thanks to a regimen of Pilates and *whoosh* . . . 6.22 seconds! Sweet goddess Nike! A full half second shaved!

The next day, Coach Gibbs was back on the *NFL Total Access* set and I was bursting at the seams to tell him the good news. Roll that tape!

"Yeah," Gibbs said. "A little better, but I still think you need to work on that form a little bit."

Still, an improvement, I noted. Cut to the 2007 NFL Scouting Combine. Two days in and, strangely, not a single one of The Evaluators had asked me when I would run my 40. Could the novelty have worn off after just two years? Or maybe The Evaluators were just underestimating me. Maybe I did have that quick-twitch athlete buried deep within, after all. I announced I'd run the 40 at the Scouting Combine rather than force everyone to come to my Pro Day to watch.

Plus, I had extra motivation. *NFL Total Access* analyst and Lord of the 40 himself, Deion Sanders, was joining our broadcast the next day. It is not an urban legend, people. Back in 1989, Florida State cornerback "Neon" Deion Sanders ran the fastest 40 in the history of the NFL Scouting Combine. Our Mike Mayock said that none other than Bill Belichick confirmed the story: Deion stepped to the starting line, ran his 40 in a ridiculous 4.25 seconds and then left the building. Literally. He crossed the finish line and ran directly into the tunnel and vanished.

"No need to do anything else," Sanders said on our broadcast after Mayock told the story.

"Didn't even stick around for the bench press?" I asked.

Deion scoffed.

"I don't need to lift weights," he said. "When did I ever have to put Jerry Rice across my chest and lift him?"

Fair enough.

Go ahead. Marvel at the form. *(K. Terrell)*

So, knowing Deion himself was going to see this 40, I needed it to be special. I had to break 6.0 seconds. I waited until the last running-back drill of the day was complete and got ready. Seattle head coach Mike Holmgren was leaving his seat in the Combine stands as I took to the starting line.

"You better have that medical staff standing by," said Holmgren, pointing to two trainers on the sideline.

Undaunted, off I went!

I actually felt like I got a good start (for once!) and despite a late tie flap, really thought I had that six-second barrier snapped. I looked for a time but . . . nobody was timing! They weren't ready yet. I had just run an unnecessary first 40.

"I really liked your form there," Holmgren said, now standing at the railing.

I really believed Holmgren liked my form. Confidence was high. I walked back to the start. Had to just catch . . . my . . . breath. Once I did . . . off I went! I crossed the finish line. I looked for a reading and got one: 6.43 seconds. I may or may not have let out an f-bomb.

I don't know what came over me, but, for some reason, I felt seriously driven to snap 6.0 seconds. I was really into it. So, not having warmed up with a single stretch before my *first* run, I strolled back to the starting line to run the 40 for a *third* time. Silly rabbit.

Midway through my third run, pain flashed out from the back of my right thigh and went straight to my temples. It was as if a sniper had taken aim from the upper deck. I grabbed the back of my leg and everyone watching thought it was a joke. No joke, I had pulled my hamstring. As in: needing to lie down on a training table and get immediate treatment.

What an idiot.

Deion, however, loved it. So did fellow NFL Network analyst Dick Vermeil and especially Mayock, who noted that word of my injury-marred 40 had spread and said, "Five or six scouts in the stands told me they want to see it on the big Jumbotron here." The Evaluators were back on board.

It never made it to the big screen, but after we aired it on NFL Network, somebody put it on YouTube. I never thought Deion Sanders and Dick Vermeil narrating the blowing out of my hamstring would ever exist on the Internet, but there you have it.

**National Invitational Camp
RCA Dome Workout Injury Report**

Name: _Rich Fisen_ Event #: _Anchor - NFL Network_

Date: _2/25/07_ Time: _5:00 p.m._

Athletes Ph. # _____

School: _____ Athletic Trainer: _____

Body Part / Injury: _(R) Hamstring_

How injury happened: _Patient was on his third attempt at 40 yard dash when he felt a pull in his (R) hamstring_

Exam: _Pt. stated he felt a pull. Pt. painful over middle 1/3 of muscle belly upon palpation. AROM 1/5 knee flk for pain. MMT 0/5 strength. Pt. presents with noticeable limp. No defect palpated._

Action Taken: _Pt. was iced for 20 min. Pt. was given compression sleeve to wear and Advil was given. Pt. was given empty ice bags to use to ice down in hotel. Re-eval. tomorrow 2/26/07_

Athletic Trainer: _____ ATC
Eric Laudano ATC_

I limped off the RCA Dome turf with the head trainer, and that's when it hit me: I had now injured myself at both the Pro Bowl and the NFL Scouting Combine. At how many more NFL events will I require medical attention? The annual Owners' Meeting was one month away.

THE OWNERS'
MEETING

Ah, spring.

The time when the NFL goes into hibernation and Major League Baseball, the Masters, and the NCAA basketball tournament rule the sports day. Once upon a time, maybe—not anymore.

How's this for March Madness? In March 2007, 91 different NFL players switched teams during the first month of free agency with contracts totaling nearly one *billion* dollars in value. And that's just for the guys changing uniforms. During the same time period, 86 players re-signed with their old teams for the proverbial "terms not disclosed." Add in those figures and you're nearing the gross national product of Lichtenstein. Now, unlike virtually every other professional sport, not all dollars in an NFL deal are guaranteed. Regardless, it's apparent that NFL ownership is shelling it out.

Come to think of it, the NFL owners own March. Well, to be honest, many of them are wealthy enough to own any month. *I'll take November because the gemstone matches my Grey Poupon!* But, in all seriousness, on the NFL calendar, March is clearly the month of ownership. It comes in like a lion with free agency and ends with the annual NFL Owners' Meeting, where the only lamb in sight is served grilled with rosemary mint sauce.

The places where the owners hold their yearly March gathering have no red roofs. The three-day-long NFL Annual Meeting, as it's officially known, boasts of a Cy Young–like three-site rotation: The Breakers in Palm Beach, Florida (2004), the Grand Cypress in Orlando, Florida (2006), and the Frank Lloyd Wright–designed Arizona Biltmore in Phoenix (2007). When the league mixes in a new spot, it doesn't scrimp on Michelin stars; the 2005 Annual Meeting took place at the Ritz Carlton Kapalua in Maui, Hawaii. There was a nine-hole putting course shaved into the lawn overlooking the Pacific Ocean next to the *NFL Total Access* set. Terrell Davis and I busted out the flat stick during breaks.

Despite the posh surroundings, business does get accomplished. A bevy of league committees meet on their own before the affair to discuss what proposals or changes, if any, should be forwarded to The Membership during the General Session that lasts all three days. Or two and a half days, if the owners are getting antsy to bolt for home (which they usually are) and have other matters to attend to (which they usually

Yes, me and TD were actually putting on the job at the Owners' Meeting.
(*Joann Kamay*)

have). If you're scoring at home, some of the more prominent committees include:

> **Broadcasting Committee,** Broncos owner Pat Bowlen, chair-
> man
> **Stadium Committee,** Panthers owner Jerry Richardson, chair-
> man
> **Finance Committee,** Saints owner Tom Benson, chairman
> **Workplace Diversity Committee,** Steelers owner Dan Rooney,
> chairman
> **Competition Committee,** Falcons team president Rich McKay
> (son of the great coaching legend John McKay) and Ten-
> nessee Titans head coach Jeff Fisher, cochairmen.

Yes, most of the head coaches attend the NFL Annual Meeting, too. If
The Membership is going to vote on Competition Committee–suggested

Titans head coach Jeff Fisher and NFL vice-president of officiating Mike Pereira stop
by *NFL Total Access* at the 2006 Owners' Meeting. *(Joann Kamay)*

changes on matters like holding penalties and celebration rules and the number of instant-replay challenges during a game, you can bet dollars to donuts that the head coach wants a say in all that. Same goes for the general managers. They're also there, as are most team presidents. It's a top-of-the-flow-chart hootenanny.

Presiding over it all is, of course, the NFL commissioner. He kicks off the meeting Monday morning with his State of the League address to The Membership (including a six-minute video review of the previous season put together by NFL Films) and brings it to an official close with a Wednesday press conference. In between, the commissioner sits at the front of the massive General Session meeting room, moving the process along, cajoling parties to compromise, and settling disputes behind the scenes. It's a fascinating process to watch unfold. Some of the more famous faces in professional sports follow Robert's Rules of Order to conduct the business of the most popular sport in America as well as to set parameters for the competition between teams on the field of play. It's a lot like your fantasy football league. Except this isn't fantasy, and nobody's team is called something like "The Nipsey Russells."

Just like the Scouting Combine in February, the NFL Annual Meeting in March attracts its share of media and agents. And just as they do at the Scouting Combine, they're all at the Owners' Meeting milling outside an off-limits area—the General Session room—waiting to buttonhole anyone coming out for a breather.

Only NFL owners, club members (team presidents, financial officers, lawyers, GMs, coaches, etc.), and league staffers are allowed inside the General Session room. At times, however, the owners are limited as to who they can bring inside. Certain sensitive league matters are discussed during something called a "one owner, one member" session. For such top-secret powwows, even the most influential owners in the league are limited to one member guest only. You should see the number of NFL power brokers cooling their heels out in the hallway with the media horde during those sessions, which also happen to be quite off-limits to certain NFL personnel, including your humble narrator.

However, I have been fortunate to gain admittance to the General Session inner sanctum on occasion. Every time I'm inside, I can't help but think of the scene from *Superman* where General Zod is found guilty and then cast into space in that mirror thingie. In this bizzaro scenario,

I'm Zod and the NFL owners are the judges. Maybe I'm sharing too much and need to work this out with a therapist? My general meaning is this: The sheer power in the room hits you smack in the face. Plus, the blue lighting cast upon three NFL shields that hang from the curtain behind the commissioner adds to the science fiction atmosphere.

The General Session ballroom has the same setup every year—owners sitting at tables in the form of what looks like one big gothic letter E. Whichever committee is addressing The Membership sits at a long table in the front—the long side of the E—with The Membership sitting at three perpendicular tables shooting out like, if you will, three arms of an E. The commissioner sits right in the middle of the long table for all three days; the different presenting committees rotate in and out of the seats on either side of him.

One other person has the same prominent seat at every Owners' Meeting, every year—that's Al Davis. The owner of the Oakland Raid-uhs sits at the very end of the table that forms the bottom arm of the E, perched in the only chair in the whole room with arms on it. It's from this back-of-the-room throne that Davis throws out several nuanced questions to the presenting committees. A total silence falls so Davis can be heard. Others take to microphone stands placed throughout the room from where they make impassioned pleas against a rule change or rousing speeches in favor of it. When shown on NFL Network, it comes across more like NFL C-SPAN.

But don't take my word for it. Let me take you into the General Session as *NFL Total Access* has exclusively taken its viewers for every Annual Meeting since 2004. That year at The Breakers, Commissioner Tagliabue allowed NFL Network to first put cameras in the rear of the General Session. It pulled back the curtain on the genteel debate that had been going on for decades among The Membership. It also revealed the subtle diplomacy a commissioner must occasionally employ to get something done. The subject up for debate: the Competition Committee's unanimous recommendation that the use of TV instant replay to review on-the-field calls by referees be made a permanent fixture in the NFL. Despite its immense popularity with the fans, instant replay still had many detractors in The Old Guard portion of The Membership, which, as a whole, also had two other options—extend instant replay for a period of five more years or just kill it altogether. It was a momentous vote. Flanked at the front table by the Competition Committee, Tagliabue brought the meeting to order.

2007 NFL ANNUAL MEETING
PENALTY FOR SPIKING BALL ON FIELD OF PLAY

Chiefs head coach Herman Edwards makes a point to The Membership.
(*NFL Network*)

TAGLIABUE: The fans have always been the big supporters of replay and have always been tremendously interested in replay, so we are experimenting with this discussion with a taped coverage by the NFL Network of the discussion of replay, which, happily, does not appear to be as controversial as it's been in some prior years. I think the way to proceed, Rich [McKay], would be to start with the committee's recommendation that replay be adopted in its current form, but on a permanent basis. I guess the key point there is that this would be permanently in place rather than only in place for five years. Does anyone want to speak to permanence versus five years?

BROWN: Paul, I would.

Bengals owner Mike Brown got up from his seat and walked to a microphone. Son of the legendary Paul Brown, Mike Brown hails from The Old Guard.

TAGLIABUE: Yes, Mike.

BROWN: I would say to you that I think it's wishful thinking to say that instant replay does all that it is said to do. It really has a lot of faults. It has error built into it. It's run by human beings. Just as the officials are human beings on the field, the people up above are human beings, and they make mistakes.

Jim Irsay, son of the late Bob Irsay and current owner of the Indianapolis Colts, seconded Brown's emotion.

IRSAY: The original thought of replay, I thought, was to improve upon the officiating, avoid a serious error in a big game. My understanding was it has to be irrefutable evidence [to overturn an on-the-field call]; that we would never come here and say: "A call was overturned and it shouldn't have been overturned." Because, now, that's exactly what's been happening and what we're doing [with replay] is layering human error over human error.

Rich McKay, the cochairman of the committee that recommended permanence for instant replay, snapped on his microphone.

McKAY: To Mr. Irsay's point, he's absolutely right. [Instant replay] is not perfect, and it's not going to be perfect. Although the point of [needing] irrefutable visual evidence [to overturn a call] can't be [stressed] enough times to the officials 'cause that is the league's standard. But we felt like, if we're gonna make this system better and have an opportunity to talk in coming years about how the system could be tweaked, changed, and improved, the rule ought to go in a permanent fashion.

COMMITTEE MEMBER AND SEATTLE HEAD COACH MIKE HOLMGREN: It was our feeling as a committee this year, in particular, that if we could get this passed on a permanent basis, *then* [we can] focus all our energies to making the other parts of instant replay better—the people that are actually working the machines, the observers, the communication between the field and upstairs, which at times has been a frustration for all of us. And I don't want to downplay that. That's real.

COMMITTEE COCHAIR JEFF FISHER: The officiating department has asked that the replay assistant become part of the officiating crew and travel with them on a week-to-week basis to improve the communication process that takes place between the assistant in the booth and the referee. We think that just that small little issue like that can help to improve it.

All very nice spiels. But Vikings owner Red McCombs, who would sell his team two years later, still wasn't sold on the idea of making replay permanent.

McCOMBS: If you vote for [the five-year option], *that's* going to put additional pressure to all the people working to improve it, get better, keep it working. So in my opinion, I think this vote for permanency, those of you that wanted the permanency, I think you've somewhat missed the boat, in my opinion.

At that point, Mike Brown stood up again and asked to amend the resolution to limit the extension of replay to just five years. McKay then called the roll and the vote to amend failed. Permanence was still on the table. But so was killing replay completely. Sensing a turning tide, the commissioner decided to keep the two sides talking.

TAGLIABUE: I think, at this point, we should probably focus our discussion on the merits of replay and also the subject of a third challenge versus two challenges.

Under the rules of instant replay, each coach gets to challenge two calls by officials during the span of a game. If the conclusive video evidence proves the coach wrong, the ruling on the field stands and the team loses a time-out. If the coach gets his challenge right, no time-out is taken away and the ruling on the field is changed. (The major flaw with replay, in the mind of some owners and many head coaches, is that even if the challenging coach appears right but the video offers no irrefutable evidence otherwise, the coach is still deemed wrong and loses a time-out.) The Competition Committee was now suggesting that The Membership allow head coaches a third challenge during the game—but only if his first two challenges were right.

> **McKAY:** Why not give an additional challenge if the coach gets the first two right? Last year [in 2003], that only happened one time in the entire season.

AUTHOR TIME-OUT. By mentioning that it only happened once, McKay was implying a third challenge would not lengthen the time of the game, something The Membership hates. They want NFL games to move briskly. But the real reason I pause here is to point out the incredible: Would you believe that in all 256 regular-season games during the 2003 season, only one NFL head coach got both his instant-replay challenges correct? That would be John Fox of the Carolina Panthers, who were obviously blessed in '03, what with also making the Super Bowl and all. TIME-IN.

> **McKAY:** Now, could it happen more if we were to make this amendment? Yes. I don't think it would be a great deal more, but it could happen more because, then, coaches would be more willing to use that second challenge as opposed to having to hold it in their pocket.

New England head coach Bill Belichick then got up from his seat and walked to a microphone in defense of the status quo.

> **BELICHICK:** If I understand the rule correctly, really, what you're saying is, if you have a close play, let's say, in the first half of the game, you know, key turnover or something, and you challenge the play as a critical play in the game and lose the challenge, then, in effect, you're really losing two challenges, not one. Because then you would lose the right to a third challenge. So then, the question becomes, whether you really want to challenge that [first] play at all—it's a close play, you know, you think you got a shot at it, but, you know, it's not a two-foot putt with no break.
> **FISHER:** If there are two events that take place on the field that were out of my control, calls that were wrong that I had to correct, then I should simply have enough challenges and another opportunity to challenge another play. I don't see [Belichick's point of view]. I don't

see it as being a situation where I'm gonna change my philosophy [whether] to challenge something early with the first call or even with the second.

After further debate revealed few others opposed to the idea of a third replay challenge, the Commissioner jumped in again and cut back to the chase.

TAGLIABUE: Who's opposed to replay on a permanent basis?

The Commissioner asked for a show of hands, as nonbinding a vote as you can get at an NFL Annual Meeting. For any resolution to pass in the NFL, you need a three-quarters majority of The Membership. I'll do the math for you: With 32 teams in the NFL, the magic number for passage is 24. The magic number for rejection is 9. When the commissioner asked for a show of hands against the resolution to make instant repay permanent, 9 very wealthy mitts waved in the air. Yikes. Good thing the commissioner didn't ask for an official vote. Had he done so, instant replay in the NFL may have gone the way of the wishbone offense.

TAGLIABUE: Well, then, I think someone better entertain an amendment to go back to five years.

The Competition Committee gladly entertained it. Certainly, it was better than fighting for permanence and losing instant replay altogether.

McKAY: It's our instant replay system for five years, Seasons 2004, '05, '06, '07, and '08, with the addition of the third challenge language, which is contained in Player Rule Proposal 1B.

It was still a significant request of The Membership, which had never approved an extension of instant replay beyond three years. A handful of speeches on the merit of replay sparked in the room, especially from the Competition Committee. One of the members, then–Texans GM Charlie Casserly, made the blunt point that the replay genie was already out of the bottle.

CASSERLY: Our game is a made-for-TV sport. If we don't have replay, we still have replay. It's gonna be in the stadium where everyone can see an obvious error, [with] no way to correct it. The networks are gonna replay it over and over again. And if we don't have a way to correct it, we're gonna be second-guessed forever.

Debate soon ended and time finally arrived for an official up-or-down vote. It appeared The Old Guard had made its point in staving off permanence; six who had voted no in the nonbinding vote switched their stance in favor of a five-year extension. The resolution passed 29 in favor and 3 opposed. That's how instant replay in the National Football League was saved from extinction.

TAGLIABUE: For those who regard this as progress, this shows that progress is slow and incremental. After ten or twelve years, you've added two years and one challenge [to instant replay].
McKAY: We're getting there.

They weren't kidding about the slowly grinding wheels of progress. It took Kansas City Chiefs owner Lamar Hunt 20 years to get the two-point conversion voted into the NFL. And he's the guy who came up with the idea to call the final playoff game of the year The Super Bowl!

As for instant replay, it essentially needed 20 years, too. The Competition Committee took another crack at permanence at the 2007 NFL Annual Meeting and the three years in between votes had apparently assuaged many concerns. It sailed through by a vote of 30–2. Mike Brown voted against it again, joined by Arizona Cardinals owner Bill Bidwell. Two teams that voted against it at The Breakers in 2004 broke the other way—the Colts and Chiefs. So, 21 years after first introducing it on a temporary basis—and 14 years after abandoning it for six straight seasons—The Membership finally made instant replay a permanent part of the NFL landscape.

One of the most valuable pieces of real estate at an Owners' Meeting is a treadmill in the hotel gym—before breakfast. Don't forget: The NFL Annual Meeting is packed to the gills with NFL head coaches, high-powered executives and 32 Masters of the Universe. These people didn't reach their positions in life by sleeping in. Thus, the hotel gym hops just after sunrise. It's fun to stroll in there and see a random collection of NFL power players breaking a sweat. Over the years, I've put on the headsets and tuned into CNN or TNT or VH-1 on an elliptical next to the likes of Colts president Bill Polian, Saints coach Sean Payton, 49ers coach Mike Nolan, Ravens GM and Hall of Fame tight end Ozzie Newsome, and NFL Commissioner Roger Goodell (when he was the league's COO under Tagliabue.) Oh, god. I never thought I'd become a workout name-dropper. Writing this book has gone to my head!

Already notoriously early risers, NFL head coaches also sweat with the roosters because, even at the Annual Meeting, their days start early. On the Tuesday and Wednesday mornings of every Owners' Meeting, the head coaches are made available to the media at breakfast. Each head coach chows down at his own circular table with the other seats reserved for anyone in the media who wants to sit down and ask questions over eggs over easy. Of course, the media can partake in the buffet as well. Yes, once again, the league is giving its media free food, and I'm not gonna lie: We love it. At the 2007 meeting, the rave of the AFC Coaches Breakfast Tuesday morning was the Arizona Biltmore oatmeal.

So, whether it's the dining room, the gym, the lobby, the elevator, the valet, the tennis courts, the golf course, the pool—you name it—you can run into absolutely anybody from the NFL anywhere at an Annual Meeting. At the 2005 gathering in Maui, it was a Who's Who in the NFL on the beach while the swing set near the *NFL Total Access* set was frequently jammed with the brood of The Membership. Oh, yes. There are wives and sons and daughters and grandchildren and nieces and nephews all over an NFL Annual Meeting, too. Especially at the 2006 meeting in Orlando, just down the street from Disney World. It's about more than just recreation; the NFL spouses also conduct business at an NFL Annual Meeting—so much so that they receive their own credentials that read SPOUSE and hold their own meetings on various football topics, like player health, and nonfootball related topics, like the environmental "greening" of the National Football League. At my first Owners' Meeting—2004 at The Breakers—I helped deliver a presentation on the advent of NFL Network at the Spouses' Meeting and found myself on the business end of a well-informed inquisition for 10 solid minutes.

With their families already on the scene, many league principals stay at the hotel a day or two after the Annual Meeting to enjoy one last respite. You see, once the meeting ends, everyone immediately goes into

the round-the-clock tank for final preparations for the NFL Draft, usually four weeks hence. For all parties involved—especially the spouses—
the weekend after the Owners' Meeting is a final moment of normalcy
before the insanity begins anew. Same goes for NFL Network hosts.

After the Annual Meeting in Maui, my wife and I did as the Ro-
mans and extended our stay at the Ritz Carlton Kapalua for a couple of
nights. Why not, right? I'm glad we did so I could pass along this story.

Remember. You never know who you might run into or where at
one of these affairs. The day after the meetings wrapped up in Maui, my
wife booked me a massage in the spa. I'm not going to lie. I love the spa.
I soak in the whole experience. I work out. I steam. I shower. I actually
use hair conditioner. I put on the white Ritz-Carlton terry-cloth
bathrobe and nestle my feet into the Ritz-Carlton white terry-cloth slippers. I'm feeling it. On this particular occasion, I was zoning out in the
men's spa waiting room awash in the zen aroma of eucalyptus when Giants coach Tom Coughlin padded into the room in his own terry-cloth
glory and sat down.

For those who may not know, Coughlin is the most stringent
taskmaster in the NFL. All coaches love discipline, but Coughlin notices
things like the length of socks on players during practice. In his first year as
Giants coach, he ruffled feathers by fining players who were *on time* to team
meetings. In Coughlin's world, being on time is showing up five minutes
early. So, when perennial Pro Bowler Michael Strahan arrived at an 8:25
A.M. meeting only two minutes early at 8:23, Coughlin fined him $1,000.

Now, here I was alone with Coughlin in the most metrosexual spot
on the Ritz-Carlton campus with only the Muzak and babbling water
from the nearby rock sculpture to break the silence.

"Hey, Coach."

"Rich."

"Taking a few days, huh?" I said, reaching for the *Esquire* on top of
the magazine stack.

"Yup. Taking a few days."

Coughlin fidgeted and looked at the clock on the wall. It was 10:45
A.M.

"Is that clock right?" Coughlin asked me.

I looked at my watch.

"It's dead on, ten forty-five."

Another pause. More easy listening oozed from the speakers above.

"What time is your massage?" he asked.

"Ten forty-five," I said.

"Me, too," said Coughlin. "I'm gonna go and see what's going on here."

With that, Coughlin walked out to the spa's front desk, presumably to fine his masseuse. A staff member of the Raiders who strolled into the waiting area midway through the discussion (in his own terry-cloth robe) looked at me. I looked back at him. Judging by his look, I knew we had to be thinking the same thing: "I guess the masseuse needed to be here by 10:40."

I don't know what happened after that. My masseuse came to collect me, and by the time my massage ended, Coughlin was nowhere to be found in the locker room. To this day, I still don't have the guts to ask him if he got a refund; I don't want to get fined.

Let's go back into the General Session again.

Before post–Annual Meeting spa time and after the media breakfasts, the head coaches meet with the Competition Committee and

See you at the spa, Coach Coughlin? *(Joann Kamay)*

receive a primer on the rules changes being presented to The Membership the next day. When it comes to massaging the NFL Rulebook, owners usually defer to the wishes of their head coaches since they're the experts on the subject. Therefore, whether a suggested playing rule change will pass or fail in General Session is occasionally decided at the coaches' prior meeting with the Competition Committee.

Of course, owners do chime in on the matter of a rule change, especially when it's connected to the issue of player safety. That's where we pick up another General Session—this one from the 2006 Owners' Meeting in Orlando, two months after Carson Palmer's knee exploded on national television.

Palmer blew out his right knee on the second play of the Bengals home Wild Card game when Pittsburgh's Kimo Von Oelhoffen collided with Palmer's vulnerable plant leg after Palmer had let go of a pass. Thus, the owners wanted to strengthen the rule protecting the quarterback's knees. Previously, a defender who nailed a quarterback low was only guilty of a penalty if he had an unrestricted path to the quarterback. In other words, any defender coming off a block (thus, a restricted path to the passer) could technically take a free shot at a quarterback's knee and be absolved of an infraction. The rule change: Defensive players coming off a block could still make legal contact with the quarterback's knee, but only if the defender had *no opportunity to avoid the quarterback.* Therefore, if you're blocked abruptly into the knee, that's not your fault, but if you got blocked and then still had the chance to avoid the low hit, you'd better stay away. The new language put the onus on the defender to avoid a quarterback's knee or shin to the best of his ability and placed responsibility on the referee to determine whether the defender had intended to go low and disregarded an opportunity to avoid the hit. All this on what usually is a bang-bang play.

Ironically, Von Oelhoffen's hit still would not have been deemed illegal under the new rule. While Bengals fans may disagree, the league deemed Von Oelhoffen could not avoid the hit to Palmer's knee. Still, some in The Membership wanted something done to strengthen the rule protecting their most prized assets. The head of NFL refs, the silver-haired Mike Pereira, a former side judge in the NFL, is the league's top liaison to the Competition Committee. He kicked off the session by explaining the new rule proposal.

PEREIRA: What the language [of the proposal] is saying is if your intent is to go low and the force of that contact is then in the knee area or below, then you have committed a foul and you're subject to a penalty or a fine. If you're coming in at the waist, and you make contact at the waist and slide down, that's no problem. It's just when the intent is to go low.

Carolina head coach John Fox, a former defensive coordinator with the Giants, threw out the first opinion.

FOX: The film that I saw [at the coaches' meeting with the Competition Committee], the major [leg] injuries that occurred that I'm aware of, this new rule would not have saved any of those players from injury. My problem is, you know, if it ain't broke, don't fix it.

Moments later, Eagles owner Jeffrey Lurie took to a nearby mic. After making the Super Bowl the previous year, Lurie's Eagles suffered a dreadful 2005 season. Their five-time Pro Bowl quarterback Donovan McNabb fought through an abdomen injury all year long, only to have it finally give way in Week 10. McNabb missed the final six weeks and the Eagles finished 6–10.

LURIE: Really, for any football franchise, the two most important assets are our head coaches and our quarterbacks. When a team—whether it's a good team, a mediocre team—loses its star quarterback, the popularity of the game it plays in goes dramatically down. If you look at the television ratings of the Eagles with McNabb and the Eagles without McNabb, no matter how good or poor we are, very, very different [ratings] nationally, locally, in every single way.

Two head coaches offered varying viewpoints. Marty Schottenheimer, then the Chargers defense-first head coach, took issue with the language that essentially required an official to determine a player's intent.

SCHOTTENHEIMER: I think it becomes an officiating nightmare. Ultimately, the key for all of us is to keep the quarterbacks, certainly, as well as other players, healthy. And in my personal view, we may have to fall on the sword for this, saying, "It's in the interest of quarterback safety," but, inherently, I don't think it's a good rule. It concerns me.

For offensive-minded Giants head coach Tom Coughlin, the new rule didn't go far enough.

> **COUGHLIN:** Why is it ever acceptable to hit the quarterback below the knees? If everything that's been said here [is true], the quarterback is the most important player on the team, on the field. The popularity of the game from franchise to franchise depends on the quarterback being able to play the game. Why is it— When and why would it *ever* be acceptable to hit the quarterback in the pocket below the knees, whether you're blocked [into him] or not? Those pictures we saw yesterday, with the extra here and here *(Coughlin made pushing motions.)* after being blocked, why is that acceptable? They're still carrying a player off the field. He doesn't play again.

> **(COMPETITION COMMITTEE MEMBER AND THEN-TEXANS GM) CHARLEY CASSERLY:** Coach, we had that discussion. We did. And you know what? You're 100 percent right. But, I always have a saying here: It's all about votes. And we're struggling and trying to get *this* one voted through. There's no way we can get *that* one voted through. Now, you're 100 percent right, Tom, okay? But, the other side of the coin is the defensive player, who is fouled into the quarterback, who is thrown into the quarterback on a penalty, okay? There's the other side of the story—that it's unfair to the defensive player to be fined and penalized when it wasn't his fault; he was fouled into [the quarterback]. So, in theory, Tom, we all agree with you. We just don't think we can officiate it. We don't think it's fair for the defense and we don't think we can get the votes.

In his final NFL annual meeting before retiring, Commissioner Paul Tagliabue then stepped in.

> **TAGLIABUE:** I think that the discussion here has confirmed that there is a problem. So, I think where we are is that this rule *has* to change. The unrestricted path [to the quarterback] language is just too much. It's too broad. And so the question is: How does it change? And I think that John Fox and Marty Schottenheimer make important points. Obviously, other coaches have a similar balancing to do. So, what we want to do here is see if there are the votes to pass this, we'll

vote. If there are still reservations either about language or about how it would be officiated, we'll take it up again and bring it back at the May meeting. But something has to change here. Some rule has to change, and even if it came down to do it for 2006 only—I just think something has to be changed here.

RICH McKAY: Let's go to a show of hands up to all those that would oppose the rule as written. Only one person per team can vote no. *(Laugh.)* Be nice now.

Only seven hands went up. Two hands shy of scuttling the change. The new rule passed 25–7.

One week before the 2006 Annual Meeting in Orlando, Paul Tagliabue announced his retirement as NFL commissioner after 17 legendary years on the job. Where everyone else in the media viewed the impending vacancy as a major news story, I saw opportunity.

I would run for commissioner.

Admittedly, it would be an uphill battle. I had no law degree and possessed no business acumen of any sort, but I had many things going for me. First, I had only been with the league for three years. I was a fresh face. Second, I had the power of the medium. *NFL Total Access* would be my platform from which to lay out my progressive agenda for shepherding the beloved game into the 21st century. And, third, I had moxie. While most candidates for the job quietly state their case behind the scenes, I took my message directly to the people.

I announced my candidacy on the first *NFL Total Access* of the 2006 Owners' Meeting, which Tagliabue (my would-be predecessor) opened with his final traditional State of the League Address. The Membership gave Tagliabue a standing ovation. Clearly, I had big shoes to fill. Literally. Paul Tagliabue's 584 career rebounds ranks him 23rd on the all-time list at Georgetown University, 732 behind all-time leader Patrick Ewing and 126 behind 12th place Ruben Boumtje-Boumtje.

But I digress.

I waited until Adam Schefter's midshow information segment called "Around the League" to break the news. Not exactly Schwarzenegger on Jay Leno, but it did the trick. The Membership all had NFL Network in their hotel rooms at the Grand Cypress. I had a captive audience and pounced once Schefter ticked off the names of those considered to be possible successors to Taglibue.

"There's lots of names out there," Schefter summed up from his side of the split screen, "But it still looks like Roger Goodell versus the rest of the field."

"There's one name that you've left out, Adam. I'm going to make a major announcement here exclusively on *NFL Total Access*," I said. "*I* am throwing my name into this ring and officially announcing *my* candidacy for the commissionership."

"And what's your stance on the G three program, Rich?" Schefter asked, referring to the NFL's plan to assist its clubs in financing a portion of the cost of constructing new stadiums. It's real heady, commissioner-type stuff.

"I have staff for that, Adam." I said. "I have staff for that."

"Good. That's the way it should be."

"But the bottom line is, as you know, I believe I'm a uniter not a divider. And I might be able to fill these shoes."

"I'll second that, Rich. I'll second that."

"Thanks, I appreciate that. Let's just have that marinate around the meeting now that it's out in the open."

Out in the open, indeed. A groundbreaking first step. The Membership frowns on open politicking. Conventional wisdom holds that the absolute sure-fire way to ensure you're *not* the next commissioner is to openly state that you *want* to be the next commissioner. My campaign strategy was to go in the exact opposite direction. It was a calculated roll of the dice.

I immediately had to build consensus. When Colts head coach Tony Dungy and Chiefs coach Herman Edwards (close friends off the field) paid a joint visit to *NFL Total Access* the next day, Tuesday, I ended the interview in search of an endorsement.

"It's the last Owners' Meeting for Commissioner Paul Tagliabue. I don't know if you guys know, but I've announced my candidacy."

"We are behind you a hundred percent," Coach Edwards said.

"Thank you."

"You have our vote," said Coach Dungy.

Two men of character. A solid start. But, there's a saying in politics: It takes a village. Strolling around the hotel, I felt no groundswell. I sensed very little momentum outside of the General Session. No one in the media was abuzz about my campaign. With only one more day remaining in the

On the campaign trail with Herman Edwards and Tony Dungy. (*Joann Kamay*)

Annual Meeting, I realized I needed someone in The Membership to back me. Fast.

That Tuesday night, I had dinner at one of the property restaurants with Schefter, NFL Network steadicam operator James Lytle, and editor Dave Goldstein. Returning to the hotel lobby, we ran into Baltimore Ravens owner Steve Bisciotti standing outside smoking a cigar. All three of us spent the next three hours in the fabulous company of the native Baltimorian talking Baltimore sports—from the Ravens to the old Colts to the Orioles, of which Bisciotti is a huge fan. Bisciotti is cool. He's genuine. He is what one would call a *man's* man. I determined he was the guy in The Membership to give my campaign some much needed swagger.

Plus, Bisciotti had already agreed to make a rare media appearance on *NFL Total Access* the next day on Wednesday, the wrap-up of the Annual Meeting. It was a perfect setup. I even knew an unassuming way to bring up the subject with him. Ravens team president Dick Cass was one of those mentioned as a leading potential candidate for the job, so, during the interview, I asked Bisciotti about a possibility of losing Cass to the promotion.

"I think that there are plenty of good candidates out there, and as these meeting have indicated, we're just starting to consider that," Bisciotti said. "There's going to be a lot of names that come up in the next few months and I think Dick will end up staying with the Ravens."

There was my opening.

"Has my name come up at all in that discussion?" I asked.

"Actually it did, Rich," Biscotti said. "In the meeting today [it came up], and it seemed to be a clear consensus. So it's going to be interesting, you know."

"Yes," I said, nodding. "I can see why."

"I just hope that it doesn't thwart the process."

"I just want to know that I can, maybe, count on your vote."

"Oh, yeah. You've got it," Biscotti said, adding. "I think you got that at the bar last night. Remember? You bought that Bud Light for me."

Laugh-out-loud funny. Didn't think he would go there. On the campaign front, I was equally enthused. One vote down, only 31 more to go.

Two hours later, the last guest in our coverage of the 2006 NFL Annual Meeting stepped on the set—the outgoing commissioner himself. I

Currying favor with Ravens owner Steve Bisciotti. *(Joann Kamay)*

I don't think Paul Tagliabue took my candidacy seriously. (*Joann Kamay*)

had last interviewed Tagliabue at an Annual Meeting back in 2004 at The Breakers, where The Membership gave him his last contract extension. Now, here he was on the set as a future retiree. Toward the end of the interview I brought up the elephant in the room.

"As you go through this process of finding a successor, I don't know if there's been a groundswell yet, but I think you know I announced my candidacy on this show two days ago, Commissioner. Is there any advice that you could give to me as I try to fill your very large shoes?"

Tagliabue didn't blink.

"I would say, don't get your expectations too high too early," he said. "Pace yourself, peak at the right time, and if you lose, look forward to the job you have."

"This is superb, I'm very pleased by that," I said. "But openly politicking is frowned upon, right?"

"Openly politicking in this context has usually been counterproductive."

Unfortunately, it was too late to turn back. I went home to Los Angeles with a sense of confidence. My wife, Suzy, made up buttons that read RICH FOR COMMISSIONER and I handed them out to various NFL players who appeared on *NFL Total Access*.

"Tell everyone on the Chargers to spread the word," I told Pro Bowl linebacker Shawne Merriman when I handed him a button.

For weeks, I anxiously waited for the white smoke to billow out of league headquarters. Tagliabue appointed a special eight-man Search Committee to find his successor and they looked at no fewer than 185 candidates. I was never contacted. Suddenly, several new prominent names were being bandied in the press as rumored candidates, including Secretary of State Condoleezza Rice and Governor Jeb Bush of Florida. None of it was true, but reality was sinking in. On August 1, 2006, the eight-man Search Committee issued a list of five finalists for the job. Your humble narrator was not one of them. Dejected, I slumped at my computer and noticed an e-mail from one of the heavy hitters, NFL Executive Vice President Joe Browne, with the subject heading of "Jeb Bush." It was a tongue-in-cheek classic from the front office:

"As I told the Florida governor, now that the list of five finalists for NFL commissioner has been selected, it's time for you and your family to move on with your lives. There will be other jobs you covet during your career . . . you may not get those either, but at least you can covet them."

Sure, I had lost, but I was determined to lose with dignity. The next guy was going to be my new ultimate boss. He turned out to be COO Roger Goodell, who, by the way, is just as cool as Bisciotti. And I'm not just saying that because he *is* my ultimate boss. Really.

At any rate, Joe Browne wasn't the only top brass to razz me for my Mondale-like flop of a candidacy. None other than Tagliabue gave me considerable grief. It was months later on our pregame show in Canton, Ohio, at the Hall of Fame Game, the first preseason contest of the year in early August.

Goodell was taking over as commissioner at the end of the month. Concluding the interview, I took off the gold Rolex that my wife's mother gave me as a wedding present.

"Well, you're getting ready for retirement. They asked me to give you this, Commissioner. There you go."

I handed the watch to Tagliabue, who looked at it and said: "What's this for? To keep track of how long it is before you become a candidate for the commissioner's position? They don't need a wristwatch for that; they need a calendar with thirty years on it!"

Tagliabue *(far right)*, in his final appearance as commissioner on *NFL Total Access*, dashed my hopes. *(Joann Kamay)*

Suddenly, in his final moments as commissioner on NFL Network, the lawyerly Tagliabue was turning into Rodney Dangerfield.

"That's why the time on it is standing still," I said. "Be careful with the watch, my mother-in-law gave me that."

Tagliabue was still on a roll, holding the watch.

"This runs out to 2035. Yeah, you'll be in there before this runs out."

So, you're telling me there's a chance?

ROOKIES

A frequent criticism of football is that true game action occurs, on average, once every minute, and even only then in bursts of seconds. We've seen it countless times: The players huddle up on each side of the ball and stroll to the line of scrimmage. Once the ball is hiked, the play develops, and unless someone goes on a 100-yard tear the whole shebang from snap to tackle usually lasts five to ten seconds. Then they untangle the pig pile, get up, and adjust their shoulder pads. Then huddle up again for about 30 seconds. Only then another play occurs. And the next scrum. And the next huddle. Perhaps someone calls a time-out. If you add up the total running time of only the actual plays during an average three-hour NFL game, it might, when strung together, yield a mere 10 to 12 minutes of activity.

The NFL Draft, however, makes all that look like a *Terminator* movie. In the first round of an NFL Draft, each team has 15 minutes to make its selection. Your average network television situation comedy, minus commercials, lasts 22 minutes. In other words, it takes the San Diego Chargers nearly the same amount of time to decide to draft someone like, say, MVP running back LaDanian Tomlinson as it does for Jack Tripper to successfully sort through all the wacky misunderstandings between his two sultry roommates and goofy landlord Mr. Furley.

Of course, all 32 NFL franchises would be quick to point out that making a first-round selection in the NFL Draft is no laughing matter. Short of personal scandal, there's no better sure-fire way to earn yourself a lickety-split pink slip in the National Football League than by taking part in pulling the trigger on a very wrong, franchise-altering selection in the NFL Draft. Ergo, if you polled most general managers, player personnel advisers, and coaches, I'd say they would say 15 minutes isn't long enough. After months upon months of scouring campuses across our great nation to compile statistics of every sort on virtually every draft-eligible collegian in pads, followed by weeks upon weeks of broad jumps and Pro Days and interviews and physicals with those collegians, capped by endless organizational meetings and film sessions to review all of the above, nearly eight months of talent evaluation boils down to a pressure cooker the NFL sets on 15 minutes. Toss in the fact that phone lines ring the entire time with distracting and enticing trade offers from other teams hoping to swap draft positions, and it gives a whole new meaning to being "on the clock."

That's why the first round of an NFL Draft usually takes *six hours* to complete. Every team milks every last second on that 15-minute meter if necessary, and it is frequently necessary because once the NFL commissioner starts the clock, anything can happen.

Take, for instance, the Dallas Cowboys in the 2007 NFL Draft, during which they picked 22nd overall. In the previous nine drafts, the Cowboys had not drafted a single offensive player with a first-round pick—the longest such streak in modern history—and therefore, with older receivers in Terrell Owens and Terry Glenn and a banged-up offensive line, the Cowboys were solid favorites to draft someone on offense with that first-round 22nd overall pick. Plus, when Dallas's time on the clock finally arrived, the previous nine teams had selected a defensive player, preserving the offensive player pool as deep. As in: the Grand Banks in *Red October* deep. You see, top prospect Notre Dame quarterback Brady Quinn remained shockingly undrafted. For one reason or another, every team kept passing on the quarterback who set no fewer than 36 records at Notre Dame, but with Kansas City picking after Dallas at No. 23, the intrigue began to build. The Chiefs' quarterback roster was in flux, making them ripe candidates to put Quinn out of his misery (I believe Einstein once theorized: Expecting to be drafted early + not hearing your name called 21 times × 15 minute wait per

Giving my best Peter Jennings pose at the 2006 NFL Draft. *(David Drapkin)*

time = misery). The Cowboys had no interest in taking Quinn; they already had a quarterback in Tony Romo. Therefore, they would have ordinarily drafted the best player available at a position that would fill a hole on their roster. Luckily for Dallas, two circumstances had suddenly developed that no one in their right minds could have predicted:

1. The 22nd overall pick in the NFL Draft had become a valuable commodity.

2.   Brady Quinn was still available to be taken with the 22nd
         pick.

Immediately, whatever predraft strategy the Cowboys had in mind
went right out the window. America's Team was open for business. The
Cowboys' phone began to ring off the hook because, again, teams interested in Quinn knew they had to act fast with Kansas City choosing next.
Among the suitors were the Baltimore Ravens, who were picking 29th
overall and whose starting quarterback Steve McNair wasn't getting any
younger. However, another team busted through on call waiting with the
proverbial offer you can't refuse—the Cleveland Browns.

Several agonizing hours earlier (again, refer to Einstein's Theory of
Misery) the Browns had passed on taking Quinn with the third overall
pick in favor of Wisconsin left tackle Joe Thomas. Cleveland could have
made a big splash with their fan base by selecting Quinn—an Ohio
native—but the Browns decided that shoring up their offensive line was
more important. In fact, Cleveland had called Quinn and his agent the
night before the draft to say they were going in a different direction. That
was *their* predraft strategy. Now, like Dallas, that strategy required immediate retooling, because, unexpectedly, Quinn was still available at No.
22. With the Browns next picking in the second-round at 36th overall,
trading up with Dallas to pull off an NFL Draft bonanza for the ages by
getting Thomas *and* Quinn in the same first round materialized as a real
doable possibility. So Cleveland rocked and sent that second-round pick
and their first-round pick in the 2008 NFL Draft (a steep price) to Dallas for the suddenly coveted 22nd overall pick and used it to select Brady
Quinn. It produced the expected measure of hoopla. Eight days later, the
Browns trotted out both prized draft choices to a thunderous standing
ovation during halftime of the Cleveland Cavaliers playoff basketball
game against the Nets. Move over, LeBron!

Exciting stuff, indeed. Too bad none of it played out in person at
the NFL Draft.

The NFL Draft, known officially as the Annual Player Selection Meeting, is the only event on the league calendar at which the major players are not present. It's a lot like going to the Super Bowl in Miami with
the Colts and Bears playing somewhere else—and phoning in an update
every 15 minutes.

The key decision makers—a.k.a. our old friends The Evaluators—are not located in the actual NFL Draft auditorium, but at their respective team facilities, convened in various conference rooms filled with banks of television sets and equipped with multiline telephones and laptops and personal computers and DVD machines. There's sure to be a lot of hot coffee and probably a plate of bagels in there at the start, maybe even some fruit to prevent scurvy because the draft lasts so freaking long. For years, these locales were dubbed the War Room. But out of sensitivity to the current times, the nickname has been changed to simply Draft Room. At any rate, the basic point is this: All team owners and coaches and general managers and player-personnel personnel are dispersed across the country rather than at the site of the NFL Draft, which, in case you're scoring at home, has been held in New York City every year since 1965.

So, who *is* at an NFL Draft? Well, first, you've got the head honcho himself—the NFL commissioner, who officially convenes the proceedings a little after noontime on the Saturday of the two-day NFL Draft Weekend. Yes, *two days*. Again, because the first round lasts about six hours, you can only humanely fit the first three rounds of the seven-round NFL Draft in on the first day. The last four rounds take place on Sunday on Draft Weekend. (The NFL mercifully cuts the amount of clock time in the second round down to ten minutes per selection, then in every round thereafter to five minutes per selection.) When the commissioner places the first team on the clock, the crowd goes nuts. Yes, there's also a live audience, which we'll get to in a bit.

You've also got a handful of top prospects on the scene, handpicked by the league with a little help from longtime Cowboys personnel man Gil Brandt. He helps identify the prospects that deserve the invite to the Big Apple. Only the cream of the draft crop gets that invite, for two reasons: one, because the league only wants to show off the best and brightest and, two, because they only want players on hand who are likely to get drafted quickly. No one wants to subject a prospect to Einstein's Theory of Misery in person. Just ask former Cal quarterback Aaron Rodgers. He accepted the league invite to the 2005 NFL Draft only to get selected 24th overall, stewing in the backstage green room for nearly five hours, his profound disappointment beamed to a national TV audience after each and every pick. The next year, as he unexpectedly dropped down the draft, quarterback Matt Leinart decided he wouldn't be the next Rodgers and bolted the green room to avoid the cameras until the Arizona Cardinals selected him 10th overall. In 2007, nearly two hours into the Brady Quinn free fall, Commissioner Roger Goodell personally decided he had seen enough of the distraught Notre Dame quarterback squirming on television. After the Dolphins passed on him with the ninth overall pick, Quinn got up from the green room to hit the restroom. (Believe me, I wish I had the same opportunity. More on that in a moment, too.) Commissioner Goodell stopped Quinn en route and invited him to watch the rest of the draft from the commissioner's green room, where no cameras are allowed. Quinn chilled there from picks 10 through 22 in complete seclusion, spared two-and-a-half more hours of public indignity by order of the NFL commissioner.

(Quick aside: While TV cameras may pose a nuisance to the invitees, they provide a helpful hint to you, the viewer, as to who's about to get drafted. Here's a tip: If you see a prospect talking on his cell phone, he's the next draft pick. For sure. Lock it in. You see, virtually every coach in the league likes to place a phone call to the kid he's about to draft. You know, break the news before the commissioner makes the announcement and give him a rah-rah type speech at the same time. It goes something like this:

Brady Quinn (center) looks comfortably numb on our set after going through the ringer at the 2007 NFL Draft. (*Joann Kamay*)

Son, are you ready to play for the Tampa Bay Buccaneers? *Yes, sir.*
Because we're about to pick you. We're not making a mistake are we?
   No, sir.
Good. We're going to work you hard. *Yes, sir.*
You're going to have to earn your way. *Yes, sir.*
All right, then. Congratulations. Your ass now belongs to me. *Yes, sir.*

So, whenever a prospect is seen on TV taking a call during the NFL Draft, he's about to get his name called from the podium. In fact, supersly überagent Drew Rosenhaus used this trick o' the trade to his advantage during the 2003 NFL Draft. His client, running back Willis McGahee, had left college early even though he blew out his knee during the Orange Bowl four months before. Many people thought McGahee had made a terrible mistake in bypassing his senior year because no NFL team risks a first-round pick on a guy rehabbing a catastrophic injury. Midway through the first round, however, a surprising shot appeared on TV— McGahee at home at his family draft gathering, talking on the cell phone. Could it be a team was about to gamble on him after all? Actually, no. It was Rosenhaus on the other end calling McGahee to make any team watching TV at that moment think there was interest in his client. In fact, when Rosenhaus called McGahee's cell, he was sitting right next to him on the couch. Perhaps it worked. The Bills eventually chose McGahee in the first round with the 23rd overall pick. Here endeth the aside.)

   It should come as no surprise that the commissioner runs the show at the NFL Draft. When not doling out green room hall passes to plummeting prospects, he takes care of his more traditional duties—announcing each and every first-round pick from a podium placed at center stage. He does so with a staccato reading from the same Mad Lib–like script handed down through the years from Rozelle to Tagliabue and now to Goodell:

"With the _____ *pick in the* _____ *NFL Draft, the*
              [ordinal number]   [year]
_____ *select*_____, _____,
[name of NFL franchise]   [name of player] [position of player]

_____. _____
[school or university of player] [Name of next team in the draft order]
is now on the clock."

The commissioner reads the crucial information off a card handed to him by one of the scores of NFL front-office employees who staff the Draft. The card touches many hands before it touches his. It initially comes from the Draft Floor where every one of the 32 NFL teams has its own spartan setup in the form of a rectangular bridge table with a telephone. A maximum of three club employees may staff the Draft Desk on the Draft Floor and, because all The Evaluators are in the Draft Room, those working the Draft Desk usually have zero to do with football operations. It's frequently a perk for team employees who work on the business side or for, quite frankly, a little bit of nepotism. Current Falcons president Rich McKay often manned the Buccaneers Draft Desk while in high school and college when his father and legendary coach John McKay was with Tampa Bay. Rich McKay's own son, Hunter, has recently performed Draft Desk duty for the Falcons. Who knows? Maybe Hunter's kid will one day be on the clock.

Their job is critical, but outrageously simple. The phone rings. They pick it up. It's someone from the Draft Room with precious information—the name of the team's draft choice. The Draft Desk minion then writes the name of the player on two Draft Cards and hands one each to the two Draft Runners who flank the Draft Desk the entire time that team is on the clock. One Draft Runner takes the card and heads immediately for the Draft Pit in front of the stage. The Draft Pit is a more upscale version of a Draft Desk. It's manned by several NFL management types (Draft Pit Bosses?) and has computers in addition to a bank of telephones. Posh digs! Now, with all those modes of communication, you'd think the Draft Room would just ring up the Draft Pit with the name of its draftee and cut out the middlemen. But no. The only time the Draft Pit phones ring is when a Draft Room is calling to report a trade to league officials who need to vet the particulars. So, if you're ever at the NFL Draft and see the Draft Pit Bosses on the phone, a trade is about to be announced. Either that or they're just extremely hungry and are ordering out for pizza—but that's highly unlikely.

Now to that other Draft Runner we left standing at the Draft Desk while the other bolted for the Draft Pit. He or she takes the other card bearing the name of the soon-to-be announced draftee to the Draft Desk of the team picking next so those working that particular Draft Desk can immediately report back to their Draft Room which player is no longer available for consideration. You see, once the pick is received in the Draft Pit for processing, the clock instantly begins anew on the team choosing next. That's why you sometimes see the clock reset on your television screen before the commissioner makes the official announcement from his podium as to who is the newest rookie in the National Football League. And if you also suspect that the television networks know the name of the pick before the commissioner's announcement, you'd be correct. Once the pick arrives in the Draft Pit, two things happen. First, someone makes sure the name on it is spelled phonetically if necessary so the commissioner pronounces it correctly from the podium. (Commissioner Tagliabue once proudly proclaimed he messed up only one name in his 16 years commanding the NFL Draft.) Second, a league employee calls out to the NFL Network and ESPN control room trucks parked outside Radio City on 51st Street and tells them who is about to get drafted. We require that 20 seconds of heads-up time so all the accurate graphics and proper videotape can be ready at the instant for you—the viewer at home—at the moment the commissioner makes it official. Now, I can safely assure you that we on the NFL Network draft set insist we be kept in the dark just like you at home until the commissioner makes the announcement. During our preshow meeting prior to our first Draft broadcast in 2006, our Draft expert Mike Mayock sounded like one of the banditos from *Blazing Saddles:* "Names? We don't need any names. We'll be just fine reacting to it." Enough said.

When it's all said and done or, rather, when Commissioner Goodell reads the Draft Card at his podium, it caps a terribly arcane way of relaying crucial information. No doubt it will all one day be done via Internet—Jon Gruden pointing and clicking a mouse to select his newest franchise quarterback—but for the moment the NFL, as it usually does, remains old school by using paper pads, telephones, and messengers to move the NFL Draft along.

Now, as for those fans at the NFL Draft. I've got to be honest. They need help. I know their passion and their zeal provides the backbone for the success of the National Football League, but these people are such insane diehards that they make everyone from The Ramones to Ron Jeremy look soft core. They scream and yell like it's an NFL Sunday. They also dress like it. They come in jerseys. They come in face paint. They come in masks and helmets and with notebooks and clipboards to record every single draft pick announced from the stage. The fact that they come at all in the final weekend of April to sit indoors all day and watch a clock

NFL Network executive producer Eric Weinberger *(gesturing)* with Mike Mayock in a pre-Draft show meeting. *(Joann Kamay)*

drip down from 15 to 0 every 15 minutes (and that's just the first round!) is astounding in itself. To offer a better glimpse of who attends an NFL Draft, I have personally transcribed the following message left on my voicemail box at NFL Network on April 17, 2006:

Beep!

Hey there, Mr. Eisen! My name is Mike Randall with a group called The Charlie's Fryes down in Cleveland, Ohio. [TIME-OUT. For those in need of a refresher, quarterback Charlie Frye was the Browns third-round pick in the 2005 Draft out of the football hotbed of Akron University. When Cleveland's then-starting quarterback Trent Dilfer got hurt late in the 2005 season, the rookie Frye started five games, winning two of them. While two-out-of-five falls shy of Meat Loaf's definition of what ain't bad, it was still good enough to generate a Frye Fan Club that, fittingly, also pays homage to fast food. TIME-IN.] I'm a big Cleveland Browns fan. Just wanted to let you know that we're big fans of the show and that we're coming to the NFL Draft at Radio City Music Hall. We're coming on actually the 28th along with our good friend John "Big Dawg" Thompson . . . [AN-OTHER TIME-OUT. John "Big Dawg" Thompson is a luminary of sorts in NFL fandom. He is the lead dog, if you will, in the Browns infamous end-zone cheering section known as The Dawg Pound. Amid the frenzied biscuit-wielding throng, Big Dawg stands out as the particularly portly fellow who wears a number 98 jersey and rubber hound-dog mask. Other Thompson information of note: Big Dawg, also known as the Canine in Chief, has, in fact, legally changed his name to John "Big Dawg" Thompson and has been mentioned on the floor of the U.S. House of Representatives by Ohio Democrat and 2004 and 2008 presidential candidate Dennis Kucinich, who on October 5, 1999, placed the following into the *Congressional Record:* "Mister Speaker, I rise today in honor of John 'Big Dawg' Thompson." TIME-IN AGAIN] . . . and we just wanted to see, you know, if well . . . we thought of a show idea of having all the different fans from the NFL, like, do a little segment on NFL Network getting ready for the NFL Draft because the NFL Draft, you know, is like our Christmas. Um, but check out our Web site www.charliesfryes.com and call me back. [MY THIRD AND FINAL TIME-OUT! A visit to the Web site reveals not only a link entitled "Steelers Suck!" but also a picture of two members of The Charlie's Fryes—Mike and his brother Dan dressed in Browns uniforms with cardboard drawings of yellow fries coming out of the shoulder pads as if Mike and his brother Dan were human french fry containers. True story. TIME BACK IN.] Like I said, Dan, myself and John "Big Dawg" Thompson will be at the NFL Draft at Radio City Music Hall all of April 29 and I look forward to meeting you. Take care.

Beep!

Unfortunately, I never crossed paths with The Charlie's Fryes. That's because my derriere is virtually nailed to my seat on the NFL Network set for the entire draft. And I mean the whole shebang. In 2007, that meant 20 and a half hours of live coverage over two days, including the longest first-round in NFL Draft history at six hours and eight minutes. Midway through a first round of an NFL Draft, I'm paying attention to two things—the proceedings at the podium and when those proceedings might hit a lull long enough to allow me to bolt for the bathroom or scarf something to eat. Real glamorous, huh? The NFL Draft is the first and only time since fifth grade when I must ask for permission to go to the bathroom. Once executive producer Eric Weinberger gives the okay from the truck, all of us on the set take off our microphones and earpieces and make a mad dash from the set to the most valuable piece of porcelain in the Art Deco jewel of Radio City Music Hall. I've made this run with some of the best—Marshall Faulk, Steve Mariucci, Mayock, etc. Security leads the way as we quickly weave through the audience seated in the orchestra section to the backstage stage door. The process repeats itself when we rush back to the set with security clearing a path for us.

It's not the only time we have interaction with fans at the NFL Draft. Our set is located in the left orchestra section directly beneath the first mezzanine. Thus, we hear it from the crowd all day and all night. After one bathroom run, I heard this as I settled back into my seat: "Yo, Rich! Did everything come out all right?"

You've got to love the New York City crowd. They certainly are raucous, especially when either the Jets or the Giants are on the clock. In 2007, the Jets weren't selecting until 25th overall, an absolute eternity in NFL Draft time. So, when Commissioner Goodell announced that the Jets had struck a trade with the Panthers to move up into the 15th overall spot, the Jets fans slumping in their seats erupted as if Chad Pennington had just hit Laveranues Coles on a 65-yard touchdown slant. They started chanting like it, too.

"J-E-T-S, Jets! Jets! Jets!"

Because of their team's spotty history at the NFL Draft, Jets fans are always on the edge of their seat when the commissioner eventually hits the podium with their newest player. No matter how good the Jets draft pick is, Giants fans love to taunt the Jets fans into thinking the draft pick stinks.

In fact, I think Giants fans have the biggest mouths at an NFL Draft. It was a fan in a Michael Strahan jersey who called out to Marshall Faulk from the mezzanine during a commercial break in the 2007 third round, deep into the wee hours of the night when only one-quarter of the original noontime crowd remained.

"Yo, Marshall. Come out of retirement and play for us! We need you!" he screamed, an obvious reference to the retirement of running back Tiki Barber.

"You don't need me. I can't run that well anymore," Marshall yelled back.

"Don't matter!" the fan bellowed. "You're still better than anybody we got!"

Marshall doubled over laughing. "What about Mariucci?"

"He can be our offensive coordinator!"

Now, I had to get involved. "Offensive coordinator? He's a head coach!"

Mariucci started turning red. It was late. We had been on the air for nine hours. I think he wanted to go home and go to sleep. Then the fan shot back, "Yeah, but he drafted Charles Rogers!"

Mariucci rolled his eyes. With the second overall pick in the 2004 Draft, the Lions took Rogers, a wide receiver who proceeded to break his collarbone twice before fizzling out of the league within three years. A bust of busts. Marshall's guffaws echoed in the half-empty auditorium.

Nothing is more hard-core than attending the second day of an NFL Draft. Day Two starts at 11:00 A.M. Sunday—or less than 12 hours after the conclusion of Day One—and it features many college players you've never heard of. The second day of an NFL Draft may attract the smallest crowd in the history of Radio City Music Hall, but then again, I didn't attend the event that took place in Radio City directly after the 2007 Draft—a Björk concert.

Actually, it wouldn't surprise me if Björk got drafted on the second day. Many NFL teams use their late draft picks on what The Evaluators call "a flier." It means, in essence, What the heck? Very few sixth- and seventh-round draft choices actually make it in the NFL, so why not take a chance on a guy you think has some ability even though he may not fit into your short-term plans? That's the way The Mother of All Second-Day NFL Draft Picks came into the NFL. Even though the New England Patriots had their franchise quarterback in Drew Bledsoe, they took a flier on a Michigan quarterback in the sixth round of the first draft of the millennium. Tom Brady, the eventual two-time Super Bowl MVP, was selected with the 199th overall pick in the 2000 NFL Draft. The rest is history. Literally.

Perhaps that's why a fan would spend the last Sunday in April sitting indoors to watch rounds four through seven of an NFL Draft. Maybe

Hours before the Steelers beat the Seahawks, ESPN's Steve Young and Tom Jackson *(standing, left to right)* crash the *NFL Total Access Super Bowl XL* set with Steve Mariucci, Ray Lewis, Terrell Davis, and yours truly *(seated, left to right).* (JOANN KAMAY)

Two of the greatest runners of their time, Terrell Davis and Curtis Martin *(center)*, join me in the *NFL Total Access Super Bowl XXXIX* studio in Jacksonville. Note the pool table at left and The Precious on display. (NFL NETWORK)

Singing karaoke with Lincoln Kennedy in Detroit the Sunday before Super Bowl XL. The song we were singing? "Ebony and Ivory." Needless to say, we brought down the house. (JOANN KAMAY)

While covering the NFC squad's practice at the 2007 Pro Bowl, Marshall Faulk and I noticed Bears placekicker Robbie Gould practicing his kicks right in front of our set. So, during a segment on live TV, Robbie and I switched places. Thankfully, I didn't hurt myself. (JOANN KAMAY)

I was part of Jerome Bettis's first beach day as a retiree when he joined *NFL Total Access* at the 2006 Pro Bowl, two days after he won Super Bowl XL. (JOANN KAMAY)

NFL Network reporter Kara Henderson, *(center)*, waits for the flyover before the 2005 Pro Bowl as Rod Woodson laughs in the background about my bum shoulder. (JOANN KAMAY)

Terrell Davis and I patiently wait for the embattled Maurice Clarett to come off the field at the 2005 NFL Scouting Combine to join us on the *NFL Total Access* set. Thankfully, we had some posh digs in an RCA Dome luxury suite. (JOANN KAMAY)

Buccaneers coach Jon Gruden, known for his legendary grimace, was all smiles when he stopped by the *NFL Total Access* set at the 2006 Owners' Meeting. (JOANN KAMAY)

No, it's not Ray Nitschke. That's just me figurative imposing my will on some poor imaginary opponent as I hit the mattress during the Upper Deck photo shoot at the 2006 NFL Rookie Premiere. Fear me. (UPPER DECK)

Commissioner Paul Tagliabue waves farewell to The Draft Ziggies in the rafters of Radio City Music Hall at the 2006 NFL Draft, Tagliabue's last as NFL commissioner. NFL Network draft expert Mike Mayock and I heard it from the Ziggies all day. (JOANN KAMAY)

Interviewing Elton John in front of Tom Brady's locker prior to his performance at the 2005 regular season kickoff in New England. Apparently, Sir Elton is a friend of Patriots owner Robert Kraft, who watched the entire interview out of frame. (DAVID DRAPKIN)

From left to right: Commissioner Paul Tagliabue, Giants defensive end Michael Strahan, Bryant Gumble, Cris Collinsworth, yours truly, Raiders defensive tackle Warren Sapp, Cardinals quarterback Matt Leinart, Saints running back Reggie Bush, Broncos safety John Lynch, and Chiefs tight end Tony Gonzalez take the stage at the end of the 2006 NFL Network presentation to advertisers in New York City. (DAVID DRAPKIN)

Steve Mariucci and I wrap up an edition of *NFL Total Access* on the front lawn of the Pro Football Hall of Fame in Canton, Ohio. NFL Network lighting director Ken Schamp is blinding me with his reflector. (JOANN KAMAY)

This is how we watch games every Sunday at the NFL Network. We put one game in the big screen on the *NFL Total Access* set and split the two side screens into quadrants to watch as many as nine games at once. On this day, Deion, Mariucci, sports TV legend Bill Creasey, yours truly, and producer Aaron Owens take in the Cowboys–Jaguars game, among others. (JOANN KAMAY)

No rest for the weary: After a Thursday night trip to Seattle and a Saturday night stay in Atlanta, Marshall, Mooch, and I are back in the Los Angeles studio for the *Monday Night Football* pregame edition of *NFL Total Access*. Two days later, we were off to Green Bay and Oakland. (JOANN KAMAY)

you'll see the next great player sneak into the NFL and be able to tell your grandkids about it one day. But it is taxing. When the NFL Draft creeps through the sixth and seventh rounds—through hours 18, 19, and 20 of the Draft Weekend—it can get pretty bleak. That's why the NFL has recently instituted an incentive plan: All fans who make it through Day Two entirely will automatically get a ticket to Day One of the following year's draft. When the doors opened on Day Two of the 2007 Draft, each fan was handed a slip of paper which he or she signs. Any fan who hands in those slips after the last draft pick is announced and signs with a matching signature receives a certificate redeemable for a ticket to the 2008 NFL Draft. It certainly makes the last few picks of the NFL Draft interesting. Like a chalupa-crazed crowd at an NBA game rooting for the home team to score over 100 points, the few remaining fans at the end of an NFL Draft cheer every final draft pick like it was the first. With each pick, they're getting closer to their Draft ticket. Then comes (finally!) the last pick of the NFL Draft, for which there is actually a wee bit of pomp and circumstance with emphasis on the word "wee."

For over 30 years now, the last player selected in an NFL Draft has been known as Mr. Irrelevant. As if a player hasn't gone through enough anxiety waiting to hear his name called the entire draft, he must now deal with this moniker. But, it's all in good fun since Mr. Irrelevant gets flown out to Southern California for a week's worth of festivities every June. I'm not kidding. It's called Mr. Irrelevant Week and it's run by a nice gentleman named Paul Salata, a former wide receiver at USC who split his only season in the NFL between the Colts and 49ers in 1950. Salata says he's a fan of the underdog and thus has hosted Mr. Irrelevant Week since 1976. So, believe it or not, the last pick in an NFL Draft goes to Disneyland. He gets a parade in Newport Beach, California, and he's feted at a banquet where he receives an award called the Lowsman Trophy since it's the opposite of the Heisman Trophy. Get it? At any rate, when the final active Draft Room makes its final call to its Draft Desk and the final Draft Card gets brought to the Draft Pit, it is then handed to Salata who steps to the podium to make the announcement himself. So for years at the NFL Draft, the first draft selection was announced by Paul Tagliabue and the last by Paul Salata.

Once Salata's work is done, the NFL Draft comes to a merciful close. The diehards remaining file out and file for their tickets for next year. We in the media then go to sleep. Like Rip Van Winkle. The 2007

Deep into the seventh round of an NFL Draft, you begin questioning your existence.
(*Joann Kamay*)

NFL Draft lasted a record 18 hours. Nighty-night. You know what I'm saying? As for the new rookies, they go right to work the *following week*. Welcome to the National Football League.

In every other major American sport, fans must wait until the following season to see what their newest additions look like in their uniforms. Not in the NFL. Most teams hold a mandatory weekend practice session for all players starting either the Friday after the draft or the Friday after that. Exactly one week after first putting on a Raiders hat and holding up a Raiders jersey at the NFL Draft with the commissioner, JaMarcus Russell put on a Raiders helmet and wore his full silver-and-black uniform while avoiding the pass rush of new teammates and Pro Bowlers Warren Sapp and Derrick Burgess during team drills. Just like that.

It's not just for the rookies. Veterans also must attend this workout, called a minicamp. By rule in the collective bargaining agreement between the league and the players' union, a team can hold one mandatory weekend-long workout session for all players each off-season. (New head coaches are allowed two to help install their system.) But it really sounds more like a creation of Mike Myers's Dr. Evil than any head coach: *It's like training camp but smaller. We shall call it . . . minicamp.*

Minicamp is where the rookies go through basic training, and get measured for shoulder pads and helmets and shoes and the like. It's also where they first receive their new playbooks, which they must not only instantly absorb but also guard with their lives. Many a rookie has gotten cut before taking part in a single drill because he foolishly left the playbook in an airport or a hotel room. In this day and age, a playbook that falls into the wrong hands can wind up on the Internet. The rookie responsible (or more appropriately, irresponsible) then winds up on the unemployment line.

Sure, it's technically a workout in early May, frequently four long months prior to kickoff of the regular season, but, as you might imagine, coaches take this stuff seriously. On the eve of the Jets minicamp two weeks after the 2007 Draft, head coach Eric Mangini was asked if the road to the Super Bowl went through New England, which acquired Pro Bowl receiver Randy Moss on the second day of the draft.

"The road to anywhere starts with the next minicamp and training camp," Mangini said. "Last year was last year. This is a process and we're starting on the process."

Nobody has more of a process than NFL rookies, and there are a whole lot of them. Once the NFL Draft ends, Draft Rooms are still alive because general managers are on the phone contacting the agents of the scores of college players who went undrafted. It's a race to get the best of this remaining lot because you never know what gem you might uncover. After the 1994 Draft, the Denver Broncos signed an undrafted wide receiver out of Missouri Southern State, a Division II school in the Mid-America Intercollegiate Athletic Association. Today, Rod Smith is the leading receiver in the history of the Denver Broncos, with the most catches, receiving yards, and touchdown receptions of any undrafted receiver in NFL history. That's why the Ravens signed 16 undrafted players immediately after the NFL Draft while the Minnesota Vikings signed 15 and the Miami Dolphins 14 and so on. Within hours of the Draft's conclusion in 2007, the Chicago Bears inked seven undrafted players, including former Florida Gator quarterback Chris Leak. Sure, they have Rex Grossman, but you never know.

NFL teams need the extra bodies to man the drills for the regulars, not only at the mandatory minicamp, but also at the so-called voluntary workouts teams hold throughout May and June. I say "so-called" because these workouts (known officially and somewhat ominously as Organized Team Activities) aren't all that voluntary. Head coaches have been known to place considerable pressure on veterans to attend these "voluntary" activities and many veterans who skip the workouts have been known to slip down the depth chart because they took the "voluntary" literally. As for rookies, there are no ifs, ands, or buts. They will be at these workouts, period. Unless they get to go to the Rookie Premiere.

What's that, you ask? It's a relatively new event created by the NFL players' union to drum up some publicity for the future stars of the game. Held in Los Angeles every year since 1996, it's a four-day shindig surrounding an age-old ritual for all the top rookies—taking a picture for their first NFL trading card. In this eBay era of collectibles, that means saying a lot of cheese. Of course, it also means bread. The 30 or so rookies selected for the Rookie Premiere receive their very first official professional paycheck.

Over the four days, the union keeps the rookies busy. They didn't get the rookies a hall pass from workouts and schlep them to Hollywood just to have them catch some rays and look for Britney. There's a Rookie Premiere youth football clinic, several autograph sessions held around

Kicking it with the top neophytes at the 2005 NFL Rookie Premiere. The infamous Pacman Jones is behind your host. *(NFL Network)*

town, and a Rookie Premiere dinner (hosted the past few years by your humble narrator), but it's all just window dressing for the two-day photo shoot held at the Los Angeles Coliseum.

Trading-card photographers from Donruss, Upper Deck, and Topps set up shop in all parts of the Coliseum while former Packers great Sterling Sharpe and I conduct interviews in the end zone for a Rookie Premiere program that appears on NFL Network. One by one the players, wearing their new uniforms, rotate from photo station to photo station; for instance, Donruss takes pictures of the rookies running with the football while Upper Deck snaps the quintessential low-angle trading card photo of the player flying toward the camera with arms outstretched. They even place a huge mattress on the field so players can land softly. I should know. One year, I hit the mattress for a photo. I sure do look ferocious. I also nearly threw out my back.

If I had thrown it out, I'd have been OK. There's a masseuse on the scene. The players' union likes to keep the rookies as happy as possible. The shoot takes two days to complete; you're bound to get some moaning and groaning with all the picture taking. So, in addition to providing a massage tent off to the side, the union pumps in earsplitting levels of hip-hop over the stadium's speakers to help the rookies find their groove as they go about the photo shoot.

My first year at the Rookie Premiere in 2005, I put on shoulder pads and the No. 17 jersey of Cleveland Browns rookie Braylon Edwards to see what it's like going through the photo gauntlet. They have smoke machines for added effect, and they have Jugs machines to fire out footballs. All the running and jumping can get you tired in the hot L.A. sun. So, of course, I hit the massage tent where I lay facedown on the table and had the shapely masseuse work my shoulder pads just for the joke of it. In the end, the joke was on me, because, in the middle of the mock massage, someone else took over. When the whole crew started laughing, I looked up and saw the person putting hands on me.

It was Pacman Jones.

Too bad he wasn't as hands-on at the next rookie event.

In late June, most often two months to the day after the NFL Draft, every single drafted rookie finds himself with all the others under one roof at the annual NFL Rookie Symposium. For four full days the collection of former BMOCs and future millionaires get a comprehensive lesson in how

The real Braylon Edwards is on the left. *(NFL Network)*

to be a professional in the National Football League. And it's apparent *real fast* that the lesson has nothing to do with recognizing the blitz or picking off a slant route.

Over the four days, each rookie attends seminars, general assemblies, and breakout sessions from dawn till dusk on such topics as personal finance, life skills, personal conduct, media policy, substance abuse, family issues, player development, football operations, NFL, security, success in the NFL, and life after football. Lest you think that bringing up that last subject with rookies is overkill: The average length of an NFL career is 4.3 years. Therefore, half the young men attending a Rookie Symposium will be searching for another line of work before their 27th birthday.

Serious stuff, indeed. Thus, the NFL does not mess around. Every drafted rookie must attend the symposium or risk a hefty fine. In 1999, Chargers quarterback Ryan Leaf made his first of many professional missteps when he left the NFL Rookie Symposium early. The NFL fined him $10,000. The league made Redskins safety Sean Taylor cough up $25,000 when he decided to skip the second day of the 2005 Rookie Symposium.

The NFL is eager to make sure that each rookie has his head screwed on as straight as possible before he signs his first professional contract and essentially becomes an extension of the game. No question is too stupid, and no issue too outlandish. The help is available for the first overall pick and for Mr. Irrelevant. Whether a player wants to find out how to set up a 401(k) or simply to learn how to balance a checkbook, he's covered at the symposium. Want to know the pitfalls in hiring an agent? Dealing with the media? Curious about sexually transmitted diseases? Ditto. The league officials who operate the four-day forum rack their collective brains to think whether they're missing anything.

Legal experts, tax experts, guidance counselors, sociologists—the league brings them all in to run the breakout sessions and hammer home the do's and don'ts. The rookies rotate from session to session grouped with fellow rookie teammates. A typical sight at the Rookie Symposium would be, say, all the Cowboys draftees going from one room to another, wearing the same blue Cowboys golf shirts, carrying the same huge looseleaf notebooks containing handout materials and notes. In the massive General Assembly room, the rookies sit in the same row as their teammates. It's also the place where a motivational speaker named Zach Minor and his merry troupe of thespians hold them captive.

Each year, Zach puts on a show. Literally. A group of actors take to the General Assembly stage and put on a series of true-to-life skits with the same running theme: Choices, decisions, and consequences. Zach's minidramas all feature sticky situations that could likely present themselves to every rookie in the room during his upcoming first professional season.

One year a skit dealt with a player who returns home from a road trip only to find his brother boasting of how he's arranged for him to get $20,000 of stolen goods for just $2,500. Another year a player in the skit tells his longtime live-in girlfriend he wants to break up. The girl says she's already spoken to a lawyer about getting half his income as a common-law wife. In each skit, just as the tension builds to a crescendo, Zach Minor grabs a microphone and screams:

"Freeze!"

The actors immediately stop in their tracks, sort of like Leslie Neilsen at the end of an episode of *Police Squad.* The lights in the room go up and Minor strolls through the aisle with a microphone. A pop quiz breaks out as Minor asks random rookies how they would handle the situation playing out before them. *You in the back! Tell me what you'd do?* Occasionally, he'll pull a rookie or two from their seats and throw them into the skit to have them *act out for the entire room* what they might do next. It leads to frequently comical and also triumphant moments. For the skit involving the live-in girlfriend, Minor yanked 6-foot-6, 375-pound Bills draftee Mike Williams out of his chair and tossed him on the stage in the role of the boyfriend. Williams handled the dicey scenario with aplomb, talking in hushed tones. At one point, when the actress playing the girlfriend began to cry, Williams threw his arm around her. His fellow rookies burst into applause.

That scene ended well, but many others do not. Either way, it perfectly dovetails into Minor's indelible message to his pupils. In fact, he repeats his mantra umpteen times throughout the course of a Rookie Symposium:

"Choices. Decisions. Consequences."

Ask any player who's been through it. Choices. Decisions. Consequences. If nothing else remains from their four-day stay in the league's custody, they'll remember those three words. Of course, the Maurice Claretts and Pacmans of the world have it go in one ear and out the other. That's why the NFL also brings in some former and current NFL players to tell the rookies what's what. Very few youngsters will tune out the wisdom future Hall of Famers Rod Woodson and Cris Carter can impart. The duo also has spoken at previous Rookie Symposiums.

Carter is the perfect guy to speak at the Symposium. He experienced serious trouble shortly after entering the league from Ohio State. Yet Carter overcame substance and alcohol abuse to produce one of the best careers in NFL receiving history. In other words, he's been there and done that. In his speech to the rookies, Carter turns preacher, with no topic off-limits. At the 2005 Symposium, Carter warned the rookies about the increasing number of women they're going to encounter. Many of them, Carter warned, are motivated by love . . . of money.

"Believe me. The ladies aren't all coming up to you because you're good-looking!" Carter bellowed from the stage. "Because most of you are not *that* good-looking!"

K eeping with their covering-all-bases approach, the league also feels it is imperative for the rookies to hear from contemporaries, too. Thus, every Rookie Symposium features a panel of second-year players who re-lay experiences from the rookie season they've just completed. It's a fasci-nating discussion for its frankness as well as its freshness. I know, because I moderate the panel every year. We talk about everything: women, money, posse, competition, agents, fame, family—you name it. It is truly no-holds-barred. Since the panelists were all in that very same General Assembly room as rookies the year before, they know the questions the current crop of rookies wants answered or *should* have answered for them.

In previous years, "Life as a Rookie" panelists have included Charg-ers linebacker Shawne Merriman (one of only two 2005 rookies to make the Pro Bowl on defense), Seahawks linebacker Lofa Tatupu (the other 2005 rookie to make the Pro Bowl on defense), Browns wide receiver Braylon Edwards (the third overall pick in the 2005 draft), Cardinals wide receiver Larry Fitzgerald (the third overall pick in the 2004 draft) and Atlanta defensive back and now perennial Pro Bowler D'Angelo Hall (the seventh overall pick in the 2004 draft.) Not all rookies, however, are bonus babies or highly touted prospects. So the NFL provides a cross sec-tion of panelists to offer up varying viewpoints on the rookie experience, players like Texans running back back Samkon Gado (undrafted out of Rev. Jerry Falwell's Division 1-AA football hotbed of Liberty University), Redskins tight end Chris Cooley (81st pick of the 2004 draft) and Jets defensive back Erik Coleman (the 143rd pick of the 2004 draft). To-gether, they sermonize and issue sage warnings to the audience of rook-ies, offering a unique window on the experience of making the biggest jump in professional sports—from college football to the NFL gridiron.

Regardless of their pedigree, the second-year players, to a man, agree on one thing: the biggest adjustment is mental rather than physical. Fans always hear about rookies having difficulty adjusting to the speed of the game at the NFL level, but it appears that NFL rookies have a bigger issue to deal with: savvy veterans hungry to keep their jobs.

"You've got guys who've been in [the league] ten to twelve years, and physically you might be better than this person. You might be big and strong and fast," Merriman told the group. "Sometimes, I go up against men that have been in the league ten, eleven years, and you see they can barely move, even just walking onto the field. I'm talking about regular walking, period. They can't move, walking around, no way they can bend down to get something. But they're gonna find a way to beat you on Sunday. I mean, they're gonna find some kind of trick. He's gonna *learn* how to beat me. That's probably the biggest difference coming for you."

Edwards concurred. "The only thing that was really different for me is the knowledge that the veterans have of the game. There are a lot of guys in this level that you'll be more advanced than in terms of size, speed, strength, and those aspects. But the guys are *smart*. You have guys that have been playing this game for ten and twelve years in the NFL, know everything, know your moves before they happen, and now you're gonna have to realize that *this* is what this game is about. So, that's the only thing that was different—just knowing that guys *know* this game. They don't just play it. They *know* it. So, get on the ball and learn."

"These veterans have kids to feed," Hall said. "They've got kids to feed, families, cars to buy, houses to buy. They're not gonna let you all come in and take their money, period, no matter what. Trust me. 'Cause I'm one of them dudes now. And there ain't nobody in here gonna come in there and take my money—for real."

By the way, D'Angelo Hall is a natural character. He's been the most entertaining "Life as a Rookie" panelist by far. People always wonder what star athletes would do with their lives if they weren't blessed with a God-given physical talent. Well, if Hall wasn't one of the best young shutdown corners in the league, he'd be traveling with the Original Kings of Comedy. He was just getting on a roll on this particular subject.

"I wish everybody would have told me just how mental this game is, you know? You can be the fastest guy in the league, the most athletic, but if you ain't in that playbook and you don't know what's going on, it don't matter. You ain't gonna get a chance to play. You know, we got guys that weren't drafted and been the league like eight, nine years and they're some of the smartest guys that I've ever seen in my life. You know, those are the kind of guys that I got myself around, picking their brain, just to try to master our defense so I can go out there and just know what's going on. So my advice for y'all is: Just learn the game, you know? Learn about guys that came before you. Don't just worry about guys that are out there right now. You gotta know the history of this game. And you definitely gotta know that playbook or you won't get a chance to play no matter where you were drafted, whether you were number one or you were a free agent. It ain't gonna matter. 'Cause, I mean, it's different out there; yo, I'm telling you. Not just game speed. Game speed gonna come to you, I'm telling you. I can't stress this enough, yo. That mental thing out there on that field, man. I'm telling you. It'll take a college All-American and get him cut the next year. That's how hard it is out there. So, I'm telling you, man. Get in that playbook, man. Don't miss any of these workouts, practices, minicamps. You know what I'm saying? Utilize being out there, being around them coaches and just try to impress them, man. Just try to *own*."

Larry Fitzgerald thought his biggest adjustment had nothing to do with football, but with something that ruins a lot of nascent NFL careers: productively filling the hours away from work. The world of college football is highly structured, from classes to study groups, with coaches looking over the players' shoulders the whole time. In the NFL, once you're done with practice, you're on your own. Therefore:

"Just have a plan in terms of time management because after practice, there's a lot of down time," Fizgerald said. "And like you guys have all been told, you've got a lot of money, you're visible, and people know who you are. With the time you have on your hands, there are a lot of times you can get into a lot of trouble not having the right things to do. So, I think that was the biggest thing for me—find things to do with my time that were productive, you know? You're in a new city. You don't have family there. You don't have anybody you know. So, you gotta surround yourself with the right people and find good things to do with your free time."

It was a remarkable soliloquy for the simple fact that Fitzgerald may just be the most squeaky-clean, well-mannered NFL draftee in recent memory. He comes from a great family. He calls everyone sir. If *he* was having trouble with his down time, imagine what issues other rookies with less solid upbringings must go through every year. Tatupu also struggled with the issue, even though he knew what was coming: He's the son of 15-year-veteran running back Mosi Tatupu.

"Manage your time knowing that this is a job. I know it's fun. And in some extents, it will seem like college all over again," the former USC star said. "But, you got to know how to manage your time and be professional about it. You're expected to show up and work hard when you're there. And, just know, it's not like you're hanging out with the boys after [practice] all the time [like in college] because a lot of [NFL players] have families. So, if you can—manage your down time wisely."

Gado, a spiritual Nigerian native, offered a simple solution.

"Find something that gets your mind off of football that's productive. Whether it's volunteering—that's actually worthwhile and that will help you stay out of trouble more than anything else. . . . It could be so many other things. Whatever your interests are that are productive to society, I think, it would be in your best interest just to get plugged in. 'Cause the NFL, it's such a high-powered corporation. They can get you plugged in to just about anything. So, you take advantage of those resources whether it's talking to your player personnel or player development leader or your coach or anything. Just find something that you enjoy doing that's productive and just plug your time into that."

Hall's solution to staying out of trouble got the room laughing.

"You're sitting at home in your big house by yourself trying to figure out what to do and that's when you get into a lot of trouble, you know? You end up going down to Buckhead in [Atlanta] or South Beach if you're in Miami. So, that free time—get a hobby, you know? I took up golf, you know? Y'all laughing now, but I tell you what, you meet a lot of people on that golf course. A *lot* of people. A lot of executives, a lot of people that's gonna help you enhance your money, enhance your image. So laugh now."

No laughing matter, as the Zach Minor skits frequently point out, are money and how the players deal with suddenly having it. I make sure to raise the topic during each "Life as a Rookie" panel because each and every rookie in the NFL gets bombarded by people looking for money, especially from parties they wouldn't expect. Listen to these stories.

MERRIMAN: Money changed a lot of people [I know], man, to be honest. I mean, you're gonna see some stuff that you probably never thought you'll see out of people in your whole entire life. I mean, I just found out in one year, so, a lot of you all are gonna go through it. I mean, you're going to see some strange stuff out of people who you wouldn't ever think would, you know, act in a certain way or ask you for a certain thing. To be honest, family's gonna be number one, because they feel like they're entitled to your money. They feel like, they changed your Pampers when you grew up, they were there when you needed some stuff for school. They're gonna bring it back up from when you were five. "Hey, remember when, you know, you wanted to go to the ice cream truck?" All the acting stuff [the Zach Minor skits] they're doing here right now, you know, I'm telling you, you might look back and say "Oh, that's corny, man. That will never happen." It happens. Trust me, it happens. It may not happen the way they're acting up here, but in a certain way, though, it does happen. So, I've just seen all that change, man. Money can do some things to people, I'm telling you. It's important for everybody to know that.

EDWARDS: You have family members that will come to you and say stuff like, "I got this idea, I got that idea." You just gotta be up front and you've got to control it yourself, man. 'Cause at the end of the day, it's *your* money. Don't let sob stories or this story or that story influence you. If there's somebody truthful that you want to help, then help them. . . . But it's hard as hell. You know, your *sister* might come up to you. Your auntie might come up to you, you know? You might have to tell your *mother* no. And I know that sounds ridiculous, you know what I'm saying? 'Cause, how can I tell my mother no? Fathers, you might have to tell *them* no. Mothers and fathers eventually will cross that line, and it might be something minuscule, but you have to be a man. You have to own your money. The checks that they sending you from your various teams, it says "Braylon Edwards." It says "Matt Leinart." It says "Vince Young." [Both players were in the audience.] These are *your* checks. The bank account is in *your* name. The car that you're gonna buy is in *your* name. The money that they're trying to come after is *yours*. That's the word you all need to remember—*yours*. So, make your own decision.

GADO: I want to add to that. It's not just the first-rounders. I was a free agent and I played half a season last year and I *still* had people coming at me. And, I mean, I'm dealing with half of minimum wage here. I mean, I didn't sign a big contract, but I echo every one of their sentiments when they say: You set the tone now. The earlier you start saying no, the easier it's gonna become. You're working hard for the money. No one else is taking heat from the coaches. It's you. And so, no one else is entitled to that. So, yeah, you take care of your family and those that you love, but, in conclusion, even the sixth-, seventh-rounders [in this room]—those that don't get paid—it's still gonna happen to you all, too.

TATUPU: I'll give [people looking for money] my financial adviser's name and number. But my financial adviser knows not to deal with anyone unless I call [my advisers] and tell them that someone's gonna be calling them. So, my advisers might get, like, ten or twelve calls in a month about things that people want to do with my money. But if I hadn't already dropped the line to my financial adviser, it's a no-go. So, there's ways around it without being confrontational and maybe, you know, upsetting some people. Go through your financial adviser, your agent, anybody. They'll help. Even your mom can tell those people no for you. Just tell them your money's tied up, come up with something. But people are gonna be out there and they're looking for your money.

D'ANGELO: Y'all gotta realize, y'all grown men. You know what I'm saying? Y'all ain't little kids no more. So when people ask y'all for money, you gotta be able to say no. You know what I'm saying? 'Cause you get yourself too extended out there, you gonna be hurting. 'Cause you gotta remember, in the NFL, you get paid after every game, but when that last game's over, you don't get paid no more. So if you're out here living it up during the season, and you think them same checks gonna come at the end of that season when it's all said and done, you're gonna be hurting. So y'all grown now. You know what I'm saying? Y'all gotta be able to tell people: No, I can't help y'all out this time. And, I mean, that's gonna be the biggest thing, just know how to say no.

FITZGERALD: Another thing, too, is, y'all don't know yet, when y'all get through signing bonus on the taxman, everything you get is cut in half. I mean, everything you earn is *not* what you taking home. They take a big chunk out of you pretty much—*real* big.

COOLEY: It truly is like *half*.

FITZGERALD: Yeah, it's ridiculous.

COOLEY: Everything you do—*like half.*

FITZGERALD: Every city you go to, they tax you.

D'ANGELO: Tax man like a pimp, yo. He gonna get his.

FITZGERALD: He gonna get his.

D'ANGELO: Straight up. He gonna get it off the front, and you mess around, he gonna get off the back, too. Like a crackhead, he gonna come back for some more. If he ain't get you right the first time, he gonna get you right the second time. For real. I hate the taxman, yo. For real, Rich. Hey, Rich, kill the taxman, yo.

Funny stuff. However, at the "Life as a Rookie" forum, if you want a real good laugh, nothing beats bringing up the subject of . . . the ladies. The panelists' eagerness to disclose their rookie experiences magically evaporates. There's lots of hemming and hawing and classic avoidance tactics like looking up at the ceiling. In 2005, the subject was broached by one of the rookies in the audience during the interactive Q&A portion of the panel:

"Temptation with the women. How do you all handle that? 'Cause, I mean, I know Larry [Fitzgerald's] out there in Arizona, getting down. And D'Angelo in the A-T-L [as in Atlanta]—"

The room broke out in hysterical laughter. Hall immediately jumped in to set the record straight.

"D'Angelo? No. No," Hall said. "D'Angelo lives forty-five minutes from the A-T-L. He stays in Brazelton. Ain't nobody ever heard about Brazelton."

"No. All I'm saying, you know, I mean, we're all young men and, you know, we all love ladies," the rookie said from the audience. "So how do you all handle that, like on a serious note. I mean, 'cause I know you all got women throwing themselves at you. Well, how do you all handle that? You know, because not every girl out there's gonna be safe."

"Well, I'm married," Hall retorted. "So you ain't gotta worry about that. Next question."

"C'mon," I said, as the laughter died down. "Is there anybody who *does* have an answer to this question?"

Erik Coleman spoke up.

COLEMAN: Well, my advice is if you go to the club to meet women, just know you're not going to meet your wife in the club, you know what I'm saying? If you're going to the club to meet someone for the night, take it for what it's worth. You're not going to find a wife in the club. They're looking for ballers; they're looking for you all with money. You guys got money, so just make the right decision. You know right from wrong. That's all I got to say.

COOLEY: I'd say I had a lot more people talk to me when I was out and they knew that I play for the Redskins. If I was out by myself or out with friends and no one knew—I mean, [then] I don't really have anyone come up and talk to me. But if I had a jersey on or if I was out and in public for my team, I had all kinds of people coming up to me. And so you kind of understand what their motives are and I think you have to know what people's motives are before you're involved.

ME: You saying you need to work on your rap a little bit, Chris?
COOLEY: Yes.

ME: Is that what you're saying?
COOLEY: Yeah.

An amusing exchange, but that's nothing compared to the following year when Samkon Gado actually tried to preach abstinence to the NFL rookie class of 2006:

GADO: I have a philosophy. I have one rule that will guarantee every single time that you will not find yourself in trouble when it comes to dealing with women. And it's strictly: Keep it in your pants.

An audible murmur came from the audience and built into outright laughter. The soft-spoken Gado pressed on.

GADO: And you just *(Laughs.)* and all I'm saying is, it's, it's, it's, no, seriously it's—
ME: Right.

GADO: It's 100 percent foolproof, 100 percent foolproof. And I know it's not what many people want to hear.

ME: Right.

GADO: And I battled whether saying it or not, but that's the truth. If you keep it in your pants, then you're not gonna get in trouble. So, it's possible. It's possible. It can be done.
MERRIMAN: I mean, that's— That's a little extremist.

Huge laughs from the audience. Merriman then told a cautionary tale that points out just how much of a target a fresh, green rookie in the NFL can be when he's out and about.

MERRIMAN: I had one incident, man. I was down in Houston and I was doing this event. And one of my best friends came over and said, "Shawne, you should walk around the counter." And I said, "For what?" "You should walk around the counter real quick. Be real slick about it, but walk around the counter, though." So I walk around the counter and I peeped over at this girl [with a laptop] on Yahoo, typing my name and finding out everything about me. Then she came over to try to talk in the lobby of the hotel. So that's the level that you're at right now.

Rookies getting Googled on the spot. Imagine if Joe Namath had to deal with that.

Armed with the knowledge stuffed into their brains from the symposium, the latest draft class gets sent back home with the NFL wringing its hands, hoping it all has sunk in. Of course, one month later, it's all about football again. Time for Training Camp and, eventually, the season.

THINGS THAT NEED TO BE IN THIS BOOK

I've noticed that a lot of sports columnists or bloggers have a random-thoughts section. All sportswriters seem to like arbitrary pithy items. Whether it's touting their new favorite show on TV (that Jack Bauer is something else!) or bemoaning the rigors of airplane travel (and then the guy next to me orders *another* tomato juice!) or the awkward declaration of manhood (Jessica Beil is *hot!*), sportswriters sure love a good slapdash collection of thoughts.

I always thought it was laziness.

Not anymore.

While writing this book and frequently agonizing over how best to work certain stories into certain chapters, I decided to stop worrying and broke the emergency "random thoughts" glass. I created a chapter of things that needed to be in the book. Thus, the name of the chapter. Suddenly, all the stories and photos with no other proper place in the book had a home. Enjoy.

THE TALE OF THE THREE DUKES: It's the most important item on the football field, yet we take it for granted. It's thrown. It's kicked. It's carried. Yet we hardly notice it as a constant source of mystery and intrigue. We think it's just a plain old football, but, in the National Football League, the ball is far more than just a ball.

Its beauty is pigskin deep.

The kids may call it a "rock" or a "pill," but did you know the NFL football actually has a proper name? It's called "The Duke," after longtime Giants owner Wellington T. Mara, whose nickname was, you guessed it, Duke—not after John Wayne but rather a great fighting Anglo-Irishman named the Duke of Wellington. When Bears founder George Halas helped Giants founder Tim Mara strike a deal with Wilson Sporting Goods Company to become the league's first official supplier of footballs in 1941, Halas suggested the NFL name the football in honor of Mara's omnipresent son. So it was suggested, so it was written, so it was used. Starting in 1941, every NFL game ball had the words "The Duke" emblazoned on it. Bart Starr threw The Duke, Jim Brown toted The Duke, and Jan Stenerud kicked The Duke. But when the NFL and AFL merged in 1969, The Duke got bounced—dropped in deference to the clean slate created by the new venture. It wasn't until 36 years later that The Duke returned. The league reinstituted the institution in 2006 as a posthumous honor to Wellington Mara.

Unlike its first incarnation, there are three Dukes this time around. There's a Home Duke, an Away Duke, and a Kicking Duke. It's a whole new NFL world, you know.

Let's start with the Kicking Duke. There's been one in every NFL game since 1999—a ball to be used only by the kickers and punters. Why? As the NFL's head of officiating Mike Periera told me, "There are two things that drove the decision—the psychology of the individuals using the football and statistics."

The league's Competition Committee compiles statistics on absolutely *everything* to discern trends or perhaps . . . something more sinister. In 1993, the committee tabulated the alarming number of touchbacks and blanched. That year, only 68.4 percent of all kickoffs were returned. That meant 32 percent of the time a kickoff returner either took a knee in the end zone or watched the ball sail out of it. In other words, *boring!* So, the Competition Committee moved the kickers back 5 yards, from the 35- to the 30-yard line and voilà! In 1994 88.4 percent of kickoffs were returned. Excitement! But wouldn't you know it . . . slowly, but surely . . . that number began to creep down again—to 80.4 percent of all kickoffs returned in 1998, still too low for the

Competition Committee's liking. What in the Wide, Wide World of Gramatica was going on?

"We were hearing," said Pereira, "kickers were basically doctoring the footballs."

Ah, yes. The psychology of the individuals using the football. Kickers and punters, whose livelihoods depend on how far they can boot The Duke. Therefore, they know all the tricks of the trade. Like bashing the ends of a football into an edge of a desk to work down the points and make it more aerodynamic. Legend has it that Chiefs Hall of Fame coach Hank Stram once told Jan Stenerud, the only kicker in the Pro Football Hall of Fame, to put helium in the football to see if it would make it go farther. It didn't. I spoke to a veteran placekicker on the very subject and asked him the strangest thing he's ever seen done to a football. He demanded anonymity. If this was the *Nightly News,* he would be silhouetted and his voice altered.

"I once saw another kicker place a 35-pound [weight] plate on top of the ball and then jump up and down on the weight," he said. "It makes the sweet spot on the ball larger."

This kicker—who shall remain nameless—also mentioned a fascinating practice of working in a football to make it nice and soft.

"Saturate the ball, soaking wet, to get the factory resin off the ball . . . and once dry you put [it] in a mesh bag with towels and throw it in the dryer and then you would put [it] in the steam room or the sauna."

The Duke taking a steambath? Is this the NFL or the Catskills?

Obviously, this aggression could not stand. In 1999, the National Football League took action. It introduced a very Lee Iacocca–sounding K-ball, the exact same football as a game football except that it has a K on it and it is only used for kicking plays. The league maintains possession of it right up to game day. In fact, the K-balls are shipped directly from Wilson to the refs' hotel and the refs bring the K-balls directly to the officials' locker room at the stadium. However, because new footballs are frequently slippery (thanks to that resin coating), the NFL allows each team to send an equipment man in to the officials' locker room to work over the K-balls for 20 minutes and not a minute longer. Yes, indeed. A proxy for the kickers is allowed pregame visitation rights to the K-balls.

I'm not making this up.

Did it work? Sure did. In 1999, the percentage of kickoffs returned spiked more than 5 percent to 85.6. In 2000, it went up even farther, to

87.1. By Jove, the K-balls got it! But wouldn't you know it . . . slowly but surely . . . that number of kickoffs returned began to creep down again—to 83.9 percent during the 2006 season. What in the name of Nedney was going on *now*?

"The best we could tell," Pereira said, "is that kickers were doing things like putting [the K-balls] in front of heaters [on the sidelines] and then saying to the equipment guy: 'This is the ball I want kicked.'"

So, now, the NFL is taking custody of the K-balls *throughout the entire game*. The league won't admit it, but many believe the last straw came in the 2006 Wild Card playoff game between Dallas and Seattle in which Cowboys holder Tony Romo had the ball inexplicably slip out of his hands as Dallas was attempting a chip-shot, sure-fire, last-second, game-winning field goal in Seattle. This, from a guy (Romo) who possessed the eye-hand coordination to nearly qualify for the field for the 2005 U.S. Open at Pinehurst. Since K-balls were being circulated into the game by the home team's equipment staff, legend now has it that somebody had busted a brand-new K-ball out of the box just in time for the Romo hold. May not be true, but it appeared to be enough for the Competition Committee to act.

Starting in 2007, the league is hiring a kicking ball guardian for every game! A member of the officiating crew plucked from the local area—employed by the league for the day—will be the person responsible for the kicking balls. This local official will travel with the rest of the crew to the stadium. He will then be in charge of K-ball security and distribution throughout the game.

So, from now on, whenever you see a kicker attempt a pedestrian 35-yard field goal or a punter boot a nondescript 40-yard punt, just know that he's using a special K-ball put into play by a special official who got them from a colleague who had the footballs directly shipped to his hotel room by Wilson Sporting Goods.

And that's just one of the three Dukes in play.

As for the Home and Away Dukes, those are the brainchildren of the NFL quarterbacks, who lobbied heavily for them. Quarterbacks are finicky creatures. They're also control freaks. They like their footballs just so. Except, for years, NFL quarterbacks could only use footballs they broke in and handled the way they preferred half the time. You see, for decades, the home teams handled all the footballs put into play in the NFL. So, at home, the footballs were, to use the Goldilocks vernacular, just right. However, on the road, quarterbacks got to feel even more out of place—using another quarterback's footballs.

"I can't tell you how many times I heard quarterbacks complaining about the balls, even during the games," Steve Mariucci told me. "Like panic in the streets."

Even worse for a quarterback, as Romo can attest, is a brand-new football. Mariucci says whenever he worked out a quarterback at a tryout he would make him throw a shiny, fully varnished football to see how he could handle it.

"Heck, you'd be lucky if you ever get a spiral out of it," Mariucci said. "That's why quarterbacks usually bring their own footballs to a workout. They hate a brand-new football, and they work it like a fiddle. They're always yelling at the ball boys to rub the balls down, even during the game."

In essence, every road quarterback in the NFL thought he was getting a new football to use from the opposing team's equipment staff while the home team quarterback sat in his comfort zone with a football he had personally aged since Pop Warner. It must have driven them nuts. Quarterbacks are borderline insane about getting the right feel on a football.

"Steve Young would bring dirt from the 49er facility," Mariucci recalled. "He'd bring a cup of dirt to the stadium just so he could put it on his fingers and he would rub it on his hands like a rosin bag just so his feel for the ball was consistent both home and away. Or maybe it was lucky dirt. I saw him do that once and asked him 'What in the world are you doing?' And he said, 'I'm getting my dirt, Mooch!'"

So, prior to the 2006 season, the quarterbacks banded together and asked the NFL to allow them to use their own footballs during a game. And when I mean banded together, I mean like Tom Brady calling Matt Hasslebeck and telling him to join the petition that Peyton Manning and several other quarterbacks had already started. True story. That happened. In college, the NCAA allows each team to use its own footballs: The home teams use footballs they prepared and the away teams do the same. Why shouldn't quarterbacks have it the same way when they go to the next level? Why should Brady have to use footballs prepared by the Miami Dolphins when he goes to Dolphin Stadium, where, surprise, he's thrown the most road interceptions of his stellar career?

The Competition Committee heard the plea, saw no downside, and shrugged. If the quarterbacks want their own Dukes, it's no pigskin off the league's nose. Thus, starting in 2006, the quarterbacks got to use their own footballs—a Duke for the home team and a Duke for the visiting team. I'll never forget the response when I brought this up on the air on *NFL Total Access* with Rod Woodson.

"Aw, isn't that sweet," Rod said, with a mock smile. "Maybe we can get them some warm milk before they go to bed."

You see, defensive players like Rod think this song-and-dance with the football is laughable. In their minds, the reason why a quarterback throws an incompletion or interception has more to do with the defense than with his "feel" for the football. Perhaps that ball came out too high because, say, a defensive lineman was in his face. And that interception had nothing to do with the fact that the quarterback didn't prepare his own football. It's because the defensive back prepared by watching film and, perhaps, picked up on the quarterback's tendency to throw late. Crying to the league to use your own football? There's no crying in football!

This is the dynamic that is playing out on both sides of the Duke every time one is snapped in the NFL.

Of course, the NFL regulates the Home and Away Dukes, but not nearly as stringently as they do the K-balls. Pereira says each team delivers a dozen Dukes to the official's locker room exactly 2 hours and 15 minutes before kickoff to each game. The Home and Away Dukes are then pressure-tested to see if they have between 12 and a half and 13 and a half pounds of pressure. If it's overpressurized, the refs take some air out. If it's underpressurized, they pump up the Dukes. Once that process is complete, the refs give the balls to the ball boys for handling during the game, during which they'll no doubt be harassed by the quarterbacks to keep working them in.

In the meantime, the NFL is working on things from its end. Pereira says the Wilson company is experimenting with a new tannery to make the football stickier coming out of the box. Those footballs will be given to the teams to try out during Training Camp 2007. If the players like it, the Home, Away, and Kicking balls in 2007 may just allow everyone to live happily ever after—but it probably won't.

And that, boys and girls, is the tale of the Three Dukes.

ROD WOODSON'S RECRUITING STORY: An instant classic. While we're on the subject of Rod, I've got to tell you this one. In case you require a quick lesson, Rod is an 11-time Pro Bowl defensive back and was one of only three active players named to the NFL's 75th anniversary all-time team in 1994. Basically, Rod is one of the best to ever lace 'em up and, back in the day, he found himself one highly recruited graduate of R. Nelson Snider High School in Fort Wayne, Indiana.

During his recruitment, Rod told me he sat in the Michigan Stadium meeting room before the Wolverines were heading out to Los Angeles to play in the Rose Bowl against UCLA. The Wolverines made the bowl even though they had lost to Ohio State, which means Bo Schembechler must have been in a foul mood. Bo stormed into the room before practice and characteristically peeled the paint off the walls. An E. F. Hutton moment broke out. Rod said you could hear a pin drop. Instantly, the laid-back Woodson thought: "Oh, no. This isn't for me."

(For fellow Michigan fans, here's another Bo recruiting story as told by Lincoln Kennedy, who eventually chose the University of Washington before enjoying a successful 10-year NFL career. Prior to Lincoln's recruiting visit to Ann Arbor, Bo sadly suffered one of his many heart attacks and wound up in the hospital. However, not even a clogged ventricle could stop Bo from his appointed rounds with a prized tackle like Lincoln. So Schembechler had Lincoln in for an adjustable bedside chat. With tubes sticking out of him and the heart monitor beeping in the background, the supine Schembechler rasped out his recruiting speech without a hitch. Lincoln said he couldn't believe it. As a Michigan Man Class of '90, I say, Way to go, Bo! Go Blue!)

Now, back to Rod.

With Purdue the early front-runner (and eventually winner) for his services, the sad-sack Indiana Hoosier football program still had to take its crack at the recently named Mr. Indiana in football. As if convincing a talent like Rod to join a squad that had won a paltry 41 games in the previous ten years wasn't difficult enough, the Indiana coach showed up to his house with quite an odd pitch.

"Son," the coach told Rod. "I've just been fired. But Indiana is still a great place to go and I hope you do."

The coach, you ask? Lee Corso. Yep. Long before he became the outrageous, popular, No. 2 pencil–wielding, mascot-head-wearing television analyst. Rod Woodson told Lee Corso, in effect, "Not so fast, my friend."

With Purdue now having the inside track and Illinois a possibility, there was still one long shot remaining with a play for Woodson—Arizona State University. It had everything that none of the other colleges in the running could offer: Sun. Fun. Pac-10. Rod flew to Arizona thinking that if one place could take him out of his Midwest comfort zone, this could be it.

Now, as we've all seen in movies, blue-chip prospects get squired around campus by a recruiting host, almost always a current member of the team who is assigned to give the recruit a taste of the, shall we say, college slice of life. So, with Rod fresh off the plane from his frigid Fort Wayne outpost and now trolling around the hopping Tempe campus of Arizona State University, guess where his recruiting host took him?

Straight to the movies. To see *Gandhi*.

Yep. The gripping saga of Mahatma Gandhi's transformation from simple lawyer to famed leader of the Indian revolts against the imperialist British through a philosophy of nonviolent protest. Directed by Sir Richard Attenborough. Total running time: three hours, eight minutes. That was the extent of Rod's first and only taste of Arizona State University campus life. After the flick, Rod said the exchange between him and host went something like this:

> **HOST:** What do you want to do next?
> **ROD:** Are you kidding me? Take me back to the hotel. I'm on the next flight outta here.

I love telling that story to every Sun Devils fan I meet. You should see the looks on their faces when they hear their school missed out on one of the greatest players in football history because of one kid's inexplicably bizarre Ben Kingsley fixation. For the life of him, Rod can't remember the name of that host. Two things for sure: Whoever that guy was, by punching his movie ticket he also punched Rod's ticket to Purdue. Secondly, he's got good taste. *Gandhi* did win Best Picture, after all.

THE MENTALITY OF AN NFL LINEBACKER: For any young man wishing to play linebacker or is currently playing the position, look no farther than the next few pages for a perfect primer. The following is from a conversation I had with Pro Bowl linebackers Ray Lewis and Takeo Spikes on our set at the Steelers-Seahawks Super Bowl in Detroit in 2006:

Ray Lewis and Takeo Spikes teaching Linebacker 101. *(Joann Kamay)*

ME: I want to know from both of you guys, what mentality does it take to play this position, in the National Football League? What does it take?

RAY: You want to answer it first?

TAKEO: No, I'm gonna let you go ahead.

RAY: Okay, Rich, honestly, and Takeo can definitely relate, people most of the time take it personal because of the mentality that we [linebackers] have when we play football, but this game is not a pretty game. This game, at my position, is physical. You're hitting linemen, three hundred-plus pounds. You hit the running backs not to just, you know, tap them on the back and say, "Good job." You're hitting them to tell them, "Don't come back through my hole again." So, your mentality has to be: I'm pissed off, at all times, by any expense. If you come at me, you're gonna get what you're not expecting to get, and a lot of people are not willing to pay that price when it comes to a football game. You know, a lot of people want to sit down, they want to be pretty, and do this [sitting on TV] right here. But when you step on that football field, you have to let somebody know, if you plan on coming across my middle or if you plan on playing football the way you think you can play football against me, you're asking to play football against the wrong person. And I think that Takeo can definitely relate to what I'm just trying to say.

TAKEO: Oh, definitely, man, 'cause when you step on that field, you want to impose your will on that opposing player. You have to. Because right on top, the hype is built up during the week and you gonna do whatever you can to win. A great example of that is [then-Steelers linebacker] Joey Porter. He's gonna find whatever he can right now throughout this Super Bowl week to get into that player's mind. It's all a mental game, and when we step on that field, I'm gonna let you know: The eyes are the window of the soul, so I want to see how bad you want it.

AUTHOR TIME-OUT. We hit the pause button on this conversation for some key background information. The verbose Porter spent much of that Super Bowl Week punking Seattle tight end Jerramy Stevens in the media as much as possible. If you recall, Jerome Bettis was the feel-good story of Super Bowl XL—Detroit native trying to win the Super Bowl in his hometown in his expected final game. Nevertheless, the brash Stevens popped off about Bettis thusly: "It's a heartwarming story and all that, but it will be a sad day when he leaves without that trophy." Porter heard the quote and was livid. "He's too soft to say something like that," Porter said. "He's going to have the opportunity to back up his words. I'm going to have the opportunity to back up my words. So it's something I'm looking forward to and I'm ready to get going." TIME-IN.

ME: So, you're saying that it's the nature of the position and it's not a shock to you guys that of all the people to have been speaking out on this whole issue of what Jerramy Stevens said is a linebacker. And not only a linebacker, but somebody like Joey Porter.

RAY: *(Nodding)* And this is the thing about what I want to tell the world. Joey Porter said nothing wrong. Joey Porter spoke what a football game is about. If you are telling me that you're gonna win, I'm telling you, "I'm gonna win. This is the Super Bowl." When you step into the Super Bowl, you have to let them know: "Look, I'm here for business. And if you, Jerramy Stevens want to deal with me, guess what, I strap on my pants the same way you strap on your pants." So what Joey Porter said he was supposed to say, 'cause this is a physical football game where you play that position.

TAKEO: Exactly.

RAY: And that's the position me and Takeo love so much, because we know what it takes to play that position.

TAKEO: Love it. Love it. I'm telling you, right now, we got Rich ready to play. Rich is ready to play.

ME: I do want to hit somebody, and if anybody comes to my set without an answer for me, they are gonna have to deal with it.

RAY: I can get you ready to play, Rich.

ME: Was my mentality good, was that good?

TAKEO: That was pretty good.

RAY: I guess it was okay. (*Laughs.*)

ME: It was awful. But, to me, it's fascinating that there isn't an offensive lineman or D-lineman or a safety [popping back at Stevens]; it's a linebacker that's the one that's at the center of it all. And that's just because of the mentality you have to have to play this game?

TAKEO: Oh, yes.

RAY: Sometimes you have to get very intricate with things that we're talking about when you talk about football. Offensive lineman and defensive lineman—they're very close to each other when they usually collide, you know, so you very rarely get the bang-on-bang of heads. Linebackers, you're coming from five, six yards, sometimes ten yards away from a person and you land . . . you're taking *all of your power*— how much you weigh right now?

TAKEO: Two hundred and forty-two.

RAY: Two hundred and forty-two pounds, probably running a 4.4 40, one of the most gifted linebackers that I've seen play this position in a long time.

TAKEO: Thank you, sir.

RAY: Yeah. And man, this guy right here [Takeo], getting ready to hit you, just like Joey Porter—that guy's attitude is the reason why the Pittsburgh Steelers are gonna come out and play the way they're gonna play Sunday.
ME: If you play in this game Sunday and [Seattle running back and 2005 NFL MVP] Shaun Alexander gets the ball first off, what do you do? What are you trying to communicate?

TAKEO: Oh, if I'm on the other side of the ball, Shaun Alexander, I'm gonna impose my will, not only on him, but the entire offense. I'm gonna let them know how it's gonna be, when it's gonna be, and how often it's gonna be. That's what you have to do. And I think that there's one other thing that Joey Porter has done. As a linebacker, when you step out on the field, and this is something I firmly believe in, and I heard Ray say it a long time ago: The linebacker sets the tone and the tempo. They are the heartbeat of the team, the left and the right ventricle. If that doesn't pump, then no blood flows throughout the team.
ME: So, let's reverse it. What if it's The Bus coming through that hole? [Even at his listed weight of 255 pounds, Jerome Bettis is a load. His nickname isn't The Bus for nothing.]

RAY: Guess what?
TAKEO: You got to get the drop on him.

RAY: Or else you gonna get the same thing.
TAKEO: You *got* to get the drop on him.

RAY: He pulls on his pants one leg at a time. The same way I do. So, yeah, it don't matter how much you weigh or anything like that. When you play the position of linebacker, you got to deal with whoever comes through that hole with the ball, period.

Here endeth the lesson.

DANCING WITH THE TRIPLET: One week before winning the 2006 championship on *Dancing with the Stars,* Emmitt Smith returned to

Dancing with Alex and Emmitt. (*Joann Kamay*)

NFL Total Access and gave me a lesson in the cha-cha. NFL Network reporter and former flamingo dancer Alex Flanagan lent a helping hand. Eat your heart out, Mario Lopez!

WILDEST WORK WEEK: Without question, the five days between Weeks 3 and 4 of the 2006 NFL regular season. It began with a 1:00 A.M. flight out of Los Angeles International Airport. I had no idea such flights existed, but Steve Mariucci and I needed to be on one right after midnight

Sunday. Otherwise, we'd never have made it to New Orleans in time for the official reopening of the Louisiana Superdome on *Monday Night Football.*

We couldn't fly out earlier. Every Sunday night after *Sunday Night Football,* I host a highly entertaining and informative (of course) highlight show with Deion Sanders and Steve Mariucci called *NFL GameDay.* After we finished the Week 3 edition of the show, Steve and I immediately headed to the airport and took the first flight out. Two fitful naps and one connection through Houston later, we found ourselves in New Orleans 13 months and 2 days after Hurricane Katrina. We were also only seven hours from going back on the air with two and a half hours of coverage of the pregame ceremonies. So, the first thing Steve and I did was get some shut-eye.

Of course, it was tough to get rest, what with a summer Mardi Gras breaking out in the streets of New Orleans. The return of football—after the harrowing nightmare that turned the Superdome into a festering shelter for thousands of suffering people and sent the Saints on the road for the entire 2005 season—was cause for a Grade-A Nawlins celebration. I like to walk to a stadium whenever possible. With only eight blocks separating the hotel and the Superdome, I went marching in.

It took a half hour to walk the eight blocks. Either offices closed up shop early or the entire city workforce had a case of the Blue Flu, because the streets were jammed with revelers of all shapes and sizes and in various states of dress. The stadium concourse was wall-to-wall people—five hours before kickoff. It took another 15 minutes for me to find producer Chris Weerts—and we were talking to each other on our cell phones the entire time. We've all been through The Drill at games.

"Where *are* you?!"

"I'm standing right here! Where are *you?*"

Finally inside the Superdome, Mooch and I met up with our other analyst for the night—Marshall Faulk, a New Orleans native born five minutes from the Superdome. Long before he found stardom in the NFL and at San Diego State, Marshall dazzled the bayou locals at George Washington Carver High School, which got completely wiped out by Katrina. Growing up in the Ninth Ward, Marshall couldn't afford to see the Saints—so he sold popcorn in the Superdome just to get a glimpse. Years later, he played in the building in Super Bowl XXXVI. Now, as part of

Commissioner Roger Goodell stops by our set at the Superdome reopening.
(David Drapkin)

NFL Total Access, Marshall was present for its biggest moment yet. The Superdome was back from the dead.

Fittingly, so were the Saints. Behind new head coach Sean Payton, the Saints started the season with two straight road wins for the first time ever. For good measure, the Saints were playing equally 2–0 Atlanta. Toss Michael Vick into the prime-time mix and you had yourself some must-see activity.

The pregame festivities were unforgettable. The first band on the field was from a local high school. The last bands were Green Day and U2. In between the performances, the crowd swelled, and soon the outdoor party came inside. One dignitary after another appeared on the turf—Commissioner Roger Goodell, his predecessor Paul Tagliabue, and my old buddy from Houston, President George H. W. Bush, who presided over the coin toss.

Our first three guests on *NFL Total Access* were Falcons owner Arthur Blank, Commissioner Goodell and Louisiana governor Kathleen

Blanco, whose interview got interrupted by one of the loudest pregame cheers in memory.

You see, Reggie Bush had just come on to the Superdome turf in a Saints uniform for the first time.

"Our people have been working so hard. They've suffered so much, lost so much," the governor said as the din rose. "So to come out here is just a visual. It's the reality that we can put our lives back together. And the importance of it is an emotional importance, a psychological importance."

Suddenly, famed director Spike Lee appeared. NFL Network operations chief Mike Konner buttonholed him and invited him to appear as a guest. Spike agreed and soon sat in the same seat the governor had sat in minutes before, offering his unique take on the occasion.

"Well, this is huge. This is like the Super Bowl," Spike said. "It's amazing. A great spirit here, but it still has to be tempered a bit. Because when the game's over, the Lower Ninth Ward still is not gonna have gas. Still not have electricity. Still not gonna have water. So for four hours it's gonna be great."

With five minutes remaining before Green Day and U2 rocked the house, we shoehorned in one last guest—Archie Manning, the greatest

Marshall, Spike, me, and Mooch in the Big Easy. *(Michael Konner)*

Saint of them all, the quarterback of the team that Marshall sold pop-corn to see.

"I haven't seen anything like this," Manning said. "I played in the first game here in 1975 and we had a big day here the first time the Saints made the playoffs. But I've never seen anything like today, or the excite-ment, the anticipation of the crowd. And, you know, it is emotional."

It's so rare for a sporting event to live up to the hype. But this game did. Lightbulbs popped from every corner of the stadium as John Carney booted the ball to the Falcons. Just three plays into the game, the Saints defense chased Vick out of the pocket and the ball came loose. An ear-splitting shriek came from the crowd and then . . . a collective exhale as the ball bounced out of bounds. That was just a mere appetizer for the feast that arrived on the next play: New Orleans blocked the Falcons punt for a touchdown. It took four plays for the Saints to get back on the board in the Superdome. The resulting noise nearly tore the roof off the place again.

Hands down, the loudest I've ever heard.

The Falcons had no shot on the Superdome field that night. The Saints cruised, 23–3. The first Saints home win in two years touched off a bayou bash that lasted deep into the night and made the morning wake-up call that much more troubling. At least I had a travel day Tuesday.

When I got back to Los Angeles, I reintroduced myself to my wife and grabbed an early dinner, when my cell phone buzzed with a text. It was from Deion: T.O. taken to emergency room, don't kno what hapnd but he's OK.

Holy smokes. I got home and turned on the TV but heard nothing. Deion wasn't answering his phone. Exhausted from the travel and the Big Easy revelry, I fell asleep only to have my cell phone buzz again with an-other text from Deion at 6:00 on Wednesday morning.

T.O. took 35 pills n da police askd was he tryn 2 harm himself n he said yes. Let Eric kno.

Good morning, indeed. I assumed our executive producer Eric Weinberger had a buzzing cell phone of his own at that daybreaking mo-ment. Perhaps he was also brought out of a deep REM state by the ludi-crous development that the five-time Pro Bowl receiver famous for screaming "I love me some me!" had apparently tried to off himself.

Now, you've got to give me credit here. This is a football book and it has taken this long for a detailed mention of the walking soap opera that is Terrell Owens. The man has filled many a minute on *NFL Total Access*. Since we went on the air in November 2003, Owens has done the following:

- Filed a grievance to get out of San Francisco because his agent missed a paperwork deadline to file for free agency.
- Dragged the league, three teams, and one union into a hearing and eventually got what he wanted in the spring of '04—out of San Francisco, but not to Baltimore, which had traded for Owens during the process.
- Forced his way to Philadelphia because he wanted to play with Donovan McNabb and then sullied McNabb's reputation within a calendar year. It took 16 months for Owens's relationship with the Eagles and his relationship with head coach Andy Reid to be irreparably harmed. He was suspended during 2005 Training Camp.
- In between, Owens excelled in his first Super Bowl—Philly's first in 24 years—and did so just five weeks after requiring surgery to repair a broken ankle.
- Owens then became a 2006 Dallas Cowboy, seemingly testing the patience of his notoriously old-school coach Bill Parcells with regularity. After missing much of preseason with a hamstring injury, Owens required surgery to repair a broken hand suffered the week before the Superdome Opener.

All very dramatic—and I'm not even mentioning his press conferences with agent Drew Rosenhaus that live on in YouTube infamy—but this was the topper: Thirty-five pills? Terrell Owens? Kill himself?

Now, gather around children, for I'm about to impart useful information. When it comes to Terrell Owens, there are two long-standing, simple Golden Rules of Thumb:

1. The first T.O. story is never, *ever* the whole story.
2. If you're a reporter covering that story, don't make any personal plans. Pack a lunch. Cancel dinner. As the man himself once said, "Get your popcorn ready."

Sure enough, while I deftly navigated the streets of Los Angeles to get to the studio, Deion buzzed in again.

> He didn't try 2 commit suicide . . . just spoke with him . . . not 35 pills—
> he never spoke 2 police.

Gee whiz, the first story wasn't the whole story after all. Which was a story in itself, because an official Dallas Police report had already hit the Internet stating that not only *did* Owens tell first responders he tried to harm himself, but his publicist also mentioned that Owens had told her he was depressed. I tried calling Deion again but got no answer. Deion was already at Owens's apartment, counseling the troubled receiver. At one point, Deion stepped outside to tell the gathering media throng that a press conference was to be held at the Cowboys facility in two hours.

In the intervening 120 minutes, I anchored nonstop live coverage of the affair as if North Korea had just set off another test bomb. Marshall Faulk and Rod Woodson joined me on set as we wondered what sort of pills Owens was taking (Marshall correctly suspected he took painkillers for his hand) and the effects that taking those pills have (Rod said he once took a painkiller for his knee and had an entire conversation with his mother that he subsequently didn't remember) and then there was the psychological issue. Was this a cry for help? Could Owens truly be as troubled as many suspected?

As always with Owens, the answer was: Who knows? At his press conference, a confident Owens laughed off the notion he tried to commit suicide. The painkillers he took for his hand had merely mixed poorly with his dietary supplements and caused him to pass out. He also said he had no idea why his publicist said he was depressed. He then handed the floor over to said publicist, Kim Etheridge. I immediately knew her media session would be the stuff of legend when she sat at the microphone chewing a piece of gum.

"When I see a man of his statue [sic] not responding and I know he's not feeling well, I used my judgment to call nine-one-one," she said. "I did not say that Terrell was depressed. Terrell did not say he was depressed."

Etheridge offered one final piece of evidence that Owens was not suicidal. "Terrell has twenty-five million reasons to be alive," referring to the three-year, $25 million contract Owens signed with the Cowboys. Yikes. (Owens fired her after the season, by the way.)

That "twenty-five million reasons" comment set off another flurry of commentary and indignation from Marshall and Rod. Deion chimed in via satellite from Dallas. All in all, we did three and a half hours of live television in the afternoon before hosting a new one-hour *NFL Total Access,* after which we stayed to update the later edition. As I expected, I didn't make dinner.

E very Friday during the season, we tape one of my favorite segments of the week—"Celebrity Picks," in which someone from the nearby Hollywood community comes into the studio to predict the outcome of 10 games from the upcoming week's docket. It's a seasonlong competition. The winner gets a prize of some sort. Over our first four seasons, we've had folks like the Rock, *CSI*'s Marg Helgenberger, actor Michael Clarke Duncan, Toby Keith, Wanda Sykes, and Carlos Santana try their hand at "Celebrity Picks." Only two have ever scored a perfect 10—Holly Robinson Peete and Hank Azaria. On this crazy week, our Friday guest personified it. Comedian Andy Dick, who not only knew zero about football but has also appeared on talk shows in drag or in a Vulcan outfit or apparently strung out or all of the above.

Segment producer Andy Gregg sensed my fatigue and wrote a real funny bit to keep Dick as scripted as possible. When Dick arrived (properly attired), he agreed to the script, but he also insisted on singing a serenade about his costar in the movie he was promoting—*Employee of the Month* with Jessica Simpson. Indeed, Dick brought an acoustic guitar player with him and sang from his prepared lyrics.

"This goes out to my friend Jessica Simpson," Dick said as his backup plucked away on a stool next to him. "Hopefully one day, she will lie down with me."

The song went like this:

Jessica, Jessica. I hope you appreciate the things I do.
Jessica, Jessica. I left my ninth rehab for you.
Jessica, Jessica. Let's sneak off and drink some wine.
Jessica, Jessica. We could have a real good time—and drink . . .
   red wine.

Producer Andy Gregg carefully vetted the lyrics of Andy Dick's tune prior to the taping of Celebrity Picks. (*Joann Kamay*)

You get na-ked and we drink . . . more wine.
And I promise not to get too drunk and throw up in your pretty,
pretty, pretty, pretty, pretty, pretty, pretty, blond hair.

The crew gave a round of applause.

ME: That's wonderful. I could see you really enjoyed working with her.
ANDY: Well, I love her and I hope that seals the deal with me and her.

ME: I think you can lock that in and rip the knob off, Andy. I think you got it done.
ANDY: (*Reaching for a drink of water*) Thank you. I need to get her done.

ME: Well, thankfully, everyone, that's water in his NFL Network mug.
ANDY: I asked for gin, you bitches!

I immediately moved the segment along to the picking of the games and, thus, to our scripted material. Dick nailed it perfectly, although his ad-lib of calling New York Jets coach Eric Mangini by the name of "Man-gyna" nearly gave me a heart attack. His predictions:

New England-Cincinnati: I love autumn in New England.
Oakland-Cleveland: My plumber's name is Cleveland.
Jacksonville-Washington: I lost my virginity on the East Lawn of the White House. So I'll take Washington.
Seattle-Chicago: I love Oprah, so I'm going to go with Chicago.

The comeback from Hurricane Katrina, then tropical depression Terrell, followed by an Andy Monsoon—that was my week in sports.

STEVE SABOL IS THE MAN: I'm not just saying that because he was kind enough to write the foreword for this book. Without question, the most fascinating nonplayer to be a guest on *NFL Total Access* is Sabol,

Steve Sabol on the *NFL Total Access* set in Los Angeles. (*Joann Kamay*)

president of NFL Films and son of its founder, Ed Sabol. Well, Steve might take umbrage at being called a nonplayer: He was an All Rocky Mountain Conference running back at Colorado College, bowling over linebackers like Wichita State's Bill Parcells. Sabol left college after one year to join his father in building the single greatest chronicler of American sports history. To say he's been there and done that is a severe understatement. As of the writing of this book, Sabol is only one of nine people currently walking the planet to have been to all 41 Super Bowls. His first Super Bowl experience kicks off this compilation of all his best recollections in talks with me over the years:

"I sat next to [Pittsburgh Steelers founder] Art Rooney at the very top of the L.A. Coliseum. My dad was [to my right] and Art Rooney was there. Art Rooney was supposed to go back down [to the field] but the elevator got jammed. So Art Rooney stayed up there and he actually helped me call the isolated cameras [for NFL Films coverage of Super Bowl I] and stayed with us every year until the Steelers went into the Super Bowl [eight years later]. I mean, Art Rooney was like a member of our staff [for eight years] all because he got stuck in the elevator [at Super Bowl I] and because he couldn't get down. He had a cigar. He said: 'Steve, can I sit here?' I said, 'Sure, Mr. Rooney.' And then, he said, 'What are you doing?' I said, 'Well, I'm calling the isolated cameras.' And he says, 'Well, maybe you should put a camera on that Elijah Pitts *(Laughs)* and what about Max Magee?' And I think, jeez, I'm sitting along with the patriarchs of the game, and he's turning into Cecil B. DeMille."

Smartest Player Sabol Ever Met: "The smartest player might have been Fran Tarkenton. Very, very interesting player. Had a great sense of the broad picture. I mean, everybody thinks of him as a scrambler and sort of an improviser, but he was very, very intelligent. I think he stands out. The smartest person? Bill Walsh."

Dirtiest Player: "Billy Ray Smith [Smith was a 13-year veteran defensive tackle who played in Super Bowls III and V for the Baltimore Colts.]. He used to put Atomic Balm [active ingredients: oleoresin capsicum and methyl salicilate, i.e., red-hot pepper oil and oil of wintergreen], you know, on his fingers. And the first play on the scrimmage line, he'd go right into your face and everybody would be playing would be like this. *(Sabol covered his face.)* Bob Brown [Hall of Fame offensive lineman, Class of

2004] had a thing where he would unscrew the corners of his face mask. And this was when the head slap was legal. So Deacon [Jones] or somebody would come up with the head slap and go right into the screws of Bob Brown's helmet."

Ugliest Player: "Larry Csonka. The man whose nose is so bent that he has to breathe through his ears. You know that if you ever take a look at him."

Prettiest Player: "Oh, boy. Probably in his heyday, Paul Hornung, the Golden Boy."

Best Name: "Steve Stonebreaker. Linebacker for the Colts, the Vikings, and the Saints."

Most Superstitious: "George Allen. We had George Allen miked once, you know, he was so suspicious, so superstitious that he felt that putting the microphone on was going to jinx him. So I finally convinced him to wear a mike, it was against the Cowboys, probably the early seventies. We put the mike on and I'm shooting from across the field, and I can hear [Allen] talking to himself: 'Oh, Steve, I don't know whether I should have done this, I don't know whether I should have.' And then, I think it was the Cowboys, they scored first. He's behind 7–0, and I could just see he's gonna take it off; he's thinks he's jinxed. Sure enough, the Cowboys got a field goal 10–0 and he runs off the field during the game, into the dugout [at RFK Stadium] and takes the mike off. And the next day *The Washington Post* reported that George Allen was so upset by his team's performance he became physically ill and went into the dugout and threw up! And it was really to take off the microphone."

First Coach He And His Dad Miked: "It started with a guy named Joe Kuharich [pronounced Q-harrick; Eagles coach 1964–68] and it was a game called the Playoff Bowl that was played after the championship game between the runners-up of the two conferences. Joe Kuharich was coach of the Eagles, and we put a mike on him in the Orange Bowl and this was the first time that it'd ever been done, 1965, the Eagles and the Colts. We put the mike on him and when we were testing it, it's working great. Game starts, Kuharich is screaming [at his players]

'Come on, come on!' and all of a sudden, over the headsets, you hear: 'The tuna are really biting out here in Biscayne Bay!' What had happened was our frequency had been tied in to the Miami Maritime Commission, so throughout the whole wire, we got, you know, fishermen saying, 'Well, we got some marlin out here off the Key West.' That was a mess. And then when we [miked] Lombardi, we got a cab dispatcher in Minnesota! You know, Lombardi's screaming, 'Grab, grab, grab, nobody's tackling him,' and [then we heard] 'We have a woman here on 3rd and 4th Street. Would you come please pick her up? She's got two bags of groceries.' That's all in the [NFL Films] 'Lost Treasures.'"

Biggest Character: "Joe Don Looney [running back, 1964–68] I remember going up to Connecticut, when he was with the Giants, and he was one of the first of the players who was into astrology and had to sleep facing the magnetic north. And outside of the Fairfield University dorm, there was a graveyard. And he would go out at night and lay on the grave-yards because he . . . the beds were too soft and he felt that by laying on the concrete, and facing a certain direction, everything would be OK. [Giants coach] Allie Sherman's got some great stories about Joe Don. He lasted about one year and then they shipped him out."

Best Venue He's Ever Filmed In: "Kansas City's Arrowhead Stadium. You just show up to the stadium and you smell the burgers. . . . And the whole stadium is all red, the background is all red. One of the great achievements, I think, for an executive, has been [Chiefs president] Carl Peterson. Because for so many years, after they won the Super Bowl, they never could fill a stadium. So every time there was a great pass play, you know, when our camera, following the ball up in the air, you'd follow the ball and then the stadium would be empty. And one of Pete Rozelle's cardinal rules to me was: You never show an empty stadium. So we had all these great shots of the ball, and a lot of times the pass was complete, but you'd see the ball go up, and empty stands. So when Carl took over the Chiefs I said: 'Carl, you got to fill that upper deck.' And he did and now that's the best place to shoot."

Worst Weather He's Ever Filmed In: "Well, I was at the Ice Bowl. I was at the '81 AFC Championship—the Browns and the Raiders.

That was cold. The worst weather was the 1962 Championship game in Yankee Stadium. That was before they had the wind chill. It was *cold*. And you talk to Bart Starr, and Jimmy Taylor, Ray Nitschke—they would tell you, that was worse than the Ice Bowl because of the wind. I was standing out in the field, and in the warm-ups, [quarterback] Y. A. Tittle came out. And warming up with [wide receiver] Del Shofner and [running back] Frank Gifford, the first pass that Y.A. throws, the wind just—whoosh!—takes it right into the stands. And you could see in his eyes he knew that that game, that day against the Packers, he wasn't going to play a factor and he didn't. And the Packers won. Now that was the game, if you look at our films, they had, like, these trash baskets. They didn't have heaters in those days. And they filled the trash baskets up with programs and stuff, and rags, and they actually built fires. And we have the footage in [NFL Film headquarters in] Mount Laurel, New Jersey, of the players holding their hands over the fire."

Person That NFL Films Had to Bleep Out the Most:

"Marv Levy. With a Harvard degree and everything. *[Another author* TIME-OUT: *A Hall of Fame coach most notable for his wildly successful stint with the Buffalo Bills in the early '90s, the seemingly genteel Levy may just be the last person you'd think that would require soap in his mouth. His most famous line caught by an NFL Films microphone came when he screamed this at a referee: "You overofficious jerk!" Back to Sabol.]* You know, the 'You overofficious jerk!' You should have heard what preceded that *(Laughs.)* and what followed that. You know, Marv, when we miked him it sounded like a piece of heavy equipment backing up, you know? It would be beep, beep, beep, beep, beep, beep, all the time. Yeah, Marv. In between the beeps there was always an 'overofficious' or 'a feckless official.' His vocabulary was great but for some reason, when the game started, all the f-bombs started to fly."

Best Howard Cosell Story:

"Well, boy. Yeah. What an interesting personality he was. And I spent a whole six months with him. After Super Bowl VII, my dad and I were leaving the game and we got in a cab with Howard Cosell. And in the cab back to Beverly Hills, where we were staying, Howard just took off on me: 'Sabol, you're wasting your time making films about football. Who cares about football? You should be using your talent to make films that're socially relevant, or about important people, and make some contribution to society with your talent! Because this football, you're wasting your time!' And I said: 'Well, Howard, what do you think we should do?' He said, 'You should make a film about me!' And that's what we did. We went out and I followed him through the Foreman-Frazier fight. Through a whole six months. You know, I had to get his laundry once. He was really a very, very interesting person. And the original title of [the documentary] when it went on the air was: *Howard Cosell at Large—And Getting Larger.* But [legendary ABC sports executive] Roone Arledge didn't like it. We had to change it to *Howard Cosell—What Is He Really Like?* And it's still one of the most interesting experiences I've ever had."

Favorite Director: "Claude Lelouch. He was the director that directed *A Man and a Woman.* And he had some impression on me as a filmmaker because there's a sequence in there where he shows a man and a woman falling in love. They're at a table. And there's no dialogue, and it's just music and camera movement. When I saw this in 1966, I felt, if you can show something as complex as a man and a woman falling in love, and have no dialogue, we should be able to do the same thing with football. To be able to convey the emotion and the passion of the sport without any script, without any sound, with just music and pictures. I like John Ford, too. And I love, *love,* the old westerns. *Duel in the Sun.* That's [produced by] David O. Selznick, you know, where Gregory Peck and Jennifer Jones are crawling up the mountain, and that was another influence. Always tight shots of the hands . . . and the blood coming out of Gregory Peck's face. I felt why don't we show football like that, with telephoto lenses?"

G otta love it. *Duel in the Sun.* Doesn't that just sound like something John Facenda [the voice of NFL Films] would say?

SPEAKING OF SUPERSTITIONS: George Allen and his NFL Films mike is just the tip of the iceberg. Thanks to movies like *Bull Durham,* baseball players have been glorified as the most superstitious or ritualistic athletes in all of American professional sports. I say football people are right up here.

Take the case of Eagles five-time Pro Bowl safety Brian Dawkins. The normally mild-mannered Dawkins becomes so crazed before a game that his onetime teammate Rashard Cook gave his alter ego a nickname—Idiot Man. The transformation has a process. It begins once Dawkins puts on his uniform, or, as Dawkins calls, it "the armor."

"Once the armor is put on," Dawkins said, "that's the last thing that goes on and at that point in my head I'm saying to myself, 'Brian Dawkins has now become "Idiot Man" and it's time to roll.' "

One final touch remains before heading out onto the field. Before it is, in fact, time to roll, Eagles trainer Chris Paduzzi must first apply a very special adhesive called a Breathe Right to Dawkins's nose in a very specific manner.

"One side is silver, the other side is green. He gets [a Breathe Right] and he paints both sides for me. According to him, green has to be on one side and silver has to be on another side, that's what he wants; I don't really care," Dawkins explained. "Someone took it one time and [Chris] had a fit, but we have a good time with it and that's just one of the methods that I use to turn from that mild-mannered guy to that weapon that's 'Idiot Man.' "

If that's "Idiot Man," then I don't know *what* to call whatever creature Jaguars Pro-Bowl defensive lineman John Henderson morphs into before a game. His pregame ritual is unique, to say the least. Henderson has a Jacksonville trainer slap him across the face so he can taste blood before heading out onto the field. If at first the assistant athletic trainer, Joe Sheehan, does not hit Henderson hard enough, Henderson barks at him again for another slap. And so on and so forth until Henderson feels sufficiently slapped around. At that point, he storms out of the locker room screaming at the top of his lungs about "wanting some" and the like.

The Henderson slap first aired on NFL Network in our fantastic 2005 summer series called *Inside Training Camp: Jacksonville Jaguars*. It has since been immortalized by YouTube, which, as of this writing, has received 133,648 views to witness the insanity. I encourage you to log on. It's something to behold. It's also something that gave me an idea for this book.

Through the years on NFL Network, I've collected some e-mail addresses from players past and present. I hit a few of those in-boxes with the following question: Did you or do you have a ritual or a superstition before every game? I also called a few of the responders on the phone. I now print their responses verbatim:

To: Rich Eisen

From: Willie McGinest (Three-time Super Bowl Champion Linebacker, 1994–Present)

Hey rich its willie. thanks for thinking of me! I do a few things. what I like to do is first get in the hot tub or take a warm shower to loosen up, get my ankles taped early, I go out and jog but I have to have my I-pod on my get crunk playlist, warm up while listening to up tempo songs, then I go in finish getting dressed call my mother and girls tell them I love them and prepare for war!

Big Mac 55Entertainment

Reggie Wayne (Colts Pro Bowl Receiver, 2001–Present)

The day before every game, I have to eat some type of soup, no matter if it's Chicken Noodle soup or broth soup whatever the case may be. I have to have some form of soup. We normally have soup, no matter if it's home or away, our strength coach John Torine has the soup. He always comes to me like "How's the soup?" He's always asks if it's a Top 5 soup. Some kind of way I have to have soup before a game. It's been like that for six years. If I don't eat the soup something's going to go wrong.

To: Rich Eisen

From: Jonathan Vilma (Jets Pro Bowl Linebacker, 2004–Present)

What's going on Rich. To answer your question, I eat steak eggs and pasta before each game. I never listen to music the night before or the day of the game. I like to focus in mentally and clear my head. I do grow my hair for the entire season, sort of like Sampson, and the one time I did cut it, we went 4-12. That's it for me Rich.

Speak to you soon.

To: **Rich Eisen**

From: **Lorenzo Neal (Two-Time Pro Bowl Fullback, 1993–Present)**

Rich,

I always get to the stadium 3 hours early before a game. I run 4 laps and between each lap I do 25 sit ups and 25 push ups. I then proceed to do my own workout session and drill session that I have been doing from day one! After I go and take a shower and say a prayer and I am ready for the big game!

Gary Baxter (Browns Defensive Back, 2001–Present)

I have to eat Lays potato chips. I still do the same thing. Since last year [in 2006 when he tore the patella tendons in both knees on the same play, jumping for an interception] I may have to change some things up now. I may have to eat Doritos or something I don't know. I definitely have to eat potato chips before the game, I don't know why. But I think I'm going to stick with Lays potato chips again this year. When something bad happens to you try to go back and ask "Can I change that up. Will this make a difference?" But for me, it's definitely Lay's potato chips. I've got to eat them.

To: **Rich Eisen**

From: **Drew Brees (Two-Time Pro Bowl Quarterback, 2001–Present)**

Hey, Rich. I am responding to you from Barcelona. I am out here for an awards ceremony and some R and R. I would love to contribute to your book. As far as a pregame ritual, I always wear pants, never shorts to the stadium. In San Diego I would always drive myself in the same car playing the same music, which would be a CD that I would select at the beginning of the year and stick with as long as we were winning. In NOLA, I rode with John Carney every game in his Black Mustang with the license plate JEDI 03 to every home game except for the first one—that Monday night game when I drove myself, got lost, was late to the game and vowed to never again drive myself to the game. I wear the same shorts and shirt on the field for pre-pregame, and do the same exercises from the 10 to the 30 yard line. I then stretch in the same pattern and throw the same routes in order with the receivers, always ending with deep balls that are all caught in the end zone for TD's. Then I go in and am prepared to play a hell of a game. Hope that helps. By the way, when I get back I am going to email you about a great programming idea for next offseason that I think NFL Network should get involved in, and I am definitely going to need your help. Talk soon.

—Drew

Brady Quinn (Cleveland Browns Quarterback, 2007–Present)

I usually take a big gulp of honey before the game. About twenty minutes before the game. It's kind of an old habit that started when I was really young and I've just kept it through the years. It originated from my dad and my uncle trying to get me fired up for early Pee-Wee games when they were on early Sunday mornings. So they told me to take a big swig of honey to get a sugar high and for some reason or another it kind of worked for the first couple of times. I almost gagged and puked but it stuck and never the less I still do it to this day.

And while we heard from one Notre Dame quarterback, we might as well hear from the all-time greatest.

To:	**Rich Eisen**
From:	**Joe Montana (Yes, that Joe Montana. You need any other introduction?)**

Rich

good luck with the book. can't wait to hear some of the stories. i did not but i was part of brent jones' superstition. he said three things had to happen for us to win. a large over weight woman wearing my jersey would call my name, my wife, jennifer, would come down and wave and steve young would throw a ball 3 feet over brent's head while we were standing still warming up . . . steve was not aware . . . and they happened every week. hope that helps.

Joe Montana

Because you can't have one without the other . . .

Jerry Rice (Thirteen-Time Pro Bowl Wide Receiver, Super Bowl XXIII MVP, 1985–2004)

Just my uniform. I think I really put the equipment guys through a lot because they never knew exactly what the pair of pants I wanted to wear. Sometimes I liked the pants to be a little big. Sometimes I wanted them to be more fitted. So they had about six pair of pants in my locker. Always new socks. Always new shoes. Then I had to shine my helmet all that stuff. So everything had to be in place. If you look good you play well. That's my motto. So it was a little pregame ritual for me.

And, now, on to the modern day Joe Montana . . .

To: Rich Eisen

From: Tom Brady, (Two-time Super Bowl MVP Quarterback, 2001–Present)

Hi Rich sorry for the delay in getting back to you . . . been running around the last week or so . . . seems like you're got some great guys participating. In all honesty, I don't have one pregame ritual that I can think of. Nothing I have to eat, or do, or say, of any significance. Kind of boring, I know. I wish I had something to share but we, as Wolverines, are pretty tame compared to those other schools. Best of luck, buddy. Take care.

Tony Gonzalez (Eight-Time Pro Bowl Tight End, Chiefs All-time Leading Receiver, 1997–Present)

Before every game, first I wrap my left wrist and then I wrap my right wrist. Then, on my left wrist, I write the initials of each one of my family members. After I write their initials, I give each one a kiss. And I have a lot of family members, so there's a lot of kisses. And my eyes are closed for each one, so I get a lot of guys looking over at me, watching me kissing my tape saying "What are you doing? Are you some type of freak?"

To: Rich Eisen

From: Desmond Howard (Super Bowl XXXI MVP, 1992–2002)
What's up Rich?
Good hearing from u man!
The 1 thing I always did was put my pads n my pants n the same
order and put my equipment on n the same order, more or less,
but that's about it. If I think of something else I'll let u know.
(Sent wirelessly via BlackBerry from T-Mobile.)

Marshall Faulk (Eight-Time Pro Bowl Running Back, 1994–2006)
Other than fall asleep in my locker before every game? No. When I say I'd
fall asleep, I mean I was out. Early in my career I had to have a Snickers
and a Coke just to keep me awake.

Terrell Davis (Super Bowl XXXII MVP, 1998 NFL MVP Running Back, 1995–2001)
The night before every game I had to take a bath. Not a bubble bath, but a
soak in a tub with those aromatherapy salts to sink into the muscles and
my body. Then I'd have to have a bowl of vanilla ice cream with regular
M&Ms. Not peanut, but regular M&Ms. With vanilla ice cream.

To: Rich Eisen

From: Cris Collinsworth (Three-Time Pro Bowl Cincinnati Bengals Receiver, 1981–1988)
I always acknowledged the ambulance. Not the ambulance crew,
the vehicle itself. I would talk to it as I took the field. Something
like, "Hey what's up. I know you're over there and I might be leaving
in you today, but I hope not. Take it easy." Stupid I know, but I never
left in one. You just needed to give it a little love. CC

Willie Parker (Pittsburgh Steelers Running Back, 2004–Present)
Pregame the night before I kind of just stay in the hotel and rent a movie
off the TV and watch a movie and stay away from my phone. All my
phones get shut down . . . no distractions. Wake up, eat a good breakfast
and I'm ready.

To: **Rich Eisen**

From: **Michael Strahan (Seven-Time Pro Bowl Defensive End, 1993–present)**

Rituals???

I have a few but not as many as I've had in the past. I still do everything in a certain order.

I always eat scrambled eggs, white toast, oatmeal, yogurt, a banana and strawberries. Never deviate from that!!

Always look at my socks and see which one feels like it should go on which foot. Never just put them on without that. Call me the sock whisperer!!!

Giants Stadium has the big main cargo door or a regular door that you can go thru to get in. I will always go thru the big door because I always want to see "The Big Picture." Stupid I know but from all the things we've done you should know that I'm not that sane but yet far from insane.

Hope that's some of what you needed. If not I'm sure I can come up with more. This was done on my blackberry so I have to limit my typing so that I can use my fingers later!!!

Talk to you soon

Stray

(Sent wirelessly via BlackBerry from T-Mobile.)

Rod Woodson (Eleven-Time Pro Bowl Cornerback, 1987–2003)

The night before every game I had to have apple pie a la mode and a glass of chocolate milk. Every time. And if I was on the road and the hotel didn't have apple pie, I had a cobbler of some sort. And chocolate milk. Without fail.

To: **Rich Eisen**

From: **Sterling Sharpe (Green Bay Packers All-time Leading Receiver, 1988–1994)**

i had several in running order. 1st i had to be the first player at the stadium on game day. THEN HAD TO GET A FULL SWEAT WORKOUT. Then i took a shower got in the tape chair which i had to be first and taped by the same guy the same way and he would tell me what my numbers would be for the game. Then i had to go to sleep. Then once pregame got going. NO ONE COULD TOUCH THE PALM OF MY HANDS. BUT BEFORE ALL THAT I HAD TO BE IN A HOTEL ROOM THAT HAD A 2 8 OR A FOUR ON THE DOOR. HOWS THAT

Warren Sapp (Seven-Time Pro Bowl Defensive Lineman, 1995–Present)

The number 13. I've got a thing about the number 13. I try not to travel on the 13th. I hate it. My whole life I've been running from the number 13 and right now [in 2007] I'm about to enter 13th year in the NFL. The number 13 is gonna be all over me. I never thought I would make it to season 13. My plan was just to have a 12-year career. So now it's not [season] 13, it's season one-and-three. Can't even say the number. It's one-and-three.

To:	**Rich Eisen.**
From:	**Merlin Olsen (NFL record 14-time Pro Bowl defensive lineman, Hall of Fame Class of 1982; Los Angeles Rams, 1962–1976)**

Rich,

I never thought that I was superstitious but I did have some rituals that I followed. I always wanted to be at the stadium early (first bus), and if I was driving I always drove the same route to the Coliseum. Once I got there, I would lay out my uniform and spend some time thinking about what I had to do in the upcoming game and visualizing myself making those plays. Sometimes that process would get out of hand, and I could feel my energy burning off, so I would stop and go fishing. Seeing myself standing in the cool water of one of my favorite trout streams, I could send my pulse back into a normal range and save some energy for the game itself.

As it got closer to game time I would finally put on my uniform and then tape my hands to protect them. Since I had broken or dislocated so many fingers, this was a critical part of my pregame ritual. My hands were vital tools for me and I did not want them to sustain additional injuries if I could help it. Each finger was wrapped individually and some were taped together to give them additional support.

The hardest part of game day, for me, was waiting for the game to start. All those trips to the head as my body prepared itself for the upcoming game, and then we would finally be standing there nervously, waiting to be introduced. All I could think of was, "let's get this show on the road." Then I would go looking for that first crisp hit of the game. The battle had finally begun.

Merlin

Thurman Thomas (Hall of Fame Class of 2007, 1988–2000)

I only had one. I had to be the last one out of the locker room. That was the one thing that I ever really did. Over my twelve years in Buffalo, it had to be Bruce Smith, Cornelius Bennett, Nate Odoms, Leonard Smith, and I was always the last one out of the locker room. I don't know how that started. It started in 1989 my second year in the league and how I became the last one out of the locker room I have know idea how it happened. But that's really the one superstition I had to be the last one out of the locker room that when I went to Miami that changed cause they wanted certain people on the field at certain times but that was something in Buffalo that I did for twelve years. From 89 to my last year in Buffalo that was basically it.

To: **Rich Eisen**

From: **Torry Holt (Five-time Pro Bowl Wide Receiver, 1999–Present)**

Rich,

I don't have any rituals. I just go with the flow, Rich. Good luck with the book Rich. Thanks.

Peace

Takeo Spikes (Two-Time Pro Bowl Linebacker, 1998–Present)

Spikes has a ritual that's been captured many times by NFL Films. A trainer cracks open a piece of smelling salts and waves it in front of Spikes, who takes a deep inhale and screams out at the top of his lungs. Every game. I e-mailed him to see if that's the only part of his pregame ritual:

What up, Rich! I was talking to Todd [his agent] about you yesterday about me checking in with ya! My favorite pregame ritual is the smelling salt right before the kickoff. The Salts insures me that my head is clear and the first thing I hit will not have a clear mind for the rest of the game. Just a matter of time. Talk to ya later, Bro.

To: **Rich Eisen**

From: **Larry Johnson (Chiefs Two-Time Pro Bowl Running Back, 2003–Present)**

Before every game I have to eat spaghetti And Cranberry juice (welchs only)

Away Games: I always leave on the early bus and sit in the very back (window seat) Home Games: I drive the same route to the stadium. Listen to the same CD playlist

I have to hear Jimi Hendrix "Along the Watch Tower" before leavn locker room. . . .

-L J-

www.27larryjohnson.com

To: **Rich Eisen**

From: **Steve Hutchinson (Four-Time Pro Bowl Guard, 2001–Present)**

Here is my pregame ritual (what i can remember anyway) I'm not that eccentric, so I hope this helps you.

I try to be the first (or one of the first) down for pregame meal. I DEFINITELY have to be the first one to the stadium. First I put on the shirt I wear under my pads during the game, and some shorts. Since I usually beat the training staff there, I have to wait for them to show up to tape my ankles. I then go back to my locker and put my game pants together. This is probably my biggest ritual. I put my left knee pad in first, followed by the right. Next, in goes the left thigh pad, and finally the right. Don't know why, just done it that way since high school. The next and only routine thing(s) I do is start to stretch on my own thirty minutes before pregame warmups. At fifteen minutes until warmups, I put my shoulder pads on. Right before I go out for pregame warmups, I pop an ammonia vile for a little wake-up. (I break another one right before we leave the locker room for kickoff as well) After our team is announced, and we run to the sideline before the opening kickoff, I have a little weird thing I do that I remember doing forever. I go over to the table on the sidelines where the cups of Gatorade and water are set up. I find the cup with the LEAST amount of water, and I dump it on my head. I then find the cup with the next least amount of water, take one sip, and then throw the rest of the cup away. I then pace the sidelines until kickoff.

Hope this helps. Sorry for the incoherency, I just wrote it how I remember it.

Steve

Byron Leftwich (Jacksonville Jaguars Quarterback, 2003–Present)

I don't let anything touch the palm of my right hand on Sunday. No water . . . I wash my face with my left hand. I don't let anybody touch the palm of my hand on game day. The only thing I want touching the palm of my hand is that football. Until the end of the game. You can't help but really before the game because once the game's going on I don't really think about it. I don't want anything wet. I don't want anything touching the palm of my hand. If you watch I always have my right hand balled up so nothing get's the chance to touch the palm of my hand. My teammates know about it. They know. Sometimes guys will try to get me to hi-five to see if I'll forget about it, but I never do. Especially the Quarterbacks on the team, they all know about it. But a lot of people know about it because there wondering why I'm walking around with my hand balled up.

And last, but certainly not least, perhaps the best and most extensive preparatory ritual in NFL history. Sapp concurred, telling me how he witnessed the following pregame custom at several Pro Bowls and "that dude is crazy." Whatever you might call it, it sure worked. Perhaps you might concur.

Deion Sanders (Eight-Time Pro Bowl Cornerback, Two-Time Super Bowl Champ, 1989–2005)

First of all, I couldn't have a roommate before a game. I needed peace and quiet—my own space. I also couldn't eat much and I mean barely anything. Playing on Monday Night Football was hard because I had to eat some time that day—maybe toast or cereal or something light. Then, I'd go back to my room and run a nice, hot bath. I was a huge film guy. Always had to watch film. So, I'd prop a laptop or my VHS player on the toilet and I'd get in the tub and watch film over and over and over again until I was calm, at peace and relaxed, until I knew every darn thing. Every route. Every audible. Everything. Then I'd pick out a suit of choice and trust me— depending on the game, there was a choice. After that, time to go to work. I hated to get to a game early. If I had to be at the game by 1:00, I'd show up at 12:59. I was never a big talker [before the game]—I'd put my laptop or my VHS player on a stool in my locker and hit play and watch more film. Then it was time to get dressed. For most of my career, I wore this underwear with dollar signs on it that I swear to you had big plays in them. I'd wear these under my uniform no matter what. I'd panic when my housekeeper misplaced them. Before putting on the uniform, I'd have it strategically laid out on the floor in front of my locker. Every team I played for, the equipment manager knew to give me a locker with enough room around it so I could lay myself out before a game—jersey, wristband, neckband, bandana, shoes, multiple socks all laid out on the floor exactly how I'd wear it. I'd circle [the uniform] and talk to it: "Gonna be a big day for you, baby. Gonna be a big day." It got to the point where my all my teammates knew not to cross over me, step over me or go over me. You've got to go around me. When it was time to get dressed, I'd start from the bottom up, starting with the socks. I was never a guy to get out on the field early to catch punts; I was never a stretcher. I only took one lap around the field. And I'd make sure everyone who needed to see me saw me—the receiver (I was covering), the punter (I was receiving punts from) the offensive coordinator, the coaches. I made sure they all saw me. I made sure strategically that all those guys saw me as I ran past. Then it was time to play. No talk. No hype. No yelling or screaming. No go-get-em speeches. Just time to play.

Me and T-Sizzles. Believe it. *(David Faller)*

I CAN ROCK THE BLING: Just check out me and Baltimore Ravens Pro-Bowl lineman Terrell Suggs, a.k.a. T-Sizzles. Holla at your boy one time, ladies.

CANTON: THE HALL
OF FAME

(Joann Kamay)

The first thing you notice when strolling up the steps to the Pro Football Hall of Fame in blue-collar Canton, Ohio, is the roar . . . of 18-wheelers whizzing down the Interstate 50 yards to the east. Indeed, if enshrined Pittsburgh Steelers teammates Terry Bradshaw and John Stallworth bounded out of the building, Bradshaw could hit Stallworth on a sweet post pattern but, unfortunately, Stallworth would also run the risk of getting smoked by a Bekins truck.

But, in a way, that's what makes the Pro Football Hall of Fame unique. There's absolutely not a thing quaint about it.

You want quaint? Go to Cooperstown. A trip to the Baseball Hall of Fame is like strolling through a Norman Rockwell painting. For those who haven't been there, Cooperstown is an idyllic one-stoplight hamlet nestled near picturesque Otsego Lake in upstate New York. It's gallant. Sweeping. Majestic. It makes you want to say: "Pass me a little more of that cider, won't you, Martha?" Even if you hate cider and you don't know anyone named Martha.

Then there's the Pro Football Hall of Fame, the original building of which is a squat two-story circular cookie cutter straight out of the Kennedy administration known as "The Juicer." You see, the Hall's flat steel roof and accompanying thick, fat spire actually makes the building look like it's ready to have a 2,500-pound grapefruit dropped on top of it. And, to boot, the whole complex is located directly next to Interstate 77, a four-lane highway that stretches from Columbia, South Carolina, all the way to Cleveland, Ohio. It makes you want to go hit somebody.

That's just the beginning. More differences between the two hallowed Halls:

IMMORTALIZATION: Cooperstown forever enshrines its Hall of Famers with a plaque. And on these plaques there are words. Flowery words. Documenting things like "acrobatic fielding" and "swashbuckling style" or "skilled bunter." Canton's Hall of Famers get no plaques. They get a bust. As in, If you piss him off, Dick Butkus is gonna bust you in the mouth.

APPELLATION: Cooperstown houses people named Whitey and Mickey. Canton is the home to guys like Bronko and Bruiser.

CONVOCATION: The Baseball Hall of Fame induction ceremony is held in late July in a sprawling meadow on the outskirts of bucolic Cooperstown, where fans spread out blankets and picnic through the entire proceeding. You almost expect Ray Liotta to stroll out of the tree line in a Chicago Black Sox uniform. As for Canton? Well, talk about old school: The induction ceremony goes down in a zero-frills high school football stadium built in 1924, situated directly south of The Juicer. Fans roast on metal bleachers in the brutal early August heat and cheer on the all-time gridiron greats receiving the sport's highest honor on the very same field your McKinley (H.S.) Bulldogs bolster civic pride under Canton's Friday night lights. Hard-core. At least during the five hours of acceptance speeches, fans are indeed allowed a water break.

IMMIGRATION: While baseball's genteel fans hail from all walks of life, football fans descending upon Canton come from another planet. To say they're colorful is to disserve the spectrum. When Miami Dolphins great Dan Marino got inducted in 2005, Rod Woodson (who's set for enshrinement in 2011) and I (who has not a Raiders' chance in heaven of enshrinement) watched in total amazement as scores of teal-clad Dolphin fans lined up on the steps of the Hall to take pictures with . . . a life-size cardboard cutout of Marino. Someone had schlepped the knickknack to Ohio, and its mere production in public sparked a near riot. One by one fans stepped up, threw an arm around the smiling still life of Dan, and said cheese. This went on for 10 solid minutes. I wish I had taken a picture—of Rod's jaw hitting the ground.

Then there's Sergeant Colt. He's a proud member of something called the Pro Football Ultimate Fans Association, an eclectic group of fanatics that includes the likes of Boss Hogette (Redskins), Bolthead Trish (Chargers), and famously bare-chested charter member Barrel Man (Broncos), who appears in desperate need of a *Seinfeld* manssiere. As for the good Sergeant, his real name is Danny Dillman and he attends every single Indianapolis Colts home game dressed as he did for the last—in Indianapolis Colts blue and white fatigues, sunglasses, riding boots, and a tilted drill sergeant hat planted atop his buzz-cut do. He has also attended every single Hall of Fame Weekend that I've hosted with NFL Network. And each and every time he stands beneath our set ramrod straight, arms akimbo, giving that 1,000-yard stare up into the booth. He says he's a fan of *NFL Total Access,* but, quite frankly, I think he ordered a "Code Red" on me.

ACCOMMODATION: In Cooperstown, fans attending Hall of Fame Weekend can stay in any number of bed-and-breakfasts or—if they're lucky—bunk with returning Hall of Famers and current inductees at the colonial four-star Otesaga Resort Hotel next to the glistening lake and a golf course called Leatherstocking. (Wasn't that something Dizzy Dean used to wear on his head when a train purser gave him too much De-wars?) In Canton, little mints on the pillow are for sissies. The Hall alums and current inductees get put up in the Canton Marriott. The one with the Neutrogena hand soap and all. The hotel has since received a face lift, at least in name only. It's been redubbed the McKinley Grand Hotel af-ter our 25th President who once opened a law office in Canton. As for the mere mortals attending the weekend, you've got your Red Roofs and Ra-madas and Sheraton Four Points. And if you're with the lucky few, you can stay in the out-of-town spot where the NFL houses its events staff as well as some crew members of the NFL Network. That would be the gothic Glenmoor Country Club, a private Jack Nicklaus–designed facil-ity that includes a 76-room, few-frills, Spectravision-less, dormlike hostelry straight out of *The Shining*. One night something red spilled out of the elevator but it was Grange.

Alright. By now, I think you get the point. Canton and its Pro Foot-ball Hall of Fame uniquely reflect the sentiments of the game. Not a stitch of window dressing. It's all about football. The town reeks of it and can't get enough of it. Over 4,200 volunteers from all around Ohio's Stark County area participate in the annual Hall of Fame In-duction Weekend extravaganza that serves as a celebration of life in the American Midwest as much as it does the sport we all know and love.

Take the Hall of Fame Grand Parade that runs down Cleveland Av-enue in downtown Canton. It's been held every year since 1963 on the day before the Hall of Fame induction ceremony and it sure is grand. Just like any other parade, there are marching bands, balloons, twirlers, baby-kissing public officials and, yes, floats. Even NFL Network has begun fielding a float. Of course, the Ultimate Fans Association has one too. Each year, the aforementioned Sergeant Colt and his kooky colleagues wave to fans (fans waving to fans?) in the appropriately titled 12th-Man Float. Spaced throughout the procession you'll find the true stars of the parade—each individual member of the incoming Canton class riding in top-down convertibles . . . like it's 1963.

Do you have any idea how many people show up for the Hall of

Fame Grand Parade? Try 200,000—or 120,000 more people than the United States Census Bureau says live in Canton. In 2006, John Madden received overdue induction into the Hall of Fame and told me this about the experience.

"Every time we got to a bend in the road, we thought the parade was over. But then we turned the corner and—boom—[yes, he talks that way in real life] there were twenty-thousand more people waving and going nuts, and the same thing happened when we went around the next corner."

This is not some new phenomenon born out of the burgeoning popularity of the game. It's been this way since the outset. In his acceptance speech in 1971, none other than the gruff Jim Brown was overwhelmed by it all.

"During the parade this morning, I had a fantastic time because there were about two hundred and fifty thousand people along our route and they were wonderful," Brown said. "They responded and they made me feel that I was really wanted in the area and that I was remembered and that the things that I did in football were highly respected, and it was all very natural and all very spontaneous, so I was very happy."

But we're getting ahead of ourselves here.

The whole shebang begins waaaay before the main event—in May, when scores of local lasses jam the landmarked Canton Palace Theatre to compete for the right to be called the Hall of Fame Festival Queen. I mean, with all due respect, something's got to pretty up an event that has the Jim Ottos of the world waddling around it, right? The crowned Queen and Her Court (i.e., the runners-up in the Queen Pageant) then spend the next three months, along with a full-time Canton Chamber of Commerce committee called the Pro Football Hall of Fame Festival Committee, getting ready for, you guessed it, the Pro Football Hall of Fame Festival, which lasts a near Christmas-like 11 days.

As in: On the first day of the Pro Football Hall of Fame Festival, my true love gave to me . . . the Balloon Classic Festival! (A festival within a festival!) What could better celebrate the enshrinement of, say, famed Purple People Eater Carl Eller than lighting the candle to a hot air balloon? There's also a women's fashion show luncheon, a food festival (festivals for everyone!) called the National Ribs Burnoff, two- and five-mile races (perhaps to burn off those ribs), and, finally, the Drum Corps International, a drum and bugle corps competition at Paul Brown Tiger Stadium in nearby Massillon, Ohio.

All of this before a single Hall of Fame player hits town.

Each and every August, *NFL Total Access* hits Canton four days before the events up to which the Queen Pageant, Ribs Burnoff, et al. all inexorably lead—Hall of Fame Induction Day and the Hall of Fame Game, the very first preseason game of the NFL year. You can't miss our set. It's located directly across the street from the Hall of Fame—inside a 15-foot-wide by 25-foot-long hermetically sealed box hydraulically raised 20 feet in the air. Sounds weird, but many sports fans have seen it before. It's the famed Hollywood Hotel that Fox used in its NASCAR coverage for years. If you think I'm lying, then what was Chris Myers's extra-hold hairspray bottle doing on our Hall of Fame set?

The genesis of the Hollywood Hotel goes like this: Fox wanted to place its NASCAR announcers close to the track, which obviously required a soundproof environment so that the roaring din of Tony Stewart swappin' paint with Little E wouldn't drown out the pearls of wisdom

The Hollywood Hotel in front of I-77 in Canton. (*Joann Kamay*)

being dropped on the air by Darrell Waltrip. So, some smart guy bought a metal container big enough to hold a studio set and three cameras, cut a large rectangular hole on one side, placed a thick double-paned glass window in that hole, and then soundproofed the whole kit and caboodle. Put the container atop some hydraulic lift so the announcers can see into the track and, voilà, you've got the Hollywood Hotel. And gosh darn if that steel stalag doesn't also perfectly fit our needs for *NFL Total Access* in Canton. We can raise it high enough to see the Hall of Fame through that lone window (a perfect backdrop!) and the soundproofing keeps out the noise from those big rigs toting goods from Lake Erie to the Atlantic. Otherwise, every conversation on our show would go something like this:

ME: SO, HOW DOES IT FEEL TO FINALLY MAKE IT TO THE HALL OF FAME?
JOHN ELWAY: WHAT?!

ME: IS IT A DREAM COME TRUE?
ELWAY: COME AGAIN?!

ME: HOLD ON! WAIT TILL THIS RYDER VAN GOES BY!
ELWAY: THIS IS STUPID! I'M OUTTA HERE!

It's still not all paradise inside our set. When the sun directly streams through the two-ply window, it creates a monstrous greenhouse effect. The Hotel does have air-conditioning, but its humming accompaniment causes the sound crew to insist we turn it off during interviews. On the 85-degree day on which Dan Marino got inducted in 2005, the unflappable quarterback typically got through the entire ceremony without letting us see him sweat. But after he stopped by our set postceremony, we could have put a gallon of Marino sweat on eBay. In fact, I'm still wondering why we didn't.

For three straight years, the game's all-time greats kindly indulged us and absolutely sweated bullets on our show—until one torrid afternoon when Madden refused to go on unless we turned the AC back on. And, clearly, Madden trumps sound guys. Because the interview was perfectly audible, we're now cool as a cucumber for every interview on *NFL Total Access* at the Hall of Fame, but then there's the wind shear. With those lifts jacking us 20 feet in the air, the semis blowing by our set on I-77 cause the

Even with the air-conditioning on at his request, John Madden's bust is sweating.
(*Joann Kamay*)

Hotel to sway a bit. When Don Shula came on the show with fellow Hall of Famer Bill Walsh, the winningest coach in NFL history turned to me and asked: "Is this thing moving?" Said Class of '89 enshrinee Art Shell, when he sat for an interview about an hour earlier: "It feels like an earthquake." That also applied to the set conditions when Class of '96 enshrinee Dan Dierdorf and his replaced hips waddled up the rickety, steep metal steps that run from the ground up to the door to our box-on-stilts.

Yes, when it comes to Hall of Fame Induction Weekend, we at NFL Network are all about the Hall of Famers. Like Canton's Festival Committee, we gear up months in advance. Every spring, we invite a group of Hall of Fame veterans into our Los Angeles studio to tape a Hall of Fame Roundtable Show for airing during our Hall of Fame coverage. On the 2005 show, we got some considerable football knights around our roundtable—the swift James Lofton (only Jerry Rice and Tim Brown amassed more receiving yards), pass rusher extraordinaire Deacon Jones (I mean, the man actually invented the term "sack"), pass protector extraordinaire Jackie Slater (he protected 24 different quarterbacks and blew open holes for Walter Payton in college), and the golden-armed Dan Fouts (first quarterback to post three straight 4,000-yard seasons). As usual, the voluble Jones stole the show.

The Canton Class of 2005 was basically the year of the quarterback, what with Dan Marino and Steve Young getting inducted with two posthumous honorees—Bennie Friedman, the first quarterback to utilize the forward pass more than the run, and the iconoclastic Fritz Pollard, the first African-American player, quarterback, and coach in league history. An extremely distinguished class worthy of enshrinement, but, unfortunately for Deacon, way too many of the type of player he despises.

"That's too many quarterbacks to be around at one time, so it means that's the year that I don't go to the Hall," Jones said. "They'll take all of the hotel rooms in the whole state of Ohio and they'll bring in these large entourages. So this is gonna be a great year for Canton if you're a lover of quarterbacks. I'm a hater of quarterbacks, you see. My twenty-fifth year [as a Hall of Famer] I'm going to spend it in New York."

He appeared dead serious. Deacon Jones, noted friend and supporter of the Hall, did not attend an Induction Weekend for the first time in recent memory. During one of the commercial breaks, Lofton joked with Jones that he was old enough to have played against Fritz Pollard. Since it's my job to, you know, stir the pot, I persuaded Lofton to pose that question on the air.

Jones immediately shot back with an easy litmus test on whether anybody played against him: "Just pull up his jersey and look at his chest. It says 'seven–five.'"

Of course, Deacon wore 75 back in the day. And don't tell him his day wasn't as good as the current day, with the Strahans and Peppers and Merrimans doing the thing that he, in essence, perfected under far less pampered conditions.

"When you talk about old school versus new school, you got to think about when we played it, okay? When we started out in training camp, we didn't have the luxury, you know, of a water break," said Deacon, moving up to the edge of his seat. "We didn't have the luxury of all the things that the present-day guy got. 'Cause then we were meaner and we were tougher.

"In training camp, we hit every day. Now they don't hit every day. So, we were, I think in my estimation, maybe a little more physical than what they are now."

Deacon Jones, James Lofton, Dan Fouts, Jackie Slater, and me. Guess which one isn't a Hall of Famer? *(David Faller)*

With the rest of us now mere captives, Deacon then kicked it into high gear, waving his big meat-hook hands for emphasis.

"Because you could hit the body from the top of the head to the bottom of the feet. [Deacon was the undisputed King of the Head Slap, long since outlawed by the NFL.] Nowadays, it's played between the neck and the waist—you take out the cross-body block, you understand? You know how many guys nowadays spend the off-season in the hospital? [A rhetorical question—zero.] Keep this in mind when you're evaluating eras. Because you cannot tell me that you're much better when you're playing less downs than me.

"You cannot make me believe that. You cannot tell me you are tougher than me when you won't play with the same injuries I play[ed] with. You understand what I mean? What would some football player right now be like if he stepped back into our era and he had to scrimmage in training camp? He had to play sixty minutes in exhibition games six times?"

Lofton finally broke in: "And he wouldn't have a cell phone either, huh?"

Fouts chimed in: "You know, Deacon, the one thing these poor guys who play today will never have that we all had?"

"What's that?"

"Monthly bills," said Fouts.

Fun times. Both Fouts and Lofton did what your humble narrator should have done—inject some levity to shut down the monologue, but, to be honest, Deacon can be a bit intimidating. It's like driving behind someone who makes a turn without using the turn signal. You honk at the small Yugo, but the huge-ass pickup that pulls that stunt? You just tolerate it and quietly motor on down the road. Yet, no matter how imposing Deacon may be, no Hall of Famer comes close in that department to Jim Brown.

As most of you may know, Jim Brown is a well-documented badass. From his on-field persona and off-the-field indiscretions to his star turns in *The Dirty Dozen* and *Ice Station Zebra* to *I'm Gonna Git You Sucka,* this man reeks of badass. Even at age 71, he still has this look that, if he so chose, he could take your weak, fool ass right out. I should know. Brown gave me that look when I once told him he might have to wait to tape his segment for our 2006 Hall of Fame Roundtable Show appearance. Well, he *did* arrive early and we *did* still have more segments to tape for that day's regularly scheduled broadcast.

"Jim," I said, shaking his hand. "We still have some more stuff to do—"

Insert furrowed brow here.

"—for today's show, so I would say probably in about a half hour—"

Insert aforementioned look here.

"—orrrrrrr maybe we might be able to shift things around and get to you sooner."

We got to him sooner.

That said, Brown has been an incredible friend of the program. He was the very first Hall of Famer ever to appear on *NFL Total Access*—in just our third week of existence—and in his subsequent appearances I came to realize it's not all piss and vinegar all the time with Brown. Once he flipped a lacrosse ball around the set on the air with another football and lax player, Seahawks Pro Bowl defensive end Patrick Kerney. (Brown also happened to be an incredibly gifted lacrosse player—the best in Syracuse history, according to an old Cornell goaltender named Dick Schaap.) Another time Brown joined our in-studio guest analyst John Lynch, the Pro Bowl safety of the Denver Broncos. Lynch asked Brown why he retired at the top of his game at the age of 29.

I had heard Brown asked this question countless times before but never heard him give this answer: "Football is one part of your life. After nine years, I wanted to do other things. I had prepared myself. I graduated from Syracuse in four years. I went to the service as an ROTC second lieutenant. I worked for Pepsi Cola for nine years when I played and I knew that I wanted to go into a high-profile profession, so I got into movies.

"So, it was not hard at all for me to leave at 29 years old, MVP of the league, and the last two years of my career we played for the championship. Now, why would I stay there and keep getting hit when I could be with Raquel Welch, Stella Stevens, and Jacqueline Bisset?"

Can you believe it?

Brown continued, chuckling: "I mean, that would be ridiculous if I didn't leave. And make more money! And also have somebody say: Mr. Brown, here's your jacket. Mr. Brown, would you like your car today? I mean, c'mon fellas. That's a no-brainer."

The first interview I ever conducted for NFL Network involved Brown, and it left a permanent impression of the man's toughness. Months before NFL Network hit the air in November 2003, we visited Canton because an astoundingly large number of alums—115 in all—returned to celebrate the Hall's 40th anniversary. Thus, it served as an incredibly unique opportunity to get rare interviews with some of the game's legends and build an archive in the process. We shot the Network's inaugural interviews in the Hall of Champions, the dark, mystical room where the Hall houses all the busts of its enshrined. In essence, our chats brought the busts to life. We had a quarterbacks panel—Fouts, Joe Namath, and Jim Kelly—and our coaches panel featured Shula, Marv Levy, and Mike Ditka, who ran late by about 30 minutes. Apparently, Da Coach had enjoyed a bit of Canton revelry the night before and our call to his hotel room to inquire as to his whereabouts served as a wake-up call. Our defense panel consisted of Merlin Olsen, Ronnie Lott, and

Lawrence Taylor, who sadly bailed at the last minute. So I asked the destructive duo: What was the hardest they ever hit somebody?

Lott said there were too many instances in which he "blew somebody up" to single out one particular hit. Olsen stroked the beard that had become famous more from his three-year stint as NBC's *Father Murphy* than his 15-year stint with the Rams, four of them as one quarter of the Rams' vaunted Fearsome Foursome with Deacon, Rosie Grier, and Lamar Lundy. Olsen then told a story about how Jim Brown and Cleveland once visited the L.A. Coliseum and how, on that day, Brown came out of the backfield and suddenly presented Olsen with a clear shot at him.

"And I absolutely unloaded on him. I mean *unloaded*. When I picked myself up after that hit, I assumed I would find Brown lying on the ground, with his eyes rolling around the back of his head," Olsen said, laughing. "Far from it. I looked up and saw Jim still running down the sideline, going all the way for the touchdown!"

Willy Wonka had the Golden Ticket. Canton has its Golden Jacket. Back in 1978, the NFL Alumni Association approached the Hall about borrowing traditions from other sports to spruce up the induction ceremony. Someone then came up with the idea of giving each inductee a jacket to make the enshrinement official. Since the Masters had the market cornered on green, the Canton coat had to be of a different color. Why gold? Nobody knows. Perhaps somebody in the NFL Alumni Association also worked for Century 21.

At any rate, these jackets don't just mysteriously appear on the hulking shoulders of the enshrined, and they don't just find the blazer hanging in their closet upon check-in at the downtown Marriott, either. Just like everything else during Induction Weekend, considerable pomp and circumstance surrounds the presentation of this golden garment.

Each and every year, the night before the induction ceremony and hours after the Grand Parade, the Hall of Fame and the NFL Alumni Association cohost a massive dinner party in the Canton Memorial Civic Center at which the enshrinees receive their jackets to much fanfare. The Hall of Fame Festival Committee sells 4,000 tickets to the affair and could sell another 4,000 tickets if it only had the space.

Thus, one sees dinner tables in the concourse outside the main arena of the Civic Center. And tables in the hallways of the adjoining Canton Cultural Arts Center. And tables in the atrium. Every nook and cranny of the complex has a table. And a centerpiece. And napkins and silverware and place cards. Eventually, at some point during the dinner, the incoming Canton class gets another parade—through each and every outer room to allow all the diners on the periphery to get a literal brush with fame while chowing down their salad, rubber chicken (or steak), and accompanying slice of dessert.

Again, that's all *outside* the main arena. Inside the arena (normally home to the Canton Legends, your American Indoor Football Association 2006 champions) it's wall-to-wall tables; over 100 more tables in all, surrounding a 30-foot-long catwalk in the center of the floor across from a monstrous, double-decker dais. Carved into two sections of seats, the incoming Canton class and their presenters sit on the lower level of the dais, while perched on the upper level (like the Supreme Court lording over the proceedings) sits a group of dignitaries that traditionally include the Festival Committee chairman, the mayor of Canton, the Hall of Fame festival queen (remember her?), the NFL commissioner, and the Enshrinees Dinner host, who, in the past, have included the likes of Howard Cosell, Bob Costas, Al Michaels, Chris Berman, and, in 2005, your humble narrator.

On the dais of the 2005 Enshrinees Dinner. Note Dan Marino in mid-chew at right. *(K. Terrell)*

The gig is, quite simply, an honor. Because it's basically the host's job to introduce every Hall of Famer in the room. First up, the alumni. Once dinner ends, everyone from the table hinterlands comes in from the concourse to fill the stands. With the house now completely packed, the returning Hall of Famers enter the arena and everybody basically goes nuts. One by one, each Hall of Famer (usually wearing the gold jacket given to him years before) hands the host a card and the host reads the name. Not very difficult stuff, but damn is it exciting.

"Roger Staubach!"

Roger then strolls to the catwalk, walks up the steps at the middle, waves to the wild applause, and then strolls down the steps on the other side.

"Willie Davis!"

Willie does the same.

"Dick Butkus! Lynn Swann! Don Shula!"

And so on. The year I hosted the dinner, this went on for 10 glorious minutes—and it's all just the appetizer.

When an inductee arrives in Canton, the first thing he does—after unpacking in the Marriott—is head to a members-only luncheon. Called the Ray Nitschke Luncheon—after the late, hard-nosed, acerbic middle linebacker of the legendary Lombardi Packers—this is where new enshrinees get a first taste of the world that awaits them. The returning Hall of Famers show up for the lunch and basically swap lies and tell stories and take bets on which member of the incoming class is going to be the one to break down and cry during his induction speech.

"There's lots of shouting back and forth," says the longtime Hall of Fame vice president of communication, Joe Horrigan, one of the few mortals afforded an invite to the luncheon. "It used to be just a luncheon, but Ray Nitschke then always started the luncheon with a gruff, if you will, but focused speech talking to the new Hall of Famers about the importance of behavior and 'You better start marking it on your calendar to keep coming back,' and it would fire the guys up."

Now, that has become the tradition. The essential message for the newbies: You've been voted in, but you're not a Hall of Famer just yet. As for when the inductee actually becomes one, I used to believe the official moment came when said inductee made an acceptance speech and received a bust on Induction Day. That is, until I witnessed the jacket ceremony.

When these guys get called to the catwalk in the middle of the Civic Center and get that jacket slipped on, the realization that he is now a Pro Football Hall of Famer sinks in and sinks in *fast*. More guys get choked up during that ceremony than Induction Day by a wide margin.

In 2003, the old Chiefs coach Hank Stram got inducted after a very long wait that many people feared would last too long. The famously energetic Stram had fallen ill and was so infirm that he could not make his acceptance speech in person. Once so loquacious that he was the first coach to ever wear an NFL Films wire during a Super Bowl, Stram could only deliver brief Induction Day remarks by videotape.

Sure enough, Stram was at the jacket ceremony the night before. Stram, with the help of his two sons, slowly took to the catwalk. When he slipped on that jacket, there wasn't a dry eye in the house. With Dad draped in gold, the three Strams huddled in the middle of the catwalk and had themselves a real good cry.

In that respect, Induction Day becomes a bit of an afterthought, but, of course, it really isn't. It sure isn't to the nearly 20,000 fans who pack Fawcett Stadium to listen to the speeches, some of them quite stirring and some of them, quite frankly, way too freaking long.

The way Induction Day works in Canton is this: Before each inductee receives his bust and delivers his acceptance speech, he is introduced by a person of his own choosing—a presenter. For years, the presenter was more often than not an old coach, a team owner, an old teammate, a childhood friend. In 1993, Walter Payton broke with tradition and created another of his own, with his own: Jarrett Payton indeed became the first son ever to present his father for enshrinement in Canton.

That sparked a new family tradition, which, years later, led to the so-called Grit Young Rule for Presenters. In 2005, Steve Young had his proud father, Grit, present him and after years of watching his son nearly get cut at Brigham Young, nearly get mangled with the awful Buccaneers, and nearly rot behind Joe Montana in San Francisco, Grit had a lot to get off his chest and, after 10 minutes, wasn't nearly done by a long shot.

Bless him, his blow-by-blow account of Steve's career lasted, well, almost as long as Steve's career.

Thus, as of 2006, all presenters are now required to furnish the Hall with a typewritten advance copy of his remarks, which, when read aloud, can not exceed five minutes in length. All six of the 2006 presenters complied with that request except for one—Al Davis.

One of the neater aspects to any incoming Canton class is its randomness. For instance, while John Elway built his Bronco legend and Barry Sanders wowed the free football world in Detroit, neither knew they'd one day be immortalized together as they were on Induction Day 2004. Same for Steve Young and Dan Marino in 2005.

The Canton crossroads have produced some eclectic induction classes over the years, like 1993 when Dan Fouts, Larry Little, Chuck Noll, Bill Walsh, and Walter Payton all went in together. How about the Class of 1985? Could you get more of a mixed bag than Frank Gatski, Joe Namath, Roger Staubach, O. J. Simpson, and Pete Rozelle? You've got the former World War II vet and stalwart Browns championship lineman, the first-ever playboy quarterback to rule Manhattan, the clean-cut Navy-educated All-American leader of America's Team, the inaugural 2,000-yard rusher and eventual social pariah and, finally, perhaps the most important American sports leader of the 20th century—all mixed together in one Canton class.

Of the Canton classes I've personally watched gain entry, my favorite is the Class of 2006—Troy Aikman, Rayfield Wright, Harry Carson, Warren Moon, Reggie White, and John Madden. You've got the first Cowboys quarterback to be enshrined since Staubach, the "Big Cat" offensive lineman who protected Staubach, the prideful Giants captain and inventor of the famed Gatorade Shower, the first modern day African-American quarterback to gain enshrinement, the sack king of his generation who died too soon, and, finally, the first-ever Raiders Super Bowl coach, who also followed the entire careers of his Canton classmates (save for Wright) in his now quarter-century-long role as wildly successful football TV analyst.

The class was perfectly split between first-ballot Hall of Famers and those with famously long waits. The short-wait list: Aikman, Moon (the second oldest first-ballot player ever, behind George Blanda), and White (sadly, the first-ever first-ballot player to be inducted posthumously). As for the long-wait list, you had Wright (who waited 22 years), Carson (whose 13-year wait so angered him that he once threatened to refuse enshrinement upon being offered it), and Madden, who was delighted he went in for his work as coach rather than as TV analyst or video-game impresario.

Their choice of presenters could not have been more moving.

Aikman: Norv Turner, the onetime Cowboys offensive coordinator Aikman credits for his success.

Moon: Leigh Steinberg, the sports agent who helped shepherd Moon from underappreciated Rose Bowl star to Canadian Football League wilderness (in which he only won five straight Grey Cups) to National Football League immortality.

Carson: Donald Carson, Harry's 23-year-old son, who was diagnosed with a rare blood disorder just five days after graduating college.

Wright: Stan Lomax, Wright's coach at Fort Valley State University, who, once upon a time, saw something in the tall basketball star who couldn't make his high school football team. Before graduating from high school, Wright was so inspired by a career-day speech made by an air force recruiter that Wright signed up on the spot. So Lomax made a pitch to the recruiter to let Wright out of his commitment—at a meeting at Wright's house with his mother and pastor in attendance while anxious young Rayfield waited out on the curb for the verdict. The rest is history. Canton history. By the way, Wright's 86-year-old mother was in attendance again at Induction Sunday.

White: Jeremy White, Reggie's erudite 20-year-old son, who presented his mother, the vivacious Sara White, who accepted the enshrinement on her late husband's behalf. White's 17-year-old daughter, Jacoila, sang the national anthem prior to the induction ceremony. The way the White family allowed everyone—all of Canton and all of Reggie's fans who flocked there from Philadelphia and Green Bay— to share in their joy over Reggie's enshrinement as well as their grief over his death is exactly what made the weekend extra special.

Madden: Al Davis, Canton Class of '92. The Brooklyn boy
who became manager of the general partner of the Oakland
Raid-uhs. Darth Vader himself. In presenting his first Super
Bowl coach, Davis was making a record ninth presenting
speech in Canton, with his first being in 1978, for a San
Diego Charger. Back in the day, Davis was an offensive assistant on Sid Gillman's staff in San Diego and they had a receiver by the name of Lance Alworth. Davis's mere presence
at the proceedings—and flouting of the new Grit Young
Rule—kicked the entire weekend up a notch, from memorable to classic.

So did Madden, for that matter. One could make the case that he's
the most famous person ever inducted into the Pro Football Hall of
Fame.

"If someone comes up to me and calls me 'Coach' I know he remembers me from the Raiders," Madden said. "If someone calls me
'John' I know it's from TV, and if I get 'Madden' then I know that person plays a video game."

Madden's folksiness proved a perfect complement to the more
melancholy aspects of the weekend, from White's premature death at age
44 to Harry Carson's ill son. During his acceptance speech Madden reit-
erated his long-standing belief in what happens in the Hall of Champions when the last employee turns off the lights:

"I believe that the busts talk to each other. I can't wait for that conversation, I really can't. Vince Lombardi, Knute Rockne, Reggie White,
Walter Payton, all my ex-players, we'll be there forever and ever talking
about whatever. That's what I believe. That's what I think is going to
happen, and no one's ever going to talk me out of that."

Madden then added: "These guys are going. 'Oh, no, hope I don't
have to put up with his B.S. for an eternity.'"

In just the past decade, Induction Day in Canton has gotten bigger in
virtually every way, and I don't mean the waistlines of the returning
alums. Back in the day, the induction ceremony used to be held on the
actual steps of the Pro Football Hall of Fame—with the returning Hall
of Famers in rows of chairs on the cement landing atop the steps and
their guests seated on the cement space at the bottom. Fans jammed

themselves into whatever space they could find in front of the Interstate. Acceptance speeches were frequently punctuated by truckers blowing a horn in salute.

That arrangement, however, came to an end in 2002, thanks to Jim Kelly, the popular Buffalo Bills quarterback and Pittsburgh native whose enshrinement apparently attracted half of western New York and Pennsylvania. So, now, 20,000 people fill a stadium to witness the proceedings, which also has a postgame component.

Ever since *NFL Total Access* began broadcasting from Canton on Induction Day in 2004, the Hall of Fame (along with serious cajoling from our outrageously dogged bureau producer Drew Ohlmeyer) has immediately brought every single inductee to our box-on-stilts for our postceremony program. Thus far every single inductee, without fail, has graciously complied.

Yes, Super Bowl MVPs go to Disney World. Freshly minted Hall of Famers go to *NFL Total Access*.

For those of us cooped up on the set, the anticipation and excitement is palpable. Our stage manager Joann sets up the glass table for the bronze bust and an extra chair for the newest member of the Pro Football Hall of Fame. One by one, they come to our set with their new, bronze bauble in tow: Barry Sanders, John Elway, Bob Brown, Carl Eller, Dan Marino, Steve Young, Rayfield Wright, Harry Carson, John Madden, Sara White, Troy Aikman, and Warren Moon. They've all come, and they've all said the same thing.

"Man, it's hot in here!"

Remember, it took John Madden to finally get our sound guys to turn on the air-conditioning—in our *third* year of covering Induction Day.

Regardless, they all sit down humbled, honored . . . and exhausted. For after the Nitschke Luncheon and the Grand Parade and the Enshrinees Dinner and the Jacket Ceremony and the requisite press conferences and the autograph sessions and countless handshakes and meet-and-greets . . . and *then* a five-hour-long induction ceremony, the last thing these people want to do is talk.

They want to party.

Yes, very infrequently can you find the words "party time" and "Canton" in the same sentence, but every Induction Day each new inductee holds his own evening private party somewhere in town.

In 2006, both Rayfield Wright and Troy Aikman threw separate

After a long wait for enshrinement, Harry Carson reflects with his bust on our set.
(*Joann Kamay*)

parties on the grounds of our hotel, the Glenmoor Country Club. Wright held his in a massive tent on the front lawn with Richard Street of the Temptations providing the entertainment. Check that. Street took a back seat when the two 88s of their respective Dallas generations, Drew Pearson and Michael Irvin, took the stage and banged out "My Girl." Meanwhile, inside, Aikman took over the large hall in the main building—with Irvin just plain holding court as entertainment. It was one big, fat, star-studded Cowboys extravaganza; you could see folks like Staubach, Irvin, Emmitt Smith, Tony Dorsett (Class of '94) and Cowboys owner Jerry Jones shuttle back and forth between the parties, which cooked well past midnight—another grouping of words rarely connected with Canton.

As for the NFL Network crew, we were all hunkered down in the oak-panel bar inside the Glenmoor, toasting a great week of shows. Many of us were wiped out, especially Steve Mariucci for whom the 2006 Hall of Fame Weekend served as his first full assignment with *NFL*

Total Access. We were all just beginning to get to know Mooch, who, in hindsight, had the entire crew at "hello." He was just as engaging off-air as he was in his nascent on-air work, at which he refreshingly professed an eager desire to get better. He also enjoyed mixing it up with the crew at postshow dinners and sessions at the Glenmoor bar throughout the week, but, on this night, Mooch was gassed. He no doubt experienced grueling days as coach of the 49ers and Lions, but had never experienced a day like this—a two-hour preinduction ceremony show followed by live coverage of the five-hour-long induction ceremony followed by a 90-minute postceremony edition of *NFL Total Access.* That right there is a lot of TV. Thus, Mariucci needed his arm twisted to raise one celebratory glass with us at the Glenmoor. He had, however, already accepted an invite to John Madden's party located back downtown. So Mooch nursed himself a glass of cabernet and bade his good nights.

Big mistake.

Several hours later, your humble narrator, operations manager Mike Konner, and *NFL Total Access* producer Bardia Shah-Rais had shut down the bar at the Glenmoor. The genesis for what came next remains hazy for obvious reasons, but, for some reason, we all decided good ol' Mooch needed some quality rookie hazing for failing to make it through the night. I clearly remember it was never a question of why, but of what and how.

As we strolled through the eerily quiet, double-wide Overlook Hotel–like corridors back to the elevator, we were all looking for inspiration, and there, right in front of the elevator, we found it—a large piano on wheels. Why the Glenmoor places a piano next to its second-floor elevator, I'll never know.

All I know is within minutes those ivories had been wheeled onto the elevator, taken up to the fourth floor, and placed directly in front of the door to the room of one Steve Mariucci. I took a picture of it with my cell phone and sent it to Mike and Bardia with the following caption: *Play it again, Mooch!*

Now, then. Occasionally, after nights like that, one has wake-up moments of, shall we say, realization, and the memory of our late-night stunt with Steve washed over me with a touch of fear. I mean, we had enjoyed our laughs with Steve all week, but the bottom line was that we had really just met him. One never knows how one might react to having, say, a piano placed keys first in your doorway.

Play it again, Mooch! *(Rich Eisen)*

I left my room and peeked around the corner with trepidation. The piano was still there! It was slightly pushed back from one side, as if Mariucci just wedged around the corner to get out. Immediately, I called Bardia to see if there were any repercussions. Bardia said he hadn't yet heard from Steve and was equally as nervous. I tried his cell phone and got voice mail. I didn't dare leave one. Minutes later, Bardia called to say he had finally spoken to Mooch, who said nothing of the incident until the end of the conversation.

"Uh, Bardia," Mooch said. "Someone put a piano in front of my door last night. Do you know who *may* have done that?"

"Uh, no, Coach. What are you talking about?" Bardia said.

"Well," Mariucci said. "If you *do* have any idea about that, just tell whoever did it that payback's a bitch!"

Later that day, with the Raiders in town to play the Hall of Fame Game that wrapped up the weekend, Mariucci asked the Oakland equipment manager for a huge roll of tape. He was going to stay up late and seal Bardia's door so he would be greeted by one big wall of tape—but

Mooch fell asleep before he could do it. That said, Bardia should watch out on future trips to Canton. Mariucci believes what he said about payback.

Believe it or not, the day after the induction ceremony, well after all the jackets and busts have been handed out, there is still one last dog-and-pony show in Canton—The Enshrinees Game Day Roundtable. Hours before kickoff, the enshrinees—many of them presumably still hung over from their respective induction parties the night before—convene for a 30-minute panel discussion. Where, you may ask? Why, in the Canton Memorial Civic Center again. At a lunch with the same setup as the dinner two nights before. Tables everywhere. And centerpieces and napkins and chicken and dessert. Again. And the place is packed—again! As for the '05 dinner, I was asked to serve as moderator for the '06 lunch discussion, which took place on a circular stage in the middle of the arena. Sara White was in rare form. When I asked her what she thought of her kids' performances at Induction Day, she said Reggie would have been so proud of both. Then she added, of Jacoila: "She just did an awesome job singing the national anthem. I think I probably collected, like, ten numbers from people over thirty and they said, 'What's her name?' and I said, 'Look, it's Jail Bait. She just graduated high school, OK? I don't care how she looked on that stage, she's jail . . . *bait!*'"

When the crowd laughter died down, I turned to Madden and kick-started a memorable exchange. It perfectly encapsulates the essence of the Pro Football Hall of Fame Induction Weekend, the bond it forms with the fans and the bond it forever creates within the incoming class. It began with my question of what it was like for John riding around Canton in his famed Madden Cruiser. (Madden has a famous fear of flying.)

MADDEN: The Madden Cruiser left from California on Monday. When you travel across the country by bus you have to leave a little pad [time] in there and we got here on Wednesday. So I was the first guy here, because when they tell you you're going into the Hall of Fame, I'm not going to miss it, I'm not gonna be late for it, I'm not gonna miss anything! When it really hit me, we're coming across the country. You go through Utah, Wyoming, Nebraska, Iowa, and all those places, and you finally get to the turnoff in Ohio in Canton and then it hit me—and I said, "Holy Shoot. I'm here." Whatever that feeling, it came then, and it hasn't left. I've just been taking in everything. Being on your feet and being up, I haven't been able to sleep at all.

AIKMAN: They don't let you get much sleep here.

MADDEN: No, they don't at all. And then this morning I got up after all these days, I got up and put my "give-ups" on. *(Madden pointed down to the rubber slippers on his feet.)* When you wear these shoes, these old "give-ups," you just gave up. *(Madden looked to the rafters.)* Take me!

ME: Sara, do women have "give-ups?"

SARA WHITE: Are you kidding? After walking around for three days all dressed up because I had to be cute? I don't think people realize that we have to walk around miles to see everybody in this arena just to get to the stage a couple of times. And I had on three-inch heels! This [event] was not made for women! This is why the Hall of Fame was made for men! But you know what? The next woman who represents her husband, I will have a manual for her with all the do's and don'ts.

MADDEN: You still have better-looking give-ups than I do.

Once the laughter died down, Sara picked up her microphone again and her soulful side took over.

SARA: Hey Rich, you know one thing that has impressed me this week? It's that these guys, Troy, John, Warren, Harry, and Rayfield, have been human beings and they have been wonderful to be around. And they're real. And people don't see them as being real. I think what the Hall of Fame does for Canton and the fans and the friends here is to bring realness to the people that are inducted. And that's what one of the greatest things is for me. To hear John talk about family and Warren do the same. It's all about family and so I just want to say, for me, that has touched me this week to know that they're real, they're touchable. Yes, they have a different job than others but they're touchable and they're real and they love people just as much as the people love them.

A rousing ovation came from the ground.

MADDEN: My feet haven't hit the ground yet. This is the happiest time in my life.

More applause.

ME: So, John, tonight, when you're calling the game between the Eagles and Raiders, when people tune into NBC, will they see you with your give-ups still on?

MADDEN: I'll still have my give-ups on. I'm going into this game as close to naked as I've ever done anything in my whole life.

MOON: That's not a good thought.

Mooch and I chat it up prior to the 2006 Hall of Fame Game with NBC's Bob Costas *(far right)* and Cris Collinsworth, who was just getting used to the NFL Network microphone. *(Joann Kamay)*

AIKMAN: They just lost their viewing audience. Now nobody's gonna watch the game.

ME: Who knew *Fear Factor* was going to be on NBC tonight?

With that we all headed off to the game. Oh, yeah. That's right. There's one very last dog and pony show—the actual Hall of Fame Game, the very first preseason game of the year. And that may be the best dog and pony show of all in Canton. Because it means the NFL season is just around the corner.

THE EIGHT-GAME
PACKAGE

y late November 2006, NFL Network had plum begun running out of things to do for a first time. Our obvious first occurred with our first broadcast at 8:00 P.M. E.S.T. on November 4, 2003. Eleven weeks later, we held our very first broadcast from a Super Bowl—the Patriots vs. Panthers battle in Houston. Then, one by one, the dominoes fell: *NFL Total Access* at the Owners' Meeting; *NFL Total Access* at the Rookie Symposium; *NFL Total Access* at Hall of Fame Induction Weekend; *NFL Total Access* at Kickoff 2004 in New England. Then in 2005, more milestones fell with our first coverage at the Pro Bowl and the Scouting Combine and Training Camp and another season Kickoff in New England. In April 2006, we took our Huggies off (to use the Parcells vernacular) with a major first for NFL Network—live, gavel-to-gavel coverage of (even though no one actually uses a gavel at) the NFL Draft.

None of us knew it at the time, but during each and every milestone passed along the way, we were all just merely rehearsing for The Eight-Game Package.

Sounds mysterious. Sounds like one of the subheadings from *Pulp Fiction,* like *The Bonnie Situation* or *The Gold Watch.* For years, The

Eight-Game Package did seem as mysterious and elusive, even though no one ever felt compelled to bring out the gimp.

At any rate, I'm talking about actual, real-live, bona fide regular season National Football League games. Games in which players suit up and smack each other around for three hours and the result then counts in the standings. Games like the ones you watch on NBC or CBS. Or Fox or ESPN or, once upon a time, ABC and TNT.

You see, during the first three years of NFL Network, we aired no games of that sort and in the eyes of many had no bona fide TV network of which to speak until we did. But that all changed one glorious day frozen in time (I'm beginning to sound like John Facenda) when then-commissioner Paul Tagliabue delivered the extra large proclamation from Super Bowl XL in Detroit: The league had created a new package of eight prime-time contests to air on Thursday and Saturday nights over the final six weeks of the season. Starting Thanksgiving Night 2006, the exclusive home for these games was to be NFL Network.

Now, every single one of us who hitched our respective wagons to NFL Network from the start always dreamed of the day we would have exclusive broadcast rights to NFL games that counted. Suddenly, in just three short years, the dream was reality, but not without much angst, because there were quicker turnarounds involved.

When the league awarded the new *Sunday Night Football* package to NBC in April 2005, the Peacock Network had fewer than 17 months to get ready for its first game, widely considered in the business to be a terribly short time. On the day NFL Network received official word that we, if you will, got games, we were exactly 299 days removed from kickoff.

The Eight-Game Package was born.

Atop the NFL Network flowchart, a calling-all-cars-type situation ensued. Overnight, NFL Network suddenly required a remote production unit to go with a studio production department meticulously built over three years. Two days before Tax Day, we had Remote Department Employee Number One—longtime ABC Sports producer Mark Loomis. It was now his job to fully staff eight separate 21-camera high-definition football broadcasts all to take place during a span of six weeks—an incredibly demanding schedule that, as of his hiring date, began in a mere 224 days.

Two weeks later, we had our two-man announce booth in place— Bryant Gumbel and Cris Collinsworth, who I believe collectively own one trillion Emmy Awards. However, they also owned contracts with other TV networks—Gumbel with HBO and Collinsworth with both HBO and NBC, which had already hired him to coanchor their new *Sunday Night* pregame show with Bob Costas, Sterling Sharpe (also an NFL Network analyst), and Jerome Bettis in his first post-retirement gig.

However, as I've come to learn in this business, if the titans of Sports Television wish to make a deal, they will. NFL Network execs and HBO and NBC pooh-bahs eventually made one to clear Gumbel and Collinsworth for NFL Network takeoff. Gumbel would call all eight games (five on Thursdays, three on Saturdays), but NBC commitments would prevent Collinsworth from being at two of the three Saturday games. None other than former Chiefs and Rams head coach Dick Vermeil would fill in there. Everyone was fired-up.

My role in The Eight-Game Package? Host of the pregame, half-time, and postgame shows, along with Deion Sanders, Marshall Faulk, and Steve Mariucci for all eight games . . . *on location.* Yep. We took these shows on the road. Which meant a lot of TV, a lot of travel, a lot of

Introducing the newest NFL Network employees Bryant Gumbel *(center)* and Cris Collinsworth in April 2006. *(David Drapkin)*

postgame revelry, and, occasionally, some brutally quick turnarounds to return to Los Angeles for appointed rounds on Friday and Sunday studio shows there.

Indeed, from Thanksgiving to New Year's Eve 2006, it was quite a ride.

Or to paraphrase a great TV show . . .

In the NFL Network Eight-Game Package, the sports fans are represented by two separate yet equally important groups: the four hosts of Total Access on Location *who deliver the fun and the hardworking men and women behind the scenes who make it all possible. These are our stories.*

Chung-chung!

Game 1: Broncos at Chiefs, Thanksgiving Night, 2006

Country music recording artist Jessica Harp (as she was introduced) neared the crescendo of our national anthem. Standing on the sideline on 20-yard line in Arrowhead Stadium, I looked to my right and saw Marshall Faulk giving me that *look* again. Eyebrows raised, you-know-what-eating grin as if to say: Here it comes.

O'er the land of the free and the home of the . . .

CHIEEEEEEEFFFFFSSSS!

It cascaded down from the throats of every single human in the capacity crowd of 79,409, and the rumble hit me directly in the pit. Marshall doubled over laughing. He knew I had never been to Arrowhead before, and during the entire flight out from Los Angeles he swore to me that this place was, far and away, the best and loudest venue in the National Football League. Marshall enjoys being right.

It didn't take long to understand. At first Arrowhead blush, it's apparent you're not in Kansas anymore, so to speak. (You're actually in Missouri.) Everyone at Arrowhead dresses in Chiefs red. Period. Not burgundy. Not burnt sienna. Not scarlet or crimson or maroon or vermillion. Red. It's a prerequisite for attendance. I wouldn't be surprised if those not wearing red get sent home. Then there's the whole cheering in unison thing.

Here's how that works. Let's say Larry Johnson runs for 12 yards, which happens a lot. After the play, the public address announcer bellows "Larry Johnson gains twelve yards for a Kansas City Chiefs . . ."

Pause. Cue the crowd.

FIRST DOWN!

And I mean everybody belts that one out. It is, to be honest, freaking frightening. The first time that happened Thanksgiving night, I jumped. Marshall got hysterical laughing again, and Steve Mariucci came running up to tell me how he tried desperately to incorporate that "first down screaming stuff" in Detroit when he first became Lions coach.

"But the first two times we did it, only, like, ten people screamed out 'first down' so we ditched it," screamed Mariucci, moving three inches from my ear to be heard. "There's no place like this."

Now, I know Broncos fans just began to grip this book a bit tighter. Sure, the good folks in Mile High Stadium have their own ear-splitting reputation. Plus, fans in Denver have been cheering in unison since John Elway first wet his diapers. Here's how that goes: Let's say Chargers quarterback Philip Rivers heaves one to his all-world tight end Antonio Gates and Broncos stud cornerback Champ Bailey bats it down. The public address guy then merrily takes to the loudspeaker and booms "Rivers' pass intended for Gates is . . ."

Pause. Cue the crowd.

IN-COM-PLETE!

It's impressive. Loud. Jarring. But it's also three syllables long. It might as well be an essay. The brevity of the Arrowhead bellowing that signifies a Chiefs matriculation down the field (to use the Hank Stram vernacular) has to shake the foundation of even the most worthy opponent. It's amazing the Chiefs ever lose a home game. Yet, to be fair and balanced (to use the Bill O'Reilly vernacular) the Broncos have won more home games than the Chiefs in the first six seasons this decade.

MOST REGULAR SEASON HOME WINS, 2000-2006

---

1. Baltimore Ravens   42–14
2. Denver Broncos   41–15
3. Indianapolis Colts   41–15
4. New England Patriots   40–16
5. Kansas City Chiefs   39–17

Thus, perhaps, my theory on Arrowhead is itself a tad . . . IN-COM-PLETE. But please don't blame me for losing my head. I'll always have a soft spot for Kansas City and Arrowhead. They played host to the inaugural kickoff of The Eight-Game Package.

We hit Kansas City two days before kickoff and found ourselves in the midst of a virtual heat wave, a downright balmy 60 degrees. So, that night a few of us strolled the famed Plaza (where the city holds the traditional Thanksgiving Night lighting ceremony that annually attracts a crowd of 600,000) and grabbed some dinner. We were joined by the actor Paul Rudd, a lifelong Kansas Citian and a longtime Friend of the Program. Paul was in town for the game, which was no surprise. He loves his Chiefs. One of the first celebrities ever to appear on *NFL Total Access,* Paul showed up on our set for "Celebrity Picks" draped in the red game-worn jersey of perennial Chiefs Pro-Bowl offensive lineman Will Shields. He preferred to crow about the greatness of Priest Holmes and bemoan the Chiefs' porous defense rather than discuss his upcoming movies *Anchorman* and *The 40-Year-Old Virgin.* As for his prognosticating, Paul got 7 of his 10 picks right. Then there's his addiction to fantasy football. Paul is an enthusiastic founding owner in the annual *NFL Total Access* Hollywood Fantasy Football League, fielding a team called Tastes Like Chicken. We knew our show had gained in popularity when Paul once got accosted in the men's room at a Chiefs-Ravens game in Baltimore by a man who pointed and screamed, "Hey! It's Tastes Like Chicken!" Yes, the man is quite popular, especially in his hometown. Pictures, autographs, handshakes the entire night, and Paul graciously handled each and every one.

The day before game day, we taped a segment at Arrowhead for that Wednesday's edition of *NFL Total Access.* I entered the production trailer set up in the parking lot and noticed Mariucci hunched over a laptop computer. A report had just hit the Internet stating that the struggling Arizona Cardinals had not only already decided to fire Dennis Green at season's end, but had begun preliminary talks with none other than Steve Mariucci to replace Green. While the Cardinals did eventually fire Green immediately after the 2006 season (on New Year's Day, no less!), Steve had not been contacted. You could see it in his face.

"And I would know if the Cardinals called me because Denny and I have the same agent," said Mariucci.

Now, nothing chafes a coach more than speculation about another coach's job—unless that coach's name is inaccurately mentioned in a speculative report as a possible successor. That *really* chafes a coach. Football coaches truly do belong to an unofficial fraternity and are all incredibly protective of one another. Mariucci immediately called Green to let him know the story wasn't true on his end. Later on, he eagerly refuted the report in the *NFL Total Access* segment we taped. (The Cardinals eventually hired Steelers offensive coordinator Ken Whisenhunt.)

Coordinating producer Aaron Owens and Deion Sanders having fun at the NFL Network makeshift Thanksgiving dinner. (*Joann Kamay*)

Mooch had a captive audience for his toast. (*Joann Kamay*)

That night, the entire production crew gathered for a Thanksgiving dinner at McCormick and Schmick's on the Plaza. Not exactly reminiscent of the Pilgrims' landing on Plymouth Rock, but it did the trick. All of us felt a great sense of family togetherness on this night before a momentous occasion in all of our professional lives. Turkey gravy, red wine, and good times flowed, and once dessert (pumpkin pie or lemon pie) hit the table, it was clearly time for a speech.

Your humble narrator first took the floor. I've been known to spin a yarn or two, but not quite like our boy Mariucci. I knew handing the floor over to him next could provide for some good comedy. Therefore, after raising a glass to the success of the upcoming venture, I threw it to Mooch thusly: "Now I would try and charge you up with a rousing speech, but there's someone in this room clearly more experienced in that department. Ladies and gentlemen, I now introduce to you the next head coach of the Arizona Cardinals, Steve Mariucci!"

Eruption. Standing ovation. What ensued was classic Mooch. Eyes wide. Arms flailing. Utter hilarity. The best part came when he interrupted his own heartfelt soliloquy about spending Thanksgiving with his "new family" by pausing to mention he still felt that way "even though I got pumpkin pie when I asked for lemon pie."

With Mooch still on a roll, a waiter made a show of sliding a slice of lemon pie in front of Coach. Everyone lost it.

By night's end, Cris Collinsworth took the floor. So did our executive producer and fearless leader Eric Weinberger. Unfortunately, Bryant was feeling a bit under the weather. So, he spectated more than orated. He needed to conserve energy, anyway. We all did.

So what does an NFL pregame show host and his analysts do hours before broadcasting a major first for a network? Watch football on TV. It *was* Thanksgiving Day, and our game was the third game in the tripleheader that began in the traditional NFL Thanksgiving locales of Detroit and Dallas. Still, we arrived at Arrowhead Stadium six better-safe-than-sorry hours before kickoff (production managers can be overly cautious), so your humble narrator, Deion Sanders, Mariucci, Marshall, and our information man, Adam Schefter, all scrunched into couches placed in a makeshift green room in one of the trailers in the parking lot and watched the Lions host the Dolphins.

It had been exactly one year since Mariucci coached his final game for Detroit—a 27–7 Thanksgiving Day destruction courtesy of Michael Vick and Atlanta, that led to Mooch's subsequent firing courtesy of team president Matt Millen. Now here Steve was, watching quarterback Joey Harrington, whose perennial ineffectual play helped lead to his Detroit downfall, return to the scene of the crime with the Miami Dolphins and toss a season-high three touchdowns. Mooch never once batted an eyelash (even when Deion gently needled him) and even praised Harrington for his play later on the air.

"That's my Moochie," Deion beamed.

As the second Thanksgiving Day game kicked off in Dallas and the clock ticked closer to our kickoff, I strolled outside to get some fresh air. I ran into Pat Bowlen, the eternally hip owner of the Denver Broncos.

"Where's Adam Schefter," Bowlen asked.

Schefter had been reporting that Broncos quarterback Jake Plummer's ineffectiveness had finally worn out the patience of his head coach. Schefter said that regardless of how Plummer performed in the NFL Network game, Mike Shanahan would next turn to his rookie quarterback,

Jay Cutler—a stunning move considering the Broncos were 7–4 and directly in the thick of the AFC West hunt.

"I want to know where he's getting his information," Bowlen said.

It struck me that Schefter, who had spent 10 years on the Broncos beat in Denver, had scooped the Broncos owner on the subject of his own quarterback. Schefter was inside the stadium. Bowlen sashayed that way. Within a half hour, we all followed. It was showtime.

The first time I ever walked down a tunnel to step on an NFL field came on January 15, 1995. I was covering the 1994 NFC Championship game in Candlestick Park between the Cowboys and 49ers two months into my first TV job at KRCR-TV, the ABC affiliate in Redding, California. On that day, eventual Defensive Player of the Year Deion Sanders helped Steve Young and the 49ers get over the hump against Dallas. Now, almost a dozen years later, I strolled down the Arrowhead tunnel with none other than Prime Time himself, getting ready for the biggest broadcast of my career. Before we hit the turf, Sanders turned to me and said: "Take us home tonight, Humble Host." Deion gives out nicknames to everyone he likes, including himself. He's Prime Time and, once upon a time, in his MC Hammer video days, Neon Deion. Mariucci is Moochie. Even our researcher George Li has a Deion dubbing— Puddin' Pie, as in Georgie Porgie. Now, I had a nickname. I felt like pounding shoulder pads right then and there.

The show went down without a hitch—although not without causing a ripple or two back in the league office. Toward the end of the show, during a commercial break, a lightbulb lit over Marshall's head. We should all sign a football, pitch it into the stands to some lucky fan, and then announce we'd be doing that at every stop in our eight-game tour. If people gathered in expectation of copping the prized bauble, perhaps that might create some buzz for the show. A quality all-purpose idea from the all-purpose maven. So, we got a football and a silver Sharpie and, in the next segment, Faulk announced the so-called Marshall plan.

"Is this going to be a fine from the league?" I asked Mariucci.

"I'm sure it will be. You can pay it, Rich."

"You throw it, Rich!" Deion shouted.

I mean, c'mon. We had two future Hall of Famers and Brett Favre's old position coach on the set.

"You want *me* to pitch it into the crowd?"

"Get it out there, Rich!" Marshall yelled.

So, from our set just off that 20-yard line in Arrowhead Stadium where Joe Montana and Len Dawson once slung it around, I stood up, unbuttoned my coat, cocked my arm, and uncorked a wobbling duck perfect for a skeet shoot that landed in the sea of red 20 rows up.

"Ohhhhhhh, that was ugly!" Deion yelped.

"A frozen rope, baby!" I countered.

"This is a quarterback controversy already!" said Deion, who called for Fran Charles, the anchor back in our Los Angeles studio.

We had controversy all right. One of the NFL's many risk management experts watching at home frowned upon the exercise of a league employee pitching an oblong, yet pointed object into an unsuspecting crowd on live television. Apparently, some woman was actually suing the Arena Football League because a ball flew into the stands and clocked her in the head. Needless to say, word filtered down from NFL headquarters that our souvenir stunt had achieved one-and-done status.

Unfortunately for Plummer, he didn't throw the ball much better that night. Clearly, Denver needed to remove the Arrowhead crowd from the game with a quick start, but Ty Law intercepted Plummer just three plays in. In the third quarter, our cameras caught Plummer having a

The very first NFL Network pregame show at Arrowhead Stadium.
(*Joann Kamay*)

demonstrative exchange with Mike Shanahan, the first shots of juicy controversy captured in an NFL Network broadcast. Sure enough, the start was, in fact, Plummer's last for the Broncos, and Shanahan did indeed turn to Cutler, as Schefter reported. Schefter was just beginning to find his groove in The Eight-Game Package.

Minutes after the Chiefs won, 19–10, quarterback Trent Green sat on our set still in uniform. He was a fitting first guest of our first-ever postgame show because Green also happens to be the very first in-studio guest in the history of NFL Network. Green appeared on the inaugural edition of *NFL Total Access,* an appearance made possible by the fact that he was also booked on the same day for an NFL players edition of *Wheel of Fortune,* which tapes just down the street from NFL Network's studios in Culver City, California. In this instance, Green had spent the previous 12 weeks spinning his wheels after taking a massive blow to the head in the Chiefs' season opener. Despite winning his first home game back, Green wanted to talk more about Lamar Hunt, the maverick Chiefs owner who hosted Thanksgiving Day games in his American Football League years and had spent the previous 37 years working on the game's return to Kansas City . . . only to miss this game. Hunt was in the hospital with a lung ailment that would overcome him 20 days later.

"Lamar, I hope you're feeling better," Green said. "This win is for you."

With that, Green trotted off, and we were soon to follow. We all had a plane to catch. I had to get back to L.A. to host Friday's *NFL Total Access* with celebrity prognosticator Cedric the Entertainer, who eventually got 6 of out 10 correct. So, for those keeping score at home, it went Trent Green, one, Cedric the Entertainer, two, in as many cities in a span of about 12 hours. No time to bask in the glory. We soon had another game.

Game 2: Ravens at Bengals, Thursday, November 30, 2006

Even with our first game under our collective belts, the second offered a completely new set of challenges. First off, we began arriving only one day before game day. Secondly, we were the only game in town. Thanksgiving night, Broncos-Chiefs was the last of three games on the day. This Thursday night at Paul Brown Stadium, the Baltimore Ravens, leading the AFC North versus their rival Cincinnati Bengals, served as the sum total of NFL action in America. In essence, we were kicking off Week 13 of the NFL season on NFL Network. Thirdly, but not lastly (if that makes any sense), our pregame show was about to get monstrously long. With the games stage to ourselves, our pregame show would now last three hours.

On a TV show rundown, each segment is assigned a corresponding letter. For instance, the first segment is the A-block, the second the B-block, and so on. A normal one-hour show ends with the G-block. A 90-minute program ends in the K-block. At the end of our three-hour-long pregame show, officially called *Total Access on Location,* we would literally be the new kids on Z-block.

Thus, Wednesday night, we all went straight from the Cincinnati airport to the old Cincinnatian Hotel and convened for a nice lengthy chat. As always with long meetings, catering is crucial. Thus, I asked NFL Network director of production Heather Wallace to seek out several gallons of the greatest ice cream in all the land—Graeter's Ice Cream, frozen manna from heaven churned out to satisfied customers from right there in the Queen City since 1870. The chocolate chip cookie dough is to die for. Black raspberry chip is no slouch either.

Plus, why not go for a November ice cream binge: It was 60 degrees *at night* on November 29 in Cincinnati. Another incredible stroke of weather luck, since, as someone (me) pointed out in the meeting, it was currently five degrees in Kansas City. We had gotten out of there just in time. Sadly, our weather luck was also about to strike midnight.

Halfway through the meeting, Marshall brought up the idea of tossing another football into the stands. It was then that we received the news that the curtain had been brought down on that production. Plus, even if we *could* throw a ball into the stands it was a moot point. The Bengals weren't allowing us on the field before the game.

Sure, the National Football League is one incredibly successful monolith. But it's also comprised of 32 different entities, and it becomes 32 different fiefdoms, when you're on their turf. Each team has its own idea as to what its stadium should look like on game day. Some teams apparently consider a studio desk on the field an eyesore, certainly if it's sitting under an unsightly tarplike canopy to protect against the elements. The Cincinnati Bengals are one of those teams. Thus the *Total Access on Location* set got tucked away on the plaza level concourse on the Cincinnati River side of the stadium. A perfect wind tunnel for when, say, a vicious thunderstorm blows into the area about 15 minutes before, say, a three-hour NFL pregame show hits the air.

Sure enough, a real nasty storm hit Paul Brown Stadium right around three hours before kickoff. Forty minutes into our program (the E-block for those scoring at home), the rain came down sideways while I was interviewing the league's vice president of officiating, Mike Pereira. As water pelted the side of his face, Mike said he would monitor the radar for lightning, which would mean a certain delay to the start of the game and an evacuation of the fans to the concourse.

Yikes.

Later, Cris Collinsworth, a popular former Bengal, came down from the booth for an appearance on our pregame show. He had just spoken to a weatherman friend of his in the area who said to make book that lightning was coming. Thankfully, Cris's weather guy had bad Doppler. Lightning never arrived, but that didn't mean the electrocution factor disappeared.

With one hour left in the show, Joann told all of us that we might need to bolt the set so the crew could get rid of the rainwater that had dangerously pooled on our tarp roof. We all looked up and saw the tarp hanging low in the center. If it somehow gave way on the air, it would make for quite the YouTube moment. Just as some pole-wielding crew members began poking the roof from underneath, Marshall wisely called attention to the labyrinth of electrical cords, space heaters, and lights surrounding us. Might not be such a good idea to displace the roof water after all. So, for the last hour of our show, everyone nervously watched the growing bulge hang atop our set like a liquid sword of Damocles.

The roof held better than the Ravens defense in the third quarter when Carson Palmer shocked Baltimore with a 40-yard flea-flicker to T.J. Houshmendzadeh for Cincinnati's only touchdown of the night. It was enough. The Bengals' defense had the better game, and perennial Pro Bowl receiver Chad Johnson wrapped up one of the more prolific months in NFL history—a stunning 695 yards in November.

After Cincinnati's 13–7 win, Johnson, Cincinnati's most entertaining luminary since WKRP's quirky newsman Les Nesman, joined us on the postgame set in shirtsleeves, freezing in the suddenly chilly Cincinnati night. Apparently, the ice storm that had paralyzed Kansas City and the rest of the Midwest was heading our way. As for Chad, whose dozen-large posse included his grandmother, attending a game for the very first time, he was heading posthaste to his Miami hangout. We were all heading out of Dodge the next morning. I flew east to New York City for a Friday night gala held in honor of outgoing NFL commissioner Paul Tagliabue. The next day, I rushed off to JFK Airport to get back to Los Angeles in time to host Sunday night's *NFL GameDay* with Mooch and Deion, and in my haste left my nice warm overcoat in the back of a New York City taxi, just in time for next week's visit to Pittsburgh, where the Thursday forecast called for snow.

Game 3: Browns at Steelers, Thursday, December 7, 2006

When you live out in Los Angeles for any period of time, you thin out. Sometimes literally, what with the Pilates (which I admittedly enjoy doing) and the tofu (which I still won't even eat at gunpoint) and all that crunchy granola-type stuff. Your blood thins out, too, what with the weather being pristinely perfect outdoors about 90 percent of the time. So, even with my bona fide New York City and Michigan background (born in Brooklyn, raised in Staten Island, University of Michigan Class of '90), I still wasn't prepared for what went down in Game Three of The Eight-Game Package.

Well, I tried to be prepared.

Like any good teammate, Marshall Faulk had my back. On the Monday before we took off for Pittsburgh for a suddenly meaningless Browns-Steelers contest (both teams were virtually out of the playoff race including, shockingly, the defending Super Bowl champs), Marshall got a package from the St. Louis Rams and handed me the quality goods he'd promised—Under Armour. Forget research and note cards. I must tell you the acquisition of this skintight layer of double-sided fabric was easily the best preparation I've ever undertaken. And it *still* wasn't enough. Even with a ring of space heaters around the set.

When we first braved the elements to hit the desk a little more than three hours before kickoff to Week 14 in Pittsburgh, it had already snowed for two solid hours. Poor Adam Schefter stood amid the flurries for a midafternoon live shot with our *Point After* program and got hit with snow flying from a blower.

As she did in Cincinnati, Mother Nature saved her most furious blast for *Total Access on Location*. Just like the Bengals, the Steelers would not allow us to place our desk on the field. Instead, the set location was the concourse just above the south end zone on the *open end* of Heinz

Field, overlooking what the good folks in the Steel City call the Confluence. That's where the Allegheny, the Monongahela, and the Ohio meet. In other words, we sat right on Pittsburgh's famed and mighty Three Rivers on a snowy December night for which the weather forecast included Three Dreaded Words—"feels like zero."

Holy Franco Harris, was it *cold*!

Along with the Under Armour and thick gloves, I had on ski socks. Marshall wore a ski cap every minute we weren't on the air. Deion was beside himself. During his stellar 14-season *two*-sport career, the man could have played for virtually anybody he wanted. Notice he never played for Green Bay or Chicago. He grew up in balmy Florida and went to Florida State. For him, 60 degrees is a freezing point. Now, here sat the great Deion Sanders in a snowstorm, and I thought he was going to quit on the spot. As for Mariucci, well, he's from the Upper Peninsula of Michigan from a town called Iron Mountain. Frostbite is practically his middle name. So Mooch showed up on the set with no Under Armour, no hat, no scarf, and no gloves. Tough guy. Until his wife, Gayle, called his cell phone during the first commercial break to ask him if he had lost his freaking mind. She, apparently, had taken the figurative gloves off. So Mooch literally put his on.

I can not feel my toes. Note Mariucci without gloves. He got a call from his wife after this segment. (*Joann Kamay*)

While the Steelers did not let us on the field, they did provide for our most plush green room conditions to date—the entire locker room of their Heinz Field co-tenant, the University of Pittsburgh Panthers. Located a quick walk away from the concourse door that led to the frigid set, we had full run of the place. Huge lockers to hang our coats, hot chocolate and fresh coffee, cozy leather couches placed around a large flat-screen television brought in just for the occasion. And warm. Nice and toasty warm. I nearly fell asleep during halftime. Senior coordinating producer Aaron Owens shook my shoulder right before halftime.

"Please don't make me go back out there," I begged.

The Steelers and Browns were probably saying the same thing heading *in* to their locker rooms. Thanks to the weather, the stands were only half full (I'm an optimist), and with Cleveland's starting quarterback Charlie Frye injured, Derek Anderson got his first career start—the 200th different NFL quarterback to start a game during Brett Favre's Iron Man streak. The Steelers defense ate Anderson up. Pittsburgh led a sloppy game 10–0, which meant the first 10 quarters of The Eight-Game Package had produced a grand total of 5 touchdowns.

Again. Did we *really* have to go back out there?

Thankfully, we got some excitement in the second half. Pittsburgh's Willie Parker ran for a single-game team record 232 yards, and the night nearly ended with a fistfight. With just less than seven minutes left and the Steelers winning 27–0, Browns tight end Kellen Winslow broadsided Steelers linebacker Larry Foote long after the whistle. It earned Winslow an unsportsmanlike conduct penalty and the immediate scorn of Steelers firebrand Joey Porter. No one knew at the time that the free agent-to-be Porter was in his second-to-last game in his eight-year career with Pittsburgh. At the time, the Pro Bowl linebacker needed to be held back, but nobody could hold back his tongue after the game. With cameras and tape recorders rolling, Porter foolishly called Winslow a word that rhymes with maggot. Within days, the league slapped Porter with a $10,000 fine. Within minutes, as Eric Weinberger was now telling me from the truck, Porter would be on our frigid postgame show set. In that interview, Porter was more mindful of his words but still mighty steamed.

"It was a cheap shot but that's [Winslow's] makeup," Porter said. "He says he's the best tight end in the game, but I don't see it. I lost all the little respect that I did have left for him."

While he had little remaining respect, I hardly had any circulation remaining in several of my toes. The blazing-hot space heaters no longer had any effect. I was now officially Jack Nicholson at the end of *The Shining*. Upon the show's merciful end, the crew aimed to thaw out at the hotel bar—only to find it closed. Even with an early flight to Los Angeles hours away, we found an open establishment across the street and closed it down. Why not? We had survived the snow and a dreadful 27–7 game that made it only seven touchdowns through our first three contests. Our luck had to turn. Chances of that looked good, what with The Eight-Game Package now about to pop with four games over the next two weeks.

Game 4: 49ers at Seahawks, Thursday, December 14, 2006

My cousin Robert has lived in a stunning house on Lake Washington since the early '90s and once told me that Seattle has three weather patterns: started raining, raining, and just stopped raining. Now, please believe me, I never wanted this chapter to be fixated on meteorology. I do the sports, not the weather, but I only report the story as it stands. When we arrived in Seattle to broadcast the 49ers and Seahawks kickoff to Week 15, it had rained there every day for nearly six weeks. In fact, Seattle had just witnessed the wettest November in the city's *history* and had set the record by November 16.

Then came game night.

Thanks to the Seahawks, we were back on the field, under a canopy tucked away in the southeast corner of Qwest Field. If I swiveled my seat around and took 10 large steps, I'd be standing in the end zone looking for a Matt Hasselbeck pass. Then again, I wouldn't be open. All the Under Armour would have slowed me down. I felt like the Michelin Man.

It was a chilly steady rain. Coming on the heels of Pittsburgh, it was particularly cruel and unusual. Many of us were already coming down with something. Theraflu, Cold-EEZE, and Airborne had fast become the order of the day. Kara Henderson, our field reporter who's normally a mortal lock for an aperitif or two with the crew, spent Wednesday night in bed. The weather did not help. What a total bummer. I had never been to Qwest Field. I wanted to see if Seahawks fans, known as the "12th Man," were in fact louder than those in Arrowhead, as some claim. I wanted a little Eight-Game Package comparing and contrasting. In essence, I wanted to soak in the atmosphere, not have the atmosphere soak me.

It was ridiculous, but 20 minutes before kickoff, it *really* began to rain.

I mean, a collect-the-animals-by-two-and-rush-them-onto-a-boat rain.

Coming out of a commercial break, director Jennifer Love took a shot of the upper deck of the stadium, and thick droplets hit the screen. It looked like hail and, for a few seconds, may have been. The Seahawks cheerleaders (a.k.a. the Sea Gals) ran for cover in their sweat suits—cheerleaders in the layered effect, for crying out loud! A deluge spilled over the top, with water cascading onto the field from the stands. Jen then took a hilarious shot of Deion, who had slumped down in his chair, pulled down his fedora, and closed his overcoat over his face. It was indeed time to batten down the hatches.

"A *Perfect Storm*–type squall has just hit Seattle!" I said.

Quickly, with wind whipping through the canopy around the set, Eric had me toss to a feature piece just to get into tape. Perfect timing. As soon as we hit tape, our entire set went dark. Lights. Cameras. Monitors. Done.

Mother Nature had finally succeeded in doing what she could not accomplish in Cincinnati and Pittsburgh—knock us off the air. As it turned out, *all of Qwest Field* had taken a power hit. The scoreboard screen was kaput, half the lights ringing the stadium—out. A camera guy on our set said he had lived his entire life in Seattle and had never seen it like this. Right then and there, I promised myself to get a hybrid car.

Thus, the last 15 minutes of *Total Access on Location* did not come from location. Our Los Angeles–based studio crew finished the show while everyone in Seattle sorted through the *Poseidon Adventure* that had broken out. That included the refs. The rain had inundated the field to the point that mounds had bubbled up under the field turf. Suddenly, Qwest Field looked more like Safeco Field across the street. Assured by the grounds crew that the bubbles would soon subside as the rain now had, the refs delayed the start of the game by 10 minutes, virtually unheard-of in the NFL.

Once the game started, it took some time for everyone to get into it—especially the players. The Seahawks led the 49ers 7–3 at half, which meant The Eight-Game Package now had 8 touchdowns under its belt through 14 quarters. The weather was killing us. The 49ers quarterback, Alex Smith, would quickly provide some sunshine.

Still trailing 7–3 with one play left in the third quarter, Smith uncorked a gorgeous spiral down the right sideline and hit receiver Arnaz

Battle in stride for a 53-yard gain to the Seattle 33. The proverbial light had officially gone on. Six plays later, Smith found Vernon Davis for his first of three touchdowns in the fourth quarter. The other two scores were equally impressive—a scramble-to-his-left, 20-yard touchdown pass and a stunning 18-yard bootleg that faked out all 11 Seahawks defenders.

"I've never seen one guy run to one side of the field and have the entire defense on the other side of the field," Collinsworth remarked.

Three touchdowns in one quarter! An absolute bonanza. The first career lapel-grabbing performance for the first overall pick of the 2005 draft helped make the 49ers the first road winner of The Eight-Game Package. They kept their slim playoff hopes alive by preventing Seattle from clinching the NFC West.

After the game, 49ers running back Frank Gore, 194 yards farther into his first Pro Bowl season, visited the set and we quickly wrapped up the postgame show. We had a red-eye to Atlanta for our first Saturday night game, but faced a more pressing race against time. Apparently, a storm packing *100-mile-an-hour winds* was entering the area. I kid you not that, the next day, trees, street signs, wires, and electrical poles were down all over Seattle. We barely escaped it with a fluttering, white-knuckle takeoff from Sea-Tac airport shortly before midnight. Your humble narrator popped an Ambien and bade Mother Nature a not-so-gentle good night.

Game 5: Cowboys at Falcons, Saturday, December 16, 2006

The bug-eyed official from the Atlanta Falcons could hardly catch his breath and nearly knocked me over for all the Georgia Dome to see. I immediately knew I wanted no part of this guy.

We were fast approaching halftime of our most action-packed broadcast to date. The second quarter alone featured more touchdowns than our first two games *combined*. Media magnet Terrell Owens had already caught two scores from media darling Tony Romo, and Dallas's supremely talented young pass rusher DeMarcus Ware tipped a Michael Vick pass to himself and returned it for six. Undaunted, Vick still threw for three scores to knot the game at 21 at the half. And it all happened in front of our guaranteed biggest audience of The Eight-Game Package because the entire free football world watches Dallas Cowboys football. Yet, for all that, all that Crazed Falcons Dude wanted to know was

During our pregame show in Atlanta, I reminded rap star Ludacris (in shades) how we once kicked it during Freaknik. (*Joann Kamay*)

whether we saw Owens spit in the face of Falcons cornerback D'Angelo Hall and had video of it.

"Huh?"

Clearly, we didn't. Otherwise our broadcast would have been, if you will, salivating over the incident. We had 21 cameras at the game. None of them caught it. We did capture Hall going crazy on the sideline early in the second quarter, but spitting? No. I told the guy as politely as I could that I had a halftime show to do and then weaved through a phalanx of cheerleaders and photogs on the end line to return back to our set on the opposite 20-yard line.

Upon return, Falcons Dude was already there. Was there some sort of secret passageway? Now, he was chirping at both Schefter and Mariucci about L'Affaire Loogie and wanted to know if *they* knew about any video of it. Mariucci, who has a master's degree in T.O. shenanigans, looked shocked. Sure, Mooch was the 49ers head coach when Owens whipped a Sharpie out of his sock and autographed the football he had just scored with on Monday Night Football, but even *this* would be uncharted territory for Owens.

"Hey, this guy over there says that T.O. spit in—"

"I know," I said. "I didn't see anything. Did you?"

"Nope. First I've heard of it," said Mariucci.

Suddenly, Weinberger stormed the field at a brisk pace and Schefter immediately apprised him of the spit rumor, but Eric had far more pressing matters. In his first game filling in for Collinsworth, Dick Vermeil had come down with some sort of sinus infection that completely ravaged his voice. Coach sounded like Stevie Nicks, Demi Moore, Debra Winger, and Max the Butler from *Hart to Hart* all rolled into one. Not good.

"Where's Deion?" Eric asked.

In the final minutes of the half, while I was pulled over by the Falcons' Saliva Patrol, NFL Network replaced Vermeil in the broadcast booth with Marshall Faulk, quite an ironic twist, since Vermeil won his only ring by handing it off to Marshall in that very building. In fact, neither Faulk nor Vermeil had been back in the Georgia Dome since the Rams last-second win over the Titans in Super Bowl XXXIV. Eric eventually found Deion and sent him upstairs to make it an all-world three-man booth with Bryant Gumbel—one Hall of Fame broadcaster and two future Hall of Fame football players. It also turned out to be the very first African-American three-man booth in NFL television history. *And* they called an entertaining second half.

Vick opened the half by throwing his career-best fourth touchdown pass of the game. All those scores required extra points from the only NFL player requiring carbon dating—the 47-year-old Morten Andersen, who, with those extra points, became the all-time leading scorer in NFL history. Before game's end, Vick broke Bobby Douglass's 34-year-old record for most rushing yards in a single season by a quarterback. Dallas, however, scored the last 17 points to win 38–28, dealing a crushing blow to the Falcons and embattled coach Jim Mora. At 7–7, the Falcons went into a tailspin, didn't win another game, and Mora lost his job.

The Cowboys were sitting pretty at 9–5, one win away from clinching the NFC East. But who knew? They didn't win a game the rest of the year, either, including a stunning playoff loss in Seattle sealed by the official breaking of Romo's glass slipper—a fumbled hold on a potential game-winning field goal that will live on in NFL Films lore. Fifteen days later, another Dallas stunner: Parcells retired, meaning the final win of his Hall of Fame career was brought to you by . . . The Eight-Game Package.

Deion and Marshall had felt adrenaline in that building many times before, but not from broadcasting. What a first-booth assignment—and, to boot, both guys were sensational. They were also very well aware of their role in making sports TV history. However, our night was just getting started.

Producer Aaron Owens got in all of our earpieces with the news: "Kara Henderson just interviewed D'Angelo Hall in the locker room and he told her that T.O. spit in his face. Rich, you'll toss to that in the next segment."

Mooch and I looked at each other. Did it happen? Was Crazy Falcons Dude really Paul Revere after all?

"I lost all respect for the guy," Hall told Kara. "We were kind of walking face to face, walking back to the huddle, and he just hauled off and spit in my face."

Marshall gave kudos to Hall for not getting kicked out of the game. Because, had Marshall been on the business end of even a speck of T.O. phlegm, Marshall said, "It would be on." I was eager to hear Deion's take, since Prime Time might just be Owens's most ardent supporter in the media. Deion said he was shocked and Owens should absolutely be taken to task—only if he really did it. None of us knew, but we were about to find out. Once we hit commercial, there was field producer Bardia Shah-Rais behind the wheel of a golf cart heading toward our set with Owens riding shotgun.

Immediately, I began to formulate the order of questions in my head. I had to ask Owens about Spitgate. But how to go about it? Owens's arrival snapped me out of deep thought. I shook his hand and he barely gripped it, the hand still quite swollen from the surgery that had caused him to famously mix his painkillers with his supplements and wind up in a Dallas emergency room three months before. Owens didn't make eye contact. Marshall recused himself. Neither guy apparently likes the other. So Owens sat in Marshall's seat, two chairs away from the coach who frequently fined him in their 49ers days and to whom Owens hadn't spoken a word since Mariucci left San Francisco.

No, this won't be awkward at all.

"Back in five seconds!" yelled Joann.

To get T.O. talking, I first asked if scoring in the first half for the first time all season made him feel more comfortable within the Dallas offense. A layup. A cream puff. A mere spit in the ocean. Oops. Bad choice of words.

Then I dived in headfirst.

T.O. hit our postgame set in Atlanta and sparked Spitgate. (*Joann Kamay*)

"Terrell, moments ago, D'Angelo Hall said that you spit in his face during this game. What is your reaction upon hearing that?"

Now, I've learned to never ask a question without at least trying to think about what answer it might elicit. I thought Owens would either deny that the incident took place or claim it to be an accident. I certainly didn't expect a flat-out admission—but that's what happened.

"I got frustrated and I apologize for that," a matter-of-fact Owens said. "It was just a situation where he kept bugging me and kept getting in my face and he just kept aggravating me."

Say what?

Deion jumped into the silence. "Still, T.O.," he said, choosing his words carefully, "spitting in a man's face is the most degrading thing you can do to another man. Did you know that when you did it?"

"I apologize for that, and I gotta move on."

More silence.

"I just hope you guys don't take this any further," Deion said, "because you know when something like this happens you know where that ends up."

Owens quickly grew weary of the subject.

"Well, I'm not really concerned about that. Like I said, I apologize for it, and I'm man enough to say that and gotta move on, but other than that, hey, I'm just going out and trying to play football."

Done. End of story. Mariucci then changed the subject.

"How's your hand?"

Immediately, the NFL Network PR machine no doubt was wetting itself. This was one fat, massive scoop on our hands. The game and its aftermath were clearly our finest and biggest hour and within moments T.O.'s confession got beamed to every media outlet across the country. The Owens confession put me back on ESPN *SportsCenter* for the first time in three and a half years.

It brought a wild week to a close. Seattle felt weeks rather than 48 hours removed. Also Deion, Mooch and I had a 7:00 A.M. flight back to Los Angeles, what with the rest of the Week 15 docket to cover on *NFL GameDay* Sunday night.

After that, another two-game week with trips to two storied locales—Lambeau Field and Oakland's famed Black Hole.

Back from Atlanta on the *NFL GameDay* set, having a blast. *(Joann Kamay)*

Game 6: Vikings at Packers, Thursday, December 21, 2006

The cards started tumbling fast and furious. Sitting at the very end of the table, your humble narrator had just doubled down but had no sense of anxiety. The most blessed athlete in recent days sat three seats away.

"Give him twenty-one!" screamed Deion Sanders.

Sure enough, the dealer took one card from the plastic seven-deck shoe and flipped over the necessary face card. Booyah.

Now, it must be noted here that the NFL *seriously* frowns on sports gambling. Everyone I know at NFL Network strictly adheres to the league's rules on the matter. Nobody wants to lose a fun job just because they took the Timberwolves and the points. Outside of sports gambling and other ancillary gambling don'ts, we are allowed to hit a casino and indulge in conventional games of chance. So when we checked into our hotel across the street from the Green Bay airport the night before the Vikings and Packers kicked off Week 16, it didn't take long to notice the Oneida Casino right next door.

Our meeting let out early at 7:00 P.M. and Adam Schefter tried to rally troops to head out to an Italian restaurant for dinner. However, most of us had no interest in sampling the local Wisconsin twist on chicken parmigiana and, already travel weary, decided to stay put to hit the tables. Deion led that charge.

As you might imagine, the sight of Prime Time strolling through the slots turned the heads of many patrons, most of them donning some form of Packers or Vikings gear. Soon enough we found ourselves nestled at a table in the Oneida Casino "private high-stakes area"—$25 a hand.

"Who's playing third base?" Deion asked the group, correctly noting the importance of the last seat at the blackjack table. Decisions made at the Hot Corner (whether to take a card or stick) affect the figurative and literal fortunes of the entire table. I accepted the challenge.

"Play a good third base, Humble Host," Deion said as the dealer mixed the fat deck. You could just feel the next couple of hours were going to be *fun.*

"Cut the deck?"

The dealer waved the plastic Packers-yellow cut card in my direction but I deferred to Deion. Prime Time cleaved the column of cards and a sea of red chips began to part from the dealer's stash. Within minutes, the table began to cook. Producer Chris Weerts sat to Deion's right with

Kara Henderson to his left and we quickly all had bigger stacks. The action and our accompanying loudness attracted a crowd and, thus, drew considerable interest in the two empty seats between me and Kara. None of us wanted an outsider to sit down and bust up our mojo, but time and again we got saved by this bizarre sign posted on our table: NO MID-SHOE ENTRY.

You see, at the Oneida, once the dealer begins doling out cards from a new deck or shoe, the table goes into lockdown. No new player can sit down at the table and play until the shoe is complete. If you leave during the shoe—even to go to the bathroom—you can't return until the next one. Voilà. No mid-shoe entry. We sure used it to our advantage.

Like, say, when a big fat guy from Sheboygan in a Donald Driver jersey (who Deion later referred to as the White Biggie Smalls) loitered for minutes on end and tried to sit down to play.

"Sorry, sir, no mid-shoe entry."

Nothing we could do. It was clearly out of our hands.

I began feeling my oats on the hot corner. After one particularly successful shoe in which I pushed all the right buttons, Deion began calling me Terry Pendleton because Deion said Pendleton was the best third baseman he had ever played with. As our dealer, John, got ready to start a new shoe, I stood up and proudly proclaimed another table lockdown.

"Ladies and gentlemen, once again, there is *no* mid-shoe entry," I screamed out to about seven people surrounding the table, most of them fellow NFL Networkers who had no intention of playing anyway. I went on. I suddenly liked the sound of this.

"So to repeat: just in case you wish to enter this table mid-shoe, it cannot happen and why is that, John the Dealer?" I asked.

John looked bewildered but delivered the desired response.

"Uh, because, there's no mid-shoe entry?"

"Scream it loud, Terry Pendleton!" Deion yelled.

I had earned another nickname.

After a considerable time, we all left the table (of course, not midshoe) and packed into a small private area called the Onieda Executive Club Break Room to scarf down pizza Deion had ordered. We were eating Italian after all. At one point, one of the Onieda Executive Club members came into the room to grab a beverage out of the Executive minifridge and scowled at the interlopers in his Break Room. It was a strange scene—open pizza boxes with the TV tuned in to *Blind Date*.

Believe me when I tell you that watching *Blind Date* with Deion providing commentary ranks on par with a Chris Rock performance. Our most fun night on the road to date was winding down, with everyone making me promise that I had to somehow, some way, work the following into Thursday's three-hour pregame show: NO MID-SHOE ENTRY.

When driving down Lombardi Avenue and approaching professional football's most hallowed ground from the west, the first thing you notice . . . is the Kmart. I mean, it's *directly* across the street from Lambeau Field. So, just in case a Packer fan needed, say, something from the Jaclyn Smith Collection before firing up a pregame bratwurst, they could do so at the Green Bay Kmart located at 1109 Lombardi Avenue.

As anyone from Wisconsin will tell you, tailgating is a God-given right. The Lambeau Field parking lot opens a mere five hours before kickoff, but for those who can't get in there early enough . . . well, there are options. You can go to the aforementioned K-Mart lot or the Kroll's West hamburger joint across the street or the Saranac Glove Company's World of Gloves down the road or the Ashwaubenon County Village Hall on Holmgren Way. Just to name a few. Even local churches get into the act and offer game-day parking. Yes, the Packers turn license plates into collection plates.

Then there's a guy Mariucci knows who takes this tailgating business to a whole other level. This friend of Mooch's has bought three *houses* around Lambeau Field for the *express purpose* of using them for tailgating. He lives in Chicago but bought the Green Bay property just to have his own personal party space every Packers game. To help defray the cost, the guy rents the houses out year-round to college kids and then, on game day, turns those tenants into the waiters, cooks, and car valets for the tailgate. The kids keep whatever tips they earn. Year-round tenants turned built-in waitstaff for his own personal tailgate spot and crashing pad within steps of Lambeau Field. You must admit it's genius—yet a bit frightening.

Mariucci met a lot of people during his four years as Brett Favre's first quarterbacks coach in Green Bay, a golden stint that, even a decade later, has left Mooch idolized in Packerdom. Going to Lambeau Field with Steve Mariucci is like strolling into *Cheers* with Norm. Everywhere he went, everybody gave him a hug—secretaries, security guards, scouts, front-office executives, concessionaires, and fans. Even Favre himself. During our pregame show!

We were nearing the end of another Packers season, which meant Cheesehead Nation was in full hand-wringing mode over Favre's mind-set. The previous spring, Favre took several agonizing weeks before deciding to come back for another season. With the NFL Network contest against Minnesota being the last home game on Green Bay's schedule, it perhaps represented Favre's final game at Lambeau Field. Thus, retirement talk dominated our three-hour pregame (so did the Oakland Raiders; I'll explain in a moment.) The minute Favre hit the soggy tundra (yes, it was cold and raining) for warm-ups, we hit the subject again and hit it hard, especially with such a good friend of Favre's on the set in Mariucci. Just how good friends they are became obvious for the world to see when, right in the middle of our discussion, Favre ran off the field, up to our set on the 20-yard line and gave Mooch a big bear hug. On live TV.

"Sorry to interrupt your interview," Favre said.

"You're not interrupting anything," I said.

"Get him to sit down!" Weinberger screamed in my earpiece.

Before I could even attempt that maneuver, however, Favre shook all our hands, bade farewell to Mooch, and ran off to the locker room.

"How cool was *that?*" I said out loud. Mariucci was clearly moved. He began to tear up. I asked him what Favre meant to him.

Hi, Brett! Sit and stay a while. (*Joann Kamay*)

"I love that guy, I just love him," Mariucci said, barely holding it in. Our director, Jen Love, zoomed in tight. "You know, tonight is the [third] anniversary of his father's passing—don't know if you know that. That was hard . . . that was hard for him . . . He doesn't know if he is going to [keep playing]. I hope he does."

Deion gave Mariucci a pat on the back and said, "That's why we love our Moochie." Mariucci laughed and got a second wind.

"See these gray hairs? Initially they were from Brett Favre, and lately they're from Deion," Mariucci said. "But we entered this league together. His first four years in Green Bay weren't necessarily all roses. They were hard. There was a lot of work and he never missed a day—ever. He was always working at it. There were great times and down times and always he fought through it. I enjoy seeing him enjoy the success over a long period of time right here in Green Bay because they absolutely love this guy here."

Deion jumped in.

"He's also the smartest quarterback I've ever played against in my life. I remember one year when I was in Dallas and Green Bay was coming into Texas Stadium. I was excited all week because they put in a back-side corner blitz for me and I just knew I was going have an opportunity to sack Brett Favre. In the game, it was time [for the blitz]. I crawled up to the line and starting coming. But right before I got there, he released the ball, and as he was releasing the ball—as he was *releasing the ball*—he said to me, 'I knew you were coming, Prime!' I mean, he was saying that and throwing the ball in the same motion and I just turned around and walked back to the huddle laughing my butt off."

"He did that to me here when I was coaching against him!" Mariucci laughed. "We blitzed him and he came out the backdoor and completed it to Dorsey Levens and then Favre came running over to the sideline and screamed, 'Keep bringing it, Mooch!' "

Awesome. The only thing that approached a similar fun quotient during the pregame show was when Cris Collinsworth appeared for his weekly chat segment on the field set and I introduced him thusly: "Now making a rare mid-shoe entry here in Wisconsin is Cris Collinsworth."

"Yes!" Deion screamed. Half the truck got in my earpiece laughing. I was real proud of myself for that one.

Once Favre crashed the set, the rest of the night became anticlimactic. We saw better action at the Oneida tables the night before. The Vikings gave a first-career start to rookie quarterback Tavaris Jackson, who struggled all night. Minnesota's only points came on a Fred Smoot pick of Favre returned for a score. Smoot then dared to attempt the famed Lambeau Leap—celebrating a touchdown by jumping into the stands. Smoot got summarily rejected, and Collinsworth noted it was like a Cubs fan tossing back an opponent's home run ball in Wrigley. That also served as Favre's only touchdown pass of the night. Green Bay got three field goals, including one at the final gun, to win 9–7.

Thankfully, we did our postgame show in the climate-controlled atrium the Packers built as part of the Lambeau Field renovations in 2003. Fans of all shapes and sizes surrounded our set as we sent Mariucci and Bardia down to the locker room to fetch Favre for an appearance, but when they arrived, Favre was nowhere in sight. He was in the training room, a classic veteran move by somebody who wants no part of the media. Favre obviously did not want to feed the beast with fresh meat about his potential retirement. But we had an ace in the hole—Mariucci. So Bardia sent him back to the off-limits training room to try to twist his good friend's golden arm.

A jocular member of Cheesehead Nation suffers a wardrobe malfunction.
(*Joann Kamay*)

After eating pizza with Favre, Mariucci returned to our postgame set in the Lambeau Field atrium empty-handed. (*Joann Kamay*)

Minutes ticked by and there still was no sign of Favre *or* Mariucci. Time was awasting. If we were going to get Favre, it was now or never. So Bardia boldly went where he shouldn't and breached the sanctity of the training room . . . only to find Favre eating pizza with Steve. No, they weren't watching *Blind Date,* too.

"Hey, Bardia, you want a slice?" Mariucci said.

"What's your name?" Favre asked. "Lombardia?"

Realizing now he had no shot at prying Favre away from his postgame meal for our postgame show, Bardia joined them and had a slice with Favre and Mariucci in the bowels of Lambeau Field. So, upstairs, we finished the show sans Steve and hit the airport. We had a lengthy flight across country to Oakland, where Adam Schefter had suddenly become Public Enemy No. 1 for what he had reported earlier in the night.

Game 7: Chiefs at Raiders, Saturday, December 23, 2006

Minutes before our pregame show hit air in Green Bay, I heard Adam Schefter tell Eric Weinberger in the truck that he had news on the Oakland Raiders that needed to be broken immediately. Originally, Schefter was supposed to be in the first segment (the A-block, if you will) with word on Favre's future, but he had caught wind that the dreadful 2–12 Raiders were going to fire head coach Art Shell at season's end.

Back in 1994, Raiders owner Al Davis made Art Shell, the Hall of Fame offensive lineman from Oakland's glory years, the very first African-American head coach in modern NFL history. Shell's rehiring in 2006 was equally touted by the Raiders. His firing after just one year on the job would be shocking, to say the least. And talk about *risky*: Absolutely nobody in his right mind can predict anything in regard to the mercurial Davis. Reporting the firing two weeks in advance meant that Schefter was putting a lot on the line. It would be just like Davis to keep Shell to spite a reporter. However, the man reports what he knows only from trusted sources, so Schefter went on *Total Access on Location* and dropped the Art bombshell.

It didn't take long for the Raiders to respond.

Within an hour, Weinberger got in my ear.

"Rich, the Raiders have issued a release on Adam's report," he said. "We'll get it to you so you can read it in the next segment. It's classic."

Eric wasn't overselling it. Reprinted verbatim for your entertainment:

STATEMENT REGARDING ADAM SCHEFTER REPORT

ADAM SCHEFTER HAS ALWAYS BEEN A FALSE RUMOR MONGERER [sic] WITH RESPECT TO THE RAIDERS AND ANTI-RAIDER BASED UPON HIS RELATIONSHIP WITH DENVER AND WITH MIKE SHANAHAN.

NO DECISIONS HAVE BEEN MADE RELATIVE TO THE 2007 OAKLAND RAIDERS NOR WILL THEY BE MADE FOR SOME TIME.

ADAM SCHEFTER COULD NOT HAVE GOTTEN HIS IN-FORMATION FROM A "RELIABLE SOURCE" BECAUSE

THERE'S ONLY ONE RELIABLE SOURCE AND HE DOESN'T TRUST ADAM.

The only thing missing was a notation of "Dictated but not read by Al Davis." An NFL public relations director said he heard it was the Raiders first all-caps press release since Davis sued the league in the 1980s.

Talk about both barrels. Davis was upset and went personal. Schefter had spent over a decade on the beat of the Denver Broncos and coauthored books by Davis nemesis Mike Shanahan and Super Bowl XXXII MVP Terrell Davis. Al Davis hates the Broncos with a passion. Now, he equally hated Adam, on official Raiders stationery, for the entire world to read, and even made up a word with which to smear him: "mongerer." All on Adam's 40th birthday. For real.

I read the statement on the air and turned it over to Adam.

"Well, the Raiders can attack me personally all they want, but notice at no point in that statement did they say that Art Shell will be their head coach for the 2007 season," Schefter said. "Now, of course, no one can say what Al Davis is going to do in the future, but right now the Oakland Raiders are planning to fire Art Shell."

Marshall and Deion had Schefter's back.

"That's the fastest the Raiders have played defense all year," Marshall said.

Said Deion, "I trust Adam Schefter. If Adam Schefter told me my mother was moving in, she'd be there unpacked before I got home."

The firestorm had begun. In addition to spending his 40th on the road, as he had spent much of the season, Schefter had just gotten engaged, and Eric was going to send him home to New York after the Green Bay game. But with this controversial report and the fact that our next game was in Oakland, Schefter had just bought himself a ticket out west.

The Mongerer was going to the Black Hole.

I am not going to lie. The Black Hole, as the Raiders home crowd is known, can be one frightening place. First of all, it's called the Black Hole. Just as Chiefs fans all wear red, Raiders fans wear all black, with most of them dressed like extras from a *Mad Max* movie. A mere glimpse into the stands (if you dare make eye contact) reveals a sea of Darth Vader masks, skull masks, skeletons, chain mail, spiked leather vests, silver and black face paint, and a Randy Moss jersey or five.

In other words, a perfect place to be two days before Christmas.

The Raiderettes all wear Santa caps for the occasion. Ah, yes, the Raiderettes. Your humble narrator must admit that this crop of ladies were the most, uh, fetching cheerleaders of The Eight-Game Package. Marshall would second that emotion. He told me the Raiders are the only team in the league that makes the opposition run out on to the field through the *home team* cheerleaders.

"You'd be all focused [for the game] and then you run out and you're like, 'Damn.'"

At least the Raiders realize they need to offset the rabble. Normal people become transformed in the Black Hole. Back in my Redding TV days, I drove down to Oakland to cover a Cowboys-Raiders contest and did the typical "colorful" fans feature. I found one around midfield clutching a KILL THE COWBOYS! sign and asked this person what it did for a living.

Through the bleeding skull mask came this muffled reply: "I'm a second-grade teacher."

Needless to say, Schefter was admittedly on edge traipsing into this scene after his Shell report. Because he was flying back home after the pregame show and the rest of us were staying the entire night, Schefter drove himself to the stadium in a separate car. As our car pulled through the gate first, Deion rolled down his window and called over one of the security guards.

"Tell the guy behind us that he can't come in because he's the Mongerer."

We pulled through and told the driver to stop so we could check out the fruits of our shenanigans. Deion, Marshall, Mooch, and I all craned our necks to look out the back window to watch Schefter sweat, but instead he broke out laughing. Apparently, the security guard had botched the word "mongerer." I told you it's not really a word.

Then again, the good folks in the Black Hole have a language all their own. It did not take long for Schefter to hear it. He said he heard every use of the f-word imaginable. During a commercial break, Mariucci told us a story about the one time he brought the 49ers across the Bay to play Oakland and got an earful.

"I stood out there on about the 10-yard line during warm-ups and did my best to ignore them," Mariucci said, "but at one point one guy yells out, 'Steve! Steve!' You know, normally they scream out 'Hey, Mariucci, you so-and-so,' but when this guy called out 'Steve!' for some reason that made me turn around, and so he says, 'Steve, your mother's a whore!' "

On this day, even with the Mongerer in the house, nobody heard it from the Black Hole more vociferously than Deion Sanders. Now, that shouldn't be a surprise. Throughout his career in *both* sports, Deion heard it everywhere. The Eight-Game Package journey was no exception. Deion got it loud in Pittsburgh and Seattle. The crowd grilled him in Green Bay. Come to think of it, the only place where fans didn't give Deion the business was in Atlanta, where he's like Elvis, but without exception, he ignored it all . . . until the Black Hole, where, for some reason, he fully engaged the crowd.

During commercial breaks, Deion would get out of his seat on the set (surrounded by protective netting near the tunnel off the end zone) and bantered with those who had spent the previous segment bellowing at him. Later, I tossed to a Steve Sabol feature and, while that tape was running, Deion spent the entire time doodling something on a piece of paper.

Deion had his fun with the fans in the Black Hole. (*Lee/wireimage.com*)

"What's he writing?" Weinberger asked Bardia, who was stationed on the set. "Maybe we can show it when we come out [of the piece]."

Bardia strolled over and peeked in at Prime's handiwork.

"Uh, no, I don't think so," Bardia reported back through his headset.

You see, Deion had scrawled "YO MOMMA!" in big balloon letters and autographed it "Love, Prime." Deion then folded the paper in half, walked to the stands and personally guided the missive to one loud and obnoxious fan in particular, about 20 rows back, telling people to pass the paper along until it reached his intended target. The fan appeared in total disbelief that he was receiving a personal note from Deion Sanders . . . until he looked at the paper. Then he started spewing curse words that would make George Carlin blush.

Deion beamed like a proud papa.

We all survived the pregame and Schefter left the Black Hole in one piece. As I walked behind the south goalpost and back to our green room underneath the stadium to watch the game on TV, a Raider fan screamed out my name. I turned and looked. *Oh, no. Why would I do that?* The fan reached out his arm, holding a candy cane.

"We're not all bad here, Rich" he said. "Merry Christmas."

Stunned, I turned to Joann, who didn't skip a beat.

"You're not actually thinking of eating that, are you?"

And, to all, a good night. One more game to go. The day before New Year's Eve.

Game 8: Giants at Redskins, Saturday, December 30, 2006

Normally, the Giants playing the Redskins in the final week of the season with half the league hanging on the outcome would be top story news in the nation's capital, but on the night we arrived in Washington, D.C., the NFC playoff picture wasn't the only thing hanging. Iraq had just executed Saddam Hussein and, if that wasn't enough, the whole town was preparing for the state funeral of Gerald Ford.

So much for the finale of The Eight-Game Package.

Outside the Beltway, however, our game could not have been huger.

Despite their considerable injury and team chemistry issues and every back page in New York calling for Coach Tom Coughlin's head, the 7–8 Giants were still one win away from assuring themselves of the last available playoff spot in the NFC. A loss to the Redskins would throw that spot wide open for the Packers, Rams, Panthers, or Falcons to snare.

Even with a loss to the already long-eliminated Redskins, the Giants *still* weren't out of it. The list of possible NFC playoff scenarios disseminated by the league office looked like the blackboard in *A Beautiful Mind.* Bottom line: There would be lots of interested parties tuning to NFL Network for our final game. Plus, for the first time, we had no Thursday game, which allowed everyone to enjoy bonus time at home. Our sails had some extra wind at the end of a long journey.

On game day, we all packed into an SUV and headed off to FedEx Field, the palatial home of the Redskins located in the sticks of Maryland. On the way down Constitution Avenue, we passed the IRS (Deion got a big kick out of that one), the Capitol, caught a glimpse of the Supreme Court, and, minutes later, circled the Redskins' old digs—the ancient, but incredibly intimate RFK Stadium. I'm pleased to say I went to a game there once, and it was a doozy—Cowboys-Redskins in Washington's championship season of 1991. The scene was wild. Redskins fans hanged Dallas quarterback Danny White in effigy in the parking lot even though White had last played for the Cowboys in 1988 and people had stopped hanging people in effigy in 1788. We sat in my friend's season-ticket seats two rows from the front railing in the upper deck that actually hung over the end zone. Any time Mark Rypien tossed the ball for paydirt, I remember we literally had to stand up and lean over to see what happened. When the Redskins scored, the stands physically shook.

When the Redskins moved into their massive new stadium in 1997 (then called Jack Kent Cooke stadium after the team's mercurial owner) we sat in my friend's same seats—two rows from the front railing of the upper deck. Now, though, the upper deck sat atop two tiers of luxury boxes. It was as if we were watching the game from Delaware. I thought of that whole experience driving past RFK, thinking that place *looks* small.

Even in its own right, FedEx Field is monstrously large. With a capacity of 91,704, it's the largest venue in the entire league. It also may be the stadium most splattered with advertising. When driving up to FedEx Field, the first thing you notice is the massive FedEx sign plastered to a stadium painted FedEx red, FedEx green and FedEx purple. It looks like the world's largest airbill, as if the team's current mercurial owner Dan Snyder wrapped up his stadium for priority overnight shipping. Looking at the place from a distance, you really have no earthly idea which team

The band got together one more time in our final pregame show of the season in Washington. *(Joann Kamay)*

plays inside. When you go inside, you half expect the place to be filled with bubble wrap and Styrofoam curly thingies.

Yet the team still has an incredible sense of its past. While the Redskins have retired only one number—Sammy Baugh's 33—they do have a Ring of Fame that, as the name suggests, rings the upper deck of FedEx Field. Forty players are so enshrined. The Skins also field a marching band that first tooted a note in support of the Redskins back in 1938. Heading out to the field for the final three-hour *Total Access on Location,* we ran into a trombonist who said he had been tooting out "Hail to the Redskins" since the Lyndon Johnson administration. Truth be told, he looked old enough to be from the Andrew Johnson administration but out he went with me, Mooch, Deion, and Marshall for the final NFL Network game of the year.

As in Green Bay, retirement was the topic du jour. Giants running back Tiki Barber let it slip months before that he would retire at season's end at age 31 to pursue a career in broadcasting. If the Giants lost, not only could it be Barber's final game but it would also give Barber's critics more ammunition. When Barber first mentioned retirement in October, some media folk thought it would cause a rift in the locker room, what with the team's offensive leader openly talking about his goal to become the next Matt Lauer. Not exactly on the same page with team-mates whose only goal was to become the next Super Bowl champion. Tiki also freely divulged his practice of leaving his playbook at work to place his home focus squarely on his wife and two young boys. While perhaps normal to most, that approach is unorthodox in football. Re-gardless, it worked: Barber had fashioned yet another Pro Bowl season. But with the Giants having lost six of its last seven games entering Wash-ington, Tiki needed one more big performance—unless he really had al-ready mentally checked out.

He hadn't. In fact, Tiki torched the joint. He provided New York's first touchdown with a 15-yard scamper and, shortly before halftime, stunned the Redskins with a season-best 55-yard touchdown run. For good measure, with eight minutes left, Barber busted one in from midfield to seal the game and a playoff spot for the Giants. In all, Barber broke his own fran-chise record with 234 yards rushing, the NFL record for rushing by a retiree in his final regular season game. To quote Dr. Evil, it was breathtaking.

Thus, Barber could not have been a more fitting final postgame show guest for our season.

The first question was the obvious. Did such a performance make Tiki want to rethink retirement?

Before heading off to the *Today* show, Tiki Barber could not escape the grasp of Deion and the crew. (*Joann Kamay*)

"You know what, Rich, it's good to go out on top. It's good to leave them wanting more, and I think I'm going to be able to do that," Barber said. "I'm set in what my life is going to be from now on and I'm very comfortable and satisfied with my decision."

Deion jumped in.

"I've been very critical of the things that you said and how you've said them, but tonight, going for 234 [yards], ending like that, you shut me up. You shut everybody up and I'm going take my hat off to you. But again, I've been critical of saying things like 'I don't take my playbook home' and things like that."

"Really?" said Barber, with an arched eyebrow.

"Well, definitely. I was a study, study, study guy. I studied right until I went up to kickoff. I studied my butt off."

"Well, here's the difference," Tiki said. "When you play defense it's all reactionary, so you have to know what the offensive team is doing. We are determining what the defense is doing."

"You know I don't buy that," Deion said, "I'm going to let you finish, but I don't buy that."

"Well, after I had my kids," Tiki continued, "when I go home, I want to be with them. I do my work. I stay there long hours and do my work at the stadium. And really, all it comes down to, Deion, is do you play on Sunday? And for the last three years, I've done that well and I know I have."

Marshall hit Tiki on the timing of his retirement announcement.

"Do you think because you said it [in October] the guys on the team maybe didn't look at you as their leader because you weren't going to be there anymore?"

"Not one bit did they ever think that, and you can ask them. Ask them to a man and they will tell you."

Tiki was just getting started. It's tough to comprehend sometimes, because the game is so wrought with emotion, but not everyone in the National Football League is rah-rah.

"I lead in different ways. You know, I'll go and say something to one of my teammates quietly. I won't call them out. I won't be loud, and most of my leadership is done by example. So all I ever want is opportunities to get me a chance to inspire my teammates by making a big run, by making a big play. That's how I lead."

"Well, I was inspired tonight watching you run and I'm not even your teammate," Marshall said.

"I appreciate that," Barber said.

Before Barber stepped on our set, part of me thought there was still a chance the retirement talk was just talk. But I knew Barber was done for real when Deion asked him which team he would prefer to play in the playoffs—Philadelphia or Dallas—and Tiki answered him. Usually, players wouldn't touch that with a 10-foot pole.

"You know what? Philadelphia is playing out of control [the Eagles had won four straight] so I'll say I want Dallas right now."

Everyone hooted.

"Wait a minute! Hold on," I screamed. "We're on a roll, so who do you want—*Good Morning America* or the *Today* show?"

That one he wouldn't answer. You see, he would soon be active in that profession. After the Pro Bowl, his true final game in an NFL uniform, Barber did indeed sign with NBC to tote the 30 Rock for the *Today* show. It was a great interview to bring an official close to The Eight-Game Package. Afterward, we gathered for one posterity photo and headed back to our hotel for a quick catnap. We had an ungodly 4:00 A.M. pickup to take

"Puddin Pie," "Prime Time," "Moochie," "Humble Host," Bardia, "Two Eight" and "the Mongerer" pose at the end of a long, fun ride. *(Joann Kamay)*

us to the airport for our cross-country flight back to Los Angeles, where a full New Year's Eve edition of *NFL GameDay* awaited.

As Deion and Mooch piled their belongings into the back of our car for the trip to the airport, I noticed Steve carrying a shoebox.

"What's that?" I asked as we drove away.

"Deion got them for me."

Prime had already pushed his hat down over his face to get some shut-eye on the way to Dulles Airport. But from underneath, he mustered enough strength to mumble:

"Had to get some Guccis for my Moochie."

Sure enough, the side of Steve's shoebox read "Gucci."

"Good thing your last name doesn't rhyme with adidas," I said.

I couldn't believe it was over. The six weeks between Thanksgiving and New Year's went by in a flash. As the Washington Monument blinked in the dark of morning, the thought dawned on me. The Eight-Game Package had just completed the mother of all Mid-Shoe Entries. Gucci style.

At least Mooch had quality shoes in which to take the final steps of our year's journey—into the playoffs culminating in yet another Super Bowl. But, then again, the Super Bowl is also just the start of another year at NFL Network. Maybe I needed a new pair of kicks, too.

AFTERWORD

As you've no doubt gleaned from this tome, the business of the National Football League never rests. How much so? Well, the honing of the pigskin product is so constant, this book is already outdated.

No kidding.

For instance, the NFL Draft appears destined for a considerable trimming. One of the first orders of business Commissioner Roger Goodell apparently addressed after the 2007 NFL Draft was to figure out how to make sure the 2008 NFL Draft would not run into 2009. Once the first round of the '07 Draft required a record six hours and eight minutes to complete, the first-day ran a record 11 hours, 4 minutes in length, which in turn helped create a two-day draft that lasted an absurd 18 hours and 5 minutes—another NFL Draft record. So, Commissioner Goodell phoned the NFL Competition Committee and told them to find a way to shave this puppy down an hour or three. As of this book's publication, nothing has been made official, but, at the 2008 Owners' Meeting (which returns to The Breakers in Palm Beach, by the way), The Membership is expected to reduce the amount of time a team gets to make a first-round selection from 15 minutes to 12 minutes. I'll do the math—three fewer minutes per selection multiplied by 32 selecting franchises equals a grand total savings of at least 66 minutes. That's one fewer hour to the 2008 NFL Draft right there.

But wait, there's more.

The NFL Draft may go prime-time or, more specifically, Friday Night Lights. There's an idea being floated around to hold the new, leaner first round of the 2008 NFL Draft on a Friday night and parlay the event into a full-on ratings bonanza. The second and third rounds would be held on Saturday with the rest of the draft still held on Sunday. Seven rounds, three days, one draft. In terms of approving this radical concept, The Membership could soon be on the clock.

The Pro Football Hall of Fame has already gone prime-time. The lion's share of this book had already hit the presses prior to the August 2007 Hall of Fame Induction Weekend, for which the good folks of Canton totally revamped their induction ceremony. First of all, they moved the event to the evening. Gone are the days of sitting through the long hours of presenting speeches and acceptance addresses while broiling in the hot sun. The 2007 ceremony kicked off in Fawcett Stadium next to the Hall at 6:00 PM local time, and by the time the Cowboys' famed playmaker Michael Irvin stepped to the podium to deliver the sixth and final induction speech of the ceremony at 9:00 PM, the sun had completely set and night had fallen. Irvin's incredibly emotional oratory—in which he asked forgiveness from his family, friends, and teammates for his off-the-field transgressions—was made even more powerful by the darkness that surrounded the stage. He truly had a spotlight on him and, typically, Irvin shined brightly in it. Without question, the Hall of Fame will keep this new format for the foreseeable future, which means that when Deion Sanders gets enshrined in his first year of eligibility in 2011, Prime Time will fittingly go into the Hall of Fame . . . in prime time. (And talk about a Canton class for the ages: Marshall Faulk, Jerome Bettis, and Curtis Martin are all first eligible for induction in 2011, too. Reserve your hotel rooms now, people.)

Also gone are the presenting speeches as we had come to know and dread them. You may recall from the Canton section of the book (chapter 7 for those scoring at home) that, in 2006, Hall of Fame brass began requiring all presenters to type out and hand in their speeches in advance. That way, the Hall figured they could ensure the speeches to be of proper length. Well, that experiment failed miserably because no one accounted for how deliberately the presenters might present. Delivering a speech at the Pro Football Hall of Fame in front of 20,000 people can be a daunting task. (In the midst of his acceptance speech, Buffalo Bills great Thurman Thomas apologized to those he might be forgetting to mention because "it's real scary up here right now.") Needless to say, the read time for each typewritten, prepared speech remained verrrrrrry slowwwwwww. So, starting in 2007, the Hall of Fame produced a four-minute video chronicling the career of the inductee through the words and recollections of his presenter. The idea was risky—the presenter would still be allowed to deliver remarks at the video's conclusion, but the Hall hoped the presenter would have gotten enough off his chest about the inductee during the video to keep those remarks brief. Sure enough, it worked. The videos were highly enjoyable (and I'm not just saying that because NFL Network staffers put them together), and the presenting speeches were crisp. The 2007 induction ceremony lasted a mere three and a half hours, a virtual romp in the park compared to the previous year's affair which ran *90* minutes longer despite featuring the same number (six) of enshrinees. Mission accomplished—finally.

There was also a major change in the NFL Network coverage of Hall of Fame Weekend in 2007. Thanks to the Napa Auto Parts 200 race, the Hollywood Hotel was unavailable for our use. So, for the first time, we moved *NFL Total Access* inside the Hall of Fame itself, and, quite frankly, it was better. Instead of emanating from a box on stilts with that nice view of The Juicer through a double-paned window, Fran Charles and Steve Mariucci hosted *NFL Total Access* on the Thursday and Friday of Induction Week from inside the vaunted Hall of Fame Gallery, where all those bronze busts that John Madden swears talk to each other reside. The collection of busts lit up against the dark walls sure served as a stunning set. More importantly, it was air-conditioned without Madden having to demand it be so.

Thanks to the new set up, I didn't arrive on the scene until Friday (but in time for the jacket ceremony—my favorite part of Hall of Fame Weekend), whereupon I learned about one final, stunning change to the Canton landscape. The famous Mariucci piano in the second floor elevator lobby of the Glenmoor Country Club had apparently been *nailed down* to the floor. You see, the night before, both Steve Mariucci and Adam Schefter tried to move it in front of Fran's hotel room door. It was Fran's first time covering the event—a rookie, just like Mooch the year before—and Mariucci was dying to give someone else the keyboard treatment and turn it into a tradition. However, when Fran turned in early Thursday and it came time to pull the prank, Schefter couldn't move his end of the piano.

"It wouldn't budge," Schefter said, as he recounted the story for seven of us who gathered for a Friday nightcap at the Glenmoor.

Mariucci wasn't buying it.

"My end of the piano moved. There's no way it was nailed down," Mooch scoffed. "How could they nail it down? It doesn't even have wheels!"

"Trust me," Schefter assured the rest of us, raising his right hand. "The hotel did something to that piano because it just would not move."

With NFL Network crewmembers descending upon Canton for another Induction Weekend, had the Glenmoor brass really taken preventative measures and battened down the piano for fear it would wind up on the fourth floor again? Or did Adam Schefter just not apply the proper amount of elbow grease to get the job done? Clearly we had to find out.

Now, once again, the groupthink that led to the undertaking of this piano caper remains a bit hazy due to the considerable amount of, shall we say, good cheer, but the bottom line was this: If the piano could be moved, it was decided that the piano obviously had to go across the fourth floor door mouth of one Adam Schefter, who made the unfortunate choice of turning in early.

The mystery of the immoveable piano got solved quickly. So much so, that it had already been shoved onto the elevator by my co-conspirators by the time I got there. As we hit the button for the fourth floor, there were seven hands on deck: me, Mooch, Fran, producers Bardia Shah-Rais and Chris Weerts, Operations Manager Mike Konner, and Chris Dalston, a top music agent at CAA and a friend of mine in for the weekend to watch his beloved Michael Irvin go into the Hall.

The elevator snapped open on the fourth floor and we immediately sprung into action. The sound of our muffled laughs mixed with the light scraping of the piano legs on the Glenmoor carpet. Within a minute, we arrived in front of Schefter's room and ditched the precious cargo: 88 keys of ivory with a pepper mill placed on top. For some reason, Dalston felt compelled to snag the wooden condiment dispenser from somewhere along the way and bring it with the piano. Fully satisfied, we bade each other a good night and congratulated ourselves on another job well done.

Except, this time, we didn't get off scot-free. Or so it seemed.

Cut to the next morning. Another rise-and-shine in Canton, Ohio for your humble narrator was accompanied by another realization upon awakening that another outrageously juvenile stunt had gone down in the

Chris Weerts *(far left)* reminds everyone to keep quiet as well pull of the latest late-night piano/pepper mill caper at the Glenmoor. Mike Konner, Mooch, Bardia, Fran and I were all smiles outside Schefter's door, but none of us had the last laugh. *(Chris Dalston)*

middle of the Glenmoor night. Then, around 10:00 AM, came a knock on the door:

"Guest services!" said the female voice on the other side.

I opened the door a crack and a sweetly cheerful member of the Glenmoor staff outstretched her arm.

"Here's your newspaper . . . and here's a letter for you!"

I thanked her, shut the door and put down the Induction Day 2007 edition of the Canton Repository to read the letter. Written on Glenmoor Country Club stationery, it was from The Management:

> *Mr. Rich Eisen:*
> *This letter is in regards to the furniture that was moved early this morning by yourself and several other guests of our Club that will also be receiving a similar letter. Unfortunately, the piano that was damaged was the original*

piano from Brunnerdale Catholic Seminary which Glenmoor went to great
lengths to refurbish and restore.

I spoke with our General Manager this morning and we will have an
estimate of the damage by Tuesday or Wednesday of next week. Once we
have that we will forward a copy of the repair invoice to you and the others
responsible for the repairs. Each of you will be charged equally for the repairs.
At this time I can only guess that the cost will be several thousand dollars.

If you have any questions, please contact me.

> *Daniel Kirby Jr.*
> *Director of Security*
> *Glenmoor Country Club*

Whoa.

My thoughts ran the gamut. From shame and embarrassment (The
people of Canton are so incredibly hospitable and this is how I repay
them?) to fear and concern (*several thousand* dollars?) to utter and complete horror (Could this mean I might have to stay in the Red Roof next
year?!) Then, I began getting indignant. How could the piano be dam-
aged by seven guys barely moving it a grand total of 200 feet? It also sure
didn't look like a priceless antique. And how in the world did the hotel
know I was involved? Did they have video of us? And if so, how? And
where? On the elevator? We sure didn't see any cameras in the halls.

I thought about getting this Daniel Kirby Jr. on the phone to query
the director of security about his evidence but thought better of it. If I
was going to call him, it should be to apologize and take the hit. After all,
as innocuous as it was, we *did* move the piano. And it was refurbished
from a local seminary, of all places? Goodness gracious.

It soon came time to go to work. We had a noontime pickup to head
over to the Hall of Fame for our live broadcast of the induction ceremony. I got on the elevator and looked for a security camera. There
wasn't one. I then skulked off to the lobby, thinking everyone on the
Glenmoor staff had to know about this by now.

"Good afternoon!" smiled another sweet member of the Glenmoor
staff.

"Good afternoon!" I said as cheerful as possible, desperately trying
to become a productive member of Canton society once again.

Fran then entered the lobby. We walked outside.

"Did you get a letter?" I asked.

"Yeah. I did," Fran said sheepishly. He then took out his letter from Daniel Kirby Jr., director of security for Glenmoor Country Club.

"What the hell?" I said.

"I have no idea!" Fran said laughing, even though I could tell that he, like me, was crying inside.

Then Mooch came bounding out and we showed him our letters.

"Did you get one about the piano?" Fran asked.

Mariucci didn't skip a beat.

"What piano?" he said.

"Real funny," I said.

"Did you guys move the piano again?" Mariucci deadpanned.

"C'mon Steve," Fran said.

"No, really. Tell me," Mooch said, now with a sly smile.

Schefter then bounded out of the Glenmoor front door.

"Boy is the general manager of the hotel really pissed at you guys," he said. "I mean, he is *really* hot."

Schefter then explained that when he opened his door that morning, the general manager and the security director were already in the process of moving the piano back.

They told him the Club had the whole thing on videotape and were not pleased, especially because the "sound box" on the rare piano was ruined. The bill would be hefty, and we were all going to share a piece.

Mariucci turned to me and Fran.

"So, you guys broke the piano?" he said.

"Okay, Mooch. Enough," I said. "You were there. Fran knows you were there. Daniel J. Kirby Jr. knows you were there. Everybody knows you were there."

Mariucci laughed. Schefter went back inside to collect one last thing before we all headed off to the Hall.

"Why are you being so glib about this?" I asked Mariucci.

"Because this thing's a fake," said Mariucci, now taking his own letter out of his briefcase.

"Fake?" Fran said. "How is this fake?"

"It's on Glenmoor stationery, Mooch!" I said.

"Anybody can get that. It's in the desk in your room," he said.

Mr. Rich Eisen,   08/04/2007

     This letter is in regards to the furniture that was moved early this morning by yourself and several other guests of our Club that will also be receiving a similar letter. Unfortunately, the piano that was damaged was the original piano from Brunnerdale Catholic Seminary which Glenmoor went to great lengths to refurbish and restore.

     I spoke with our General Manager this morning and we will have an estimate of the damage by Tuesday or Wednesday of next week. Once we have that we will forward a copy of the repair invoice to you and the others responsible for the repairs. Each of you will be charged equally for the repairs. At this time I can only guess that the cost will be several thousand dollars.

     If you have any questions please contact me.

Daniel Kirby Jr.
Director of Security
Glenmoor Country Club

GLENMOOR
4191 Glenmoor Road N.W.
Canton, Ohio 44718
(330) 966-3600
Fax: (330) 966-3611

Good point.

"Plus, if you look real careful at the letter something is missing," Mariucci added.

Both Fran and I immediately began scanning our letters as all three of us climbed in the back of service van waiting to take us to the Hall.

"What's missing?" Fran said.

"Yeah, I don't see too much missing here," I said.

"There's no private extension on it," Mooch said. "If this Kirby guy existed and he says we should call him with questions, wouldn't he give an extension?"

Both Fran and I rejected that out of hand.

"That's ridiculous. The number to the Club is at the bottom!" Fran said.

"Daniel Kirby Jr. does *not* exist," Mariucci insisted.

"Oh yeah?" I said, popping my cell phone open. "Let's give this guy a call then."

At that point, Schefter climbed into the shotgun seat of the car.

"This thing is a fake, right?" Mooch said. "Come on."

"What do you mean?" Schefter said, cracking a smile.

"Wait a minute!" I said. "This thing is a *fake*?!"

"Get out of here!" Fran screamed.

Schefter began cackling.

"I knew it," Mariucci said.

Schefter proceeded to spill the beans. There *was,* in fact, a Daniel Kirby Jr., and he *is,* in fact, the security director of the Glenmoor Country Club, and he and the general manager *were* in the process of taking the piano back when Schefter opened his room door that morning. Two more truths: the piano was just fine, but hotel management still was not pleased with our stunt. Schefter then provided them with a remedy: Send a letter to the rooms of Rich Eisen, Fran Charles and Steve Mariucci, Schefter suggested, and have the letter claim the piano was broken and that the hotel would send out a massive bill for the repairs.

Sure enough, the security director went back to his office, typed up the letter and even brought it down to Schefter in the basement gym for his proofreading. Schefter enthusiastically approved the letter and also showed it to a very special Glenmoor guest who was also working out in the gym as part of his weeklong stay for the World Golf Championship event at nearby Firestone Country Club: none other than Tiger Woods. Can you believe it? Apparently, he got a very good laugh out of it. And why not? It's an instant classic.

"Brunnerdale Catholic Seminary," I muttered, reading the letter in a whole new light. "A very nice touch."

"Thank you," Schefter said.

After getting the piano treatment, Schefter came back with an all-timer. I mean, a Frank Reich against the Houston Oilers–type comeback. The unique triumvirate of Adam Schefter, Tiger Woods, and Daniel Kirby Jr. combined to really put one over on me, Fran and, despite his cool demeanor, Mooch. I know he was churning inside.

Of course, on the ride through Canton, we all decided to keep the ruse going for Bardia, Konner, and Weerts upon our arrival at the Hall of Fame. If Fran and I were going to spend two hours on the griddle thinking our piano prank cost NFL Network blood and our personal treasure, then they sure were going to feel the same way for a while. We showed our letters to all three colleagues and let them think we were *all* in trouble. We kept it up for a good two hours before we let Adam spill the beans again. I mean, it was his virtuoso retort to our late-night caper. We laughed about it all day and deep into the night.

During a commercial break of our seven-hour long coverage of the induction ceremony, Mooch turned to me.

"Is this piano stuff with Schefter going to make your book?" Mooch already knew his own piano escapade from 2006 was the crown jewel of chapter 7.

"Don't you think it should?" I asked.

"Absolutely," he said.

His eyes lit up and he added: "With the rate that these types of stories happen with us, you'll have to write another book."

Heaven help me . . . and my wife. If I ever think of doing this again, she might put a piano in front of the office door in our house to keep me from my computer. Or get Daniel Kirby Jr. on my case. But, fearless readers, you never know. Stay tuned—if not to your local bookstore, then certainly to NFL Network.